T0330038

Political Pressure, Rhetoric and Monetary Policy: Lessons for the European Central Bank

Philipp Maier

Economist, Monetary and Economic Policy Department

De Nederlandsche Bank

Amsterdam, The Netherlands

Edward Elgar
Cheltenham, UK • Northampton, MA, USA

Published by
Edward Elgar Publishing Limited
Glensanda House
Montpellier Parade
Cheltenham
Glos GL50 1UA
UK

Edward Elgar Publishing, Inc.
136 West Street
Suite 202
Northampton
Massachusetts 01060
USA

A catalogue record for this book
is available from the British Library

Library of Congress Cataloguing in Publication Data

Maier, Philipp.
 Political pressure, rhetoric and monetary policy : lessons for the European
Central Bank
/Philipp Maier.
 p. cm.
 Includes index.

 1. Banks and banking, Central. 2. Banks and banking, Central–Political
aspects. 3. Banks and banking, Central–European Union countries. 4. Monetary
policy–European Union countries. I. Title.

HG1811 .M35 2002
332. 1'I–dc21

                                                        2002072180

ISBN 1 84376 157 2

Printed and bound in Great Britain by MPG Books Ltd, Bodmin, Cornwall

Contents

List of Figures

List of Tables

Acknowledgements

Many people have contributed to this book, and this is usually the place to thank at least some of them. I do not intend to make an exception to that tradition. First of all, I would like to express my deepest gratitude to my former Ph.D. supervisor Jakob de Haan, who not only provided scientific inspiration, but also motivation and 'emotional assistance' when needed. His friendly and supportive way will always be a *voorbeeld* to me. Second, I am heavily indebted to Helge Berger. He provided valuable comments at many stages of this project, which made his involvement in this research project very fruitful. I am grateful to Lex Hoogduin, Friedrich Schneider and Sylvester Eijffinger for reading the entire manuscript and providing useful comments. Furthermore, I would like to thank Otmar Issing of the European Central Bank, who helped me to clarify my views on the implications of chapters 5 and 6.

I am also indebted to Alistair Dieppe of the European Central Bank, Thijs Knaap (University of Rotterdam), Erik Leertouwer (University of Groningen) and Jan-Egbert Sturm (University of Munich) for conducting fruitful joint research projects. To reflect this fact, I use the plural form throughout the thesis. Special thanks go to the Germany Institute in Amsterdam and the graduate school SOM, who provided financial support.

Furthermore, I would like to thank the staff at the Hamburgisches Welt-Wirtschafts-Archiv, where the evidence for chapters 5 and 6 was compiled, and at the European Central Bank, where large parts of chapters 8 and 9 were written. In that context I would also like to thank many ex-trainees at the ECB (among others Ramon Maria Dolores, Roberta Serafini and Maria Myroni), who contributed to make two stays in Frankfurt truly unforgettable.

My former colleagues in the Faculty of Economics of the University of Groningen created a pleasant and productive working environment in many ways, here special thanks go to Thijs Knaap, Erik Leertouwer, Remco van der Molen and Bjørn Volkerink. Good friends and relatives have kept me from drowning; and last, but not least, I would like to thank Diane for supporting me during many years, and God for creating Italy and the marvelous Fiat *barchetta*.

1. Introduction

1.1 WHY WERE CENTRAL BANKS MADE INDEPENDENT?

At first glance the idea of making a central bank independent may seem somewhat awkward: why would a government decide to transfer monetary policy to an independent authority? What are the benefits of having an independent central bank? After all, the government gives away a powerful economic instrument. Still, in many countries recent years were marked by increases in statutory independence for central banks (i.e. New Zealand, in many European countries following the Maastricht Treaty etc.). To explain this trend two main reasons have been put forward in the literature.

First, as Posen (1993) shows, it increases the credibility of commitments to price stability and assures a higher priority for fighting inflation. This reduces the inflationary bias, which in turn translates into lower overall inflation. This inverse relationship between the level of inflation and the degree of central bank independence has been shown in many empirical studies (Berger et al., 2001 provide an overview). Inflation variability is positively correlated with the level of inflation. Therefore, as central bank independence, *ceteris paribus*, lowers the inflation rate, the variability of inflation – usually measured by the standard deviation of inflation – also shows a negative relationship to central bank independence. Low inflation and low variability of inflation, in turn, enhance growth prospects in long run. Taking these two points together, a high degree of statutory central bank independence yields an overall positive picture, as Alesina and Summers (1993) note:

> Most obviously... [our findings] suggest the economic performance merits of central bank independence.[1]

So the first reason why central banks are granted independence is better long-run growth prospects, resulting from lower inflation.

Secondly, 'the most obvious advantage a fully independent central bank has, is that of not being influenced by electoral deadlines'.[2] Alesina et al. (1997) have shown that governments may be inclined to stimulate the economy before elections to enhance their re-election probabilities. If central banks are not independent, government may force them to alter their policy stance before elections accordingly, i.e. to boost economic growth. Using monetary policy to meet short-run objectives, however, is highly undesirable, since the long and variable lags of monetary policy make accurate timing almost impossible. Independent central banks may pursue a longer time horizon: elections do not affect the way they conduct monetary policy, as governments cannot force them to pursue a certain policy stance. So, non-economic influences (e.g. electoral deadlines or the political affiliation of the central bank governor etc.) should have less impact on an independent central bank's policy stance than for example on a government's economic policy.

Besides, politicians typically have rather ambitious unemployment targets, which is why they may in some cases prefer to lower unemployment at the cost of higher inflation rates. In the terms of the theoretical framework by Barro and Gordon (1983), independent central banks have less incentives to lower unemployment by creating 'surprise inflations' – in particular not before elections.

These are the theoretical arguments for central bank independence. Yet, so far a comprehensive *empirical* study in particular on the second issue is warranted. Are less independent central banks indeed more influenced by electoral deadlines? Or, to put the question even more broadly: how do central banks react when they face (political) pressure?

Recently, this debate has gained a lot of attention. There is a considerable amount of uncertainty about the future of European monetary policy: the European Central Bank (ECB), which replaced most of Europe's national central banks in 1999, was closely modeled on the German central bank, to gain most of its credibility. Yet, it is still unclear whether this legal independence also resulted in *de facto* independence: the level of statutory independence of the European Central Bank is very high, but nevertheless the ECB has received a considerable amount of external pressure (e.g. from the former German minister of finance, Oskar Lafontaine).

In this study we examine external pressure on central banks. We check to what extent central banks' rhetoric and monetary policy are influenced by politicians or interest groups, and to what extent public support can strengthen a central bank's position.

1.2   MEASURES OF CENTRAL BANK INDEPENDENCE

As a start, we have to clarify what we mean by saying that 'conflicts' occur or that 'pressure' might be applied on an 'independent' central bank, and we have to specify the channels through which external pressure might be applied.

Independence of a central bank is viewed in a political sense. Following Grilli et al. (1991) central bank independence means 'autonomy to pursue the goal of low inflation. Any institutional feature that enhances the central bank capacity to pursue this goal will, on our definition, increase central bank independence'.[3] Practically, a high degree of central bank independence implies that a central bank can use its full range of monetary instruments to archive its operating target.[4]

Conflicts might be defined as situations, where (a) the preferred policies of the government and the central bank are not compatible, and (b) the government wants its policy implemented, while the central bank refuses to comply. Conflicts can occur over different policy stances, but also over institutional arrangements, such as the introduction of a fixed exchange rate system.

Pressure is applied if the government or other external institutions try to force the central bank to adopt its policy, e.g. by threatening to change the Bundesbank Act.[5] In this chapter we treat the government as the major source for pressure, as it undoubtedly has the best opportunities to threaten the central bank, but in a later stage (chapter 5) we will also look at other potential sources of pressure.

Ranking central bank charters by their degree of legal (statutory) independence is quite difficult. An ideal measure of central bank independence would require not just classification of a number of legal aspects, but also assessment of informal links between the government and the central bank. In many cases this assessment is not possible.

Table 1.1 presents four different measures of central bank independence, developed by Alesina (1988), Grilli et al. (1991)[8], Eijffinger and Schaling (1993) and Cukierman (1992).[9] The higher the score for the central bank, the higher its statutory independence. Although all indices are based on roughly similar approaches, for some central banks they show very different outcomes.

Still, economic researchers have been very clear about the legal position of the Bundesbank: before the introduction of the single European currency and the erection of the European Central Bank, the Bundesbank was widely regarded as being one of the most independent central banks of the world. The European Central Bank was not included in these studies, but can be considered as even more independent than the Bundesbank (see chapter 8).

The strong position of the German central bank becomes even more apparent when looking at data for public support: a survey of the German research institute Mannheim Institute for Praxis Oriented Social Research on attitudes towards public institutions reflects a high level of trust by the German population in both the Federal Constitutional Court and the Bundesbank (scoring 2.2 and 2.1, respectively, on a scale of 3). This compares favorably with the scores of the Federal Government (0.6) and the Lower House of Parliament (0.9), respectively (the survey is cited in Balkhausen, 1992)).

Country	Alesina	Grilli/Masciandaro/ Tabellini	Eijffinger/ Schaling[6]	Cukierman (LVAU)[7]
Australia	1	9 (3)	1	0.31
Austria	-	9 (3)	3	0.58
Belgium	2	7 (1)	3	0.19
Canada	2	11 (4)	1	0.46
Denmark	2	8 (3)	4	0.47
Finland	2	-	3	0.27
France	2	7 (2)	2	0.28
Germany	4	13 (6)	5	0.66
Greece	-	4 (2)	-	0.51
Iceland	-	-	-	0.36
Ireland	-	7 (3)	-	0.39
Italy	1.5	5 (4)	2	0.22
Japan	3	6 (1)	3	0.16
Netherlands	2	10 (6)	4	0.42
New Zealand	1	3 (0)	3	0.27
Norway	2	-	2	0.14
Portugal	-	3 (1)	2	-
Spain	1	5 (2)	3	0.21
Sweden	2	-	2	0.27
Switzerland	4	12 (5)	5	0.68
United Kingdom	2	6 (1)	2	0.31
United States	3	12 (5)	3	0.51
Max. score possible	4	16	5	1.00
No. of countries	17	18	12	23

Table 1.1   Legal indices of central bank independence

For the European Union similar data is collected in the Eurobarometer surveys. These surveys are carried out twice a year and present an analysis of public opinion towards the European institutions. To some extent they can also give an indication about public opinion on the European Central Bank. The data shows a rather positive trend: comparing the figures of the Eurobarometers 52-54 the European Central Bank is increasingly viewed as playing an 'important role' in the life of the European Union (approval to that statement has increased from 62 per cent of the Eurobarometer 51 to 68 per cent of the Eurobarometer 54 in autumn 2000[10]). Most importantly for the work of the ECB is that this form of 'approval' is rising continuously.

Nevertheless, it is unclear whether formal independence or public support also guarantees de facto independence. Forder (1996) argues that

... a central bank may be independent by statute, and it is nevertheless accepted – on all sides – that the government will have its wishes implemented. There need not even be the feeling amongst the actors that this is improper.
... it is quite clear that the reading of statutes is not a measure of independence in the sense required by the theory ... There is no theory that says it matters what the rules say. There is only a theory that says it matters what the behavior is.[11]

One could conjecture that the statutes of the central bank may (at least partially) shape the options for the central bank to pursue the kind of policies that it deems necessary.[12] Still, one might wonder whether the members of the Bundesbank council have indeed always been politically neutral technocrats with a strong *esprit de corps* as Marsh (1992) claims.

1.3 PURPOSE OF THE STUDY

In this study we examine to what extent government and pressure groups exert significant influences on central banks. The prime object to study is the German Bundesbank, the closest proxy available for the European Central Bank. Unfortunately, we do not have sufficient data for the European Central Bank (ECB) for meaningful estimations, but where possible we extend the research to other central banks. As the European Central Bank was closely modeled on its German counterpart, answers to the German case will also provide insight into the possible relationship between the ECB and the European governments.

Several studies on the Bundesbank have been carried out previously, especially focusing on its behavior during election times. But, as we will show in the next chapter, many of these studies are not without flaws. A reliable indicator that shows periods of high pressure on the Bundesbank misses altogether. Therefore, the evidence on the Bundesbank does not answer the questions: what *exactly* does the Bundesbank doing when political pressure is applied? Does the strong, independent Bundesbank give in during conflicts with the government, and what is the role of interest groups? Since the European Central Bank is a relatively young institution a great deal of uncertainty about its future actions exists. Studying the role of other central banks, but in particular the Bundesbank, might be helpful to reduce this uncertainty. What can we learn from the Bundesbank about the possible behavior of the ECB?

Therefore, as we progress the focus shifts more and more away from the German case to the European level. We do not only examine political pressure, but also economic diversity in the euro area, as economic factors have the potential to seriously endanger the economic project. According to Feldstein (1997), EMU could even lead to a new war in Europe, if the national governments disagree on the common economic and monetary policy. Last, but not least, we extend our focus beyond the euro area and examine the candidate countries for E(M)U accession. Here we investigate the consequences for European monetary policy, again focusing both on economic and political implications.

The questions we want to answer should also be viewed in a broader context. The concept of central bank independence, which relies on the idea that governments should not be able to interfere with monetary policy, has gained quite some popularity. But does this concept really work? If central banks are formally independent, does this translate into an independent monetary policy, independent in the sense that it is not affected by possibly short-sighted political desires? What better object to study than the most independent central bank in the world! If even the Bundesbank, this former prototype of an independent central bank, showed signs of political influence, then the whole idea of central bank independence should perhaps be reconsidered.

1.4 OUTLINE OF THE STUDY

In the next chapter we first consider popular models for external pressure on central banks, before we review the findings of other researchers and show that not all questions have been adequately answered.

One of the issues that can be improved upon is how monetary policy is measured. In chapters 3 and 4 we present alternative ways to measure what central banks are doing: in chapter 3 we use interest rates and test in a cross-country setting with 14 OECD countries the impact of elections. In chapter 4 we use a monetary policy index to measure the rhetoric of the Bundesbank and test political business model and various conflict models for Germany, Japan and the US.

In chapter 5 we take a closer look at different conflict measures. We present a new indicator for Germany that measures pressure, not only from the government, but also from interest groups. We compare this new indicator to existing indicators and estimate the impact, which not only the government had on Germany's monetary policy, but also that of other organized groups such as trade unions or the financial sector.

Having completed these points, we extend the conflict approach to allow for public support. In chapter 6 we present an indicator for public support among different parts of the population. This indicator is used to demonstrate that public support is an important component of monetary policy.

The chapters 7 and 8 focus on the European Central Bank. In chapter 7 we examine the economic situation in Europe. We investigate the degree of economic convergence and highlight potential new sources of pressure: if inflation rates differ across Europe, this might create tension among the EMU member countries, resulting in additional difficulties for the European Central

Bank. In this chapter we examine to what extent inflation rates differ and offer an explanation for existing dispersion, based on the Balassa-Samuelson framework of productivity differentials. In chapter 8 we offer an interpretation of our results so far in the European context. After a brief overview of the institutional setting of the ECB we check the likelihood for external pressure and public support at the European level.

Chapter 9 focuses on the future of the EMU. Economic performance in the candidate countries for E(M)U accession is on average much lower than in the euro area. We check to what extent EU enlargement may influence the ECB's independence or monetary policy stance on economic, institutional and on political grounds.

Finally, we summarize our main findings in chapter 10 and offer a general discussion of our results.

2. Review of the Literature

2.1 MEANS OF INFLUENCING CENTRAL BANKS

The literature has identified two main channels through which governments might put central banks under pressure:

Direct influence may force the central bank to alter its policy according to the wishes of the government.

Indirect influence might be exercised through fiscal policy: if the government increases public spending, this may create pressure on the monetary policy stance. Of interest is the extent to which the government budget deficit is accommodated by monetary policy.

If governmental influence through either of the two channels cannot be observed, then we might conclude that a central bank operates independently of the government. However, reversing this reasoning does not hold, as Lohmann (1992) notes: an independent central bank may create political business cycles, if for partisan (or other) reasons it would like to influence the chances of re-election of the incumbent government. If we observe an electoral cycle in monetary policy, it is unclear whether this is due to a dependent central bank following the wishes of government or due to an independent central bank trying to influence the election outcome in a certain direction. Only if we fail to find evidence of such a cycle we can assume that the central bank is independent.

In this study we focus mostly on direct influence. Therefore, the models presented in the next section deal exclusively with the possibility that pressure is directly exerted. However, we cannot neglect the possibility of indirect pressure, therefore in section 2.5 we also review existing research on indirect government influence on Bundesbank policies.[13]

2.2   THE MODELS

Two main approaches might be distinguished: models linked to election dates and 'conflict' models. While the first type of models directly focus on either election dates or election outcomes, the second type considers periods of divergent interests at any time. Noteworthy is that the first type of models has been developed in two distinctive phases, first featuring pre-rational expectations and then having rational expectations introduced.

2.2.1   Models linked to election dates

a)   Opportunistic models

In opportunistic models, policymakers seek to maximize their popularity and the probability of being re-elected.[14] Following Paldam (1997), a business cycle is called a 'Political Business Cycle' (PBC) when it is generated by the political system. The 'classical' opportunistic model for PBCs was developed by Nordhaus (1975). An extensive formal treatment of the model can be found in Alesina et al. (1997) we just sketch the basic assumptions: the economy can be characterized by an exploitable Phillips curve, inflation expectations are adaptive and the incumbent can directly control the rate of inflation. Politicians are 'opportunistic', i.e. only interested in re-election; voters are 'retrospective' and judge the incumbent's performance on the basis of the state of the economy (notably unemployment and inflation) during his term of office. Past observations are heavily discounted. These assumptions lead to the following (testable) implications: before elections expansionary policies are pursued to reduce the unemployment rate to enhance chances for re-election. Due to expansionary policy measures unemployment drops. After the elections the incumbent will combat inflation, which has gone up due to policy measures taken, thereby raising unemployment. Both monetary and fiscal policies could be used in this way. Due to the poor memory of the voters, this cycle might be repeated endlessly.

Rogoff and Sibert (1988) and Persson and Tabellini (1990) extended the framework to a 'rational' opportunistic model ('Rational Political Business Cycles' RPBC). Rational expectations are introduced; the voters have all relevant information except for the level of 'competence' of the policymakers. This implies asymmetric information between policymakers and voters; in order to appear 'competent' policymakers manipulate policy instruments. The testable outcome of this model is that policymakers manipulate policy instruments before elections. Note that both models are observationally equivalent when the focus is on economic instruments.

b) Partisan models

In partisan models different social parties represent different social constituencies and therefore have divergent interests. Following Hibbs' (1977) 'Partisan Theory' (PT) left-wing parties are more concerned with unemployment, while right-wing parties focus more on inflation. This assumption is based on the fact that macroeconomic outcomes have important re-distributive consequences. Each voter is aware of the partisan differences and votes according to own preferences. In Hibbs' model, inflation expectations are adaptive. This model has the (testable) implication that inflation is permanently higher and unemployment permanently lower under left-wing governments.

Alesina (1987) extended the Hibbs model to a 'Rational Partisan Theory' (RPT). The framework of his model remains the same as in the PT, except for the fact that voters behave rationally, again not having complete information about the level of competence of the different policymakers. Two assumptions are added: labor contracts are signed at discrete intervals, which do not coincide with the political terms of office, and the outcome of the election is uncertain. In the case of two political parties, the rational expectations forecast is a weighted average of the inflation rates preferred by the left-wing and right-wing party; the weights are the chances of the parties to win the elections. After the election, the voters will be surprised and due to the sluggishness in wage adjustments either a recession occurs (after the victory of a right-wing government) or a boom takes place (after the victory of a left-wing government). Both boom and recession, however, are temporary.

2.2.2 Conflict models

Conflict models are not specifically linked to election dates, but focus on periods with 'tension' between government and the central bank at any time. The difficult issue here is (a) the definition of what 'conflicts' are and (b) how they can be measured. Different models have been proposed.

Vaubel (1997) looked at the partisan framework from a different angle. He argues that one should focus on the political majority of the Bundesbank Council: the members of the Council are nominated/appointed either by the Bundesländer or by the federal government and Vaubel argues that the nominees will mirror the ideology of the appointing government. Following Vaubel, a situation might occur such that a leftist government has to cope with a 'rightist' central bank council and vice versa. He determines the political preferences of the central bankers by looking at the political color of their nominators (for details see Vaubel, 1997, pp. 51-52).

An interesting implication of Vaubel's model is that the Bundesbank might obstruct the re-election of a government: before elections, the central bank will only support the incumbent if the majority of the council shares the political views of the government otherwise it may even reduce chances of re-election by contractionary monetary policy. This approach will be called 'Party Preference Theory' (PPT).

Lohmann (1998) extends the framework outlined above. First of all, she distinguishes between partisan central bankers and technocrats. Second, Lohmann argues that the degree of independence the Bundesbank enjoys, i.e. the degree to which central bankers give in to political pressures, may vary. Several factors may be the reason for that. The popularity of the federal government, for instance, may determine who bears the costs of a conflict between the central bank and government. Another factor is whether political parties in the government also have a majority in the second chamber of parliament, the Bundesrat, since a supportive Bundesrat would facilitate changing the Bundesbank law (see appendix 10.3). Lohmann has developed a special way to measure the degree of independence of the Bundesbank: she uses the number of Bundesrat members that support the government before elections. When there is no 'independence' because both chambers of parliament are under unified party control, PBC and PT cycles will show up, no matter whether the Bundesbank council consists of technocrats or partisan central bankers. So, under this refinement of the PBC model, political business cycles only show up under certain circumstances. In the case of an 'independent' Bundesbank governed by technocrats, there will be no electoral or partisan effects. However, it is possible to have an 'independent' Bundesbank (as defined by Lohmann), while at the same time certain election cycles in monetary policy – be they supportive or obstructive – are possible. In Lohmann's model, monetary policy is set in accordance to the partisan preferences of the central bank council's median voter.

Frey and Schneider (1981) developed a framework that extends standard PBC models: it focuses on conflicts between the government and the central bank at any time, not only during election periods. In their model, the central bank is generally free to follow its own interests. A low inflation rate is the most important goal for the central bank, reflecting the wishes of the financial community.

However, during periods of conflict with the government, the central bank has to adopt the government's policy stance, because in the long run, the government has the power to overrule the central bank, ultimately by changing the central bank law. Following this reasoning it may be rational for the central bank to yield to the government not only before elections, but whenever conflicts arise.[15]

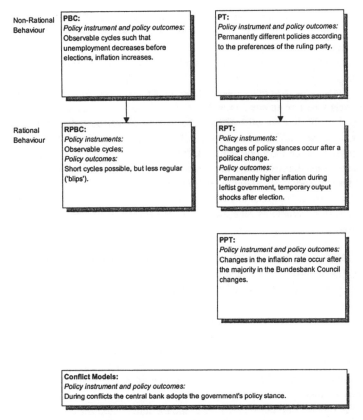

Figure 2.1   Testable implications of the theoretical models

2.2.3   Which model to chose?

Figure 2.1 summarizes the models and their testable implications. Some critical remarks to the models should be added at this stage.

Assumptions   Various authors have questioned the rather crucial assumptions of PT and RPT models: there is evidence that lower-income groups are more sensitive to unemployment levels (see for instance Mueller, 1989), but the question arises whether (supporters of) different parties have indeed different preferences with regard to unemployment and inflation. Smyth and Taylor (1992) failed to find supportive evidence for this hypothesis for the US. The same could apply for Germany, as van Lelyveld (1999) indicates.

Neumann (1993) fundamentally opposes the partisan approach since the basic assumption is not derived from analysing optimal human behavior, but it is merely claimed. Indeed, one of the first articles on systematic political influence on monetary growth rates assumed that '... low interest rates ultimately benefit the upper class, which engages in and benefits most from borrowing and investing large sums of money'.[16] This is quite different from what the PT theory assumes and shows that the theoretical foundations of empirical PT models are of an ad hoc nature.

Technical difficulties   Econometrically, partisan models are difficult to test for Germany, since only few shifts in government occurred. Moreover, the economic crisis that resulted from the oil price shocks in the 70s occurred mostly under the leadership of the Social Democrats. It is difficult to disentangle the inflationary effect or the effects of high interest rates from the economic effects of leftist governments, possibly trying to implement expansionary economic policies.

Conflict models vs. PBC/PT   The main advantage of a conflict model is that it focuses on those periods where the government's and the Bundesbank's policy stance differ, irrespective of electoral deadlines. After all, it is unlikely that every election influences either the government's or the central bank's policy. Assume, for instance, a period before an election during which the government enjoys (for various non-economic reasons) a high degree of popularity. In this case it is not necessary to stimulate the economy in order to win the next election. When such a period is included in the sample, the (R)PBC hypothesis is quite likely to be rejected. Besides, conflicts may arise at *any* time, so focusing on elections almost surely gives an incomplete description of the relationship between the central bank and government. Conflict models can be viewed as an extension of the traditional models, or, put differently, the PBC model is a special case of a conflict model, where conflicts are assumed to occur only during a fixed period before elections.

Definition of conflicts   A nice property of the (R)PBC models is that data on elections is easily available. This cannot be said for the more general conflict models: their outcome will critically depend on how conflicts are defined and measured. Frey and Schneider (1981) define a conflict as a period when fiscal policy is expansive, whereas monetary policy is restrictive. To construct their variable measuring policy conflicts they use the difference between the actual budget deficit and the 'business cycle neutral' budget deficit. If the stance of monetary and fiscal policy differ, they assume a conflict. However, the use of cyclically adjusted deficits as indicator for fiscal policy stance has a number of serious drawbacks, among them serious measurement problems.[17]

     Baum (1983), instead, compares the actual unemployment rate with the 'desired' unemployment rate, as specified in the *Jahreswirtschaftsbericht der Bundesregierung*. This seems correct as far as the desired goal value for government is concerned, but it is uncertain whether this is also the desired goal value of the central bank. Moreover, this measure may fail when unexpected external shocks occur.

On a more fundamental level, the definition of conflicts given by Frey and Schneider is not unproblematic: it may not always be justified to speak of a conflict when different policy stances are observed (see Baum, 1983). One might even imagine a situation where different policy stances do not indicate a conflict, but are a politically desired policy mix.

2.3 MEASURES OF MONETARY POLICY

Before we can proceed presenting previous empirical evidence we have to address the issue of quantifying monetary policy. If we want to estimate the effect of pressure from outside, we must first agree on a measure of what the central bank is actually doing. Monetary policy is pursued by using different instruments at the same time. How can we correctly determine the overall policy stance of a central bank?

Typically, a simple regression analysis to test for influence of external pressure on central bank policies looks like this:

$$Y_t = \alpha_0 + \sum_{i=1}^{T} \alpha_i Y_{t-i} + \sum_{j=1}^{J} \beta_j X_j + \gamma Pressure_t + \varepsilon_t,$$

where X_j denotes policy instruments or additional independent (exogenous) factors, $Pressure_t$ is the political or electoral variable and ε is the error term. While we have seen in the discussion about conflict models that measuring the political variable can be difficult, we now want to turn our attention to Y_t: we must find a way to measure the stance of monetary policy.

Monetary policy has two important components: first, what the central bank tells the public that it does, and second, what it actually does. Both components need not always correspond. Therefore, two things should be examined: the rhetoric of the central banks, and its actions.

Five possibilities exist: policy outcomes, monetary instruments, monetary aggregates, interest rates or monetary policy indices.

a) Policy outcomes
Policy outcomes such as inflation or GDP growth should not be used to test for governmental influence on the Bundesbank. Although monetary policy certainly has a strong impact on these variables, the possibility of long and

variable lags and external influences makes it impossible to attribute changes in, say, the GPD growth rate *only* to the central bank.

Therefore, policy outcomes are not very suitable indicators and variables with a narrower relationship to the central bank's policies are needed to make statements about the central bank's behavior.

b) Monetary instruments

Many studies have used one single monetary instrument of the Bundesbank in their empirical model. At first glance, monetary instruments seem to be the logical way to measure the policy stance: the instruments are fully controlled by the central bank and therefore perfectly indicate what the central bank is doing.

At second glance, however, things are a bit more complex: if we want to use monetary instruments in a regression analysis we have to identify one 'key instrument' which perfectly mirrors Bundesbank policy. This is nearly impossible: the relative weight and importance of monetary instruments changed considerably over time (see Schultes, 1996). Moreover, there were times when different instruments were used in opposite directions, e.g. the discount rate was raised, but at the same time the rediscount quotas were enlarged. This happened for instance on the 28th of June, 1984 following Bundesbank statements that it was a 'merely technical measure' to reduce the spread between the discount rate and market interest rates. Then it is difficult to determine the 'net effect', that is the direction of the monetary impulse.

It therefore comes as no surprise that different authors have come up with different instruments, which are all said to be the best way to effectively measure German monetary policy.

c) Monetary aggregates or targets

As the conduct of monetary policy of the Bundesbank has been directed towards monetary growth targets since 1975, the development of the monetary target seems the obvious choice to measure the bank's policy. However, the Bundesbank has missed its target in nearly 50 per cent of the cases.[18] The fact that targets were missed quite often indicates that German monetary policy also takes other variables into account. This has also been stressed on various occasions by the Bundesbank (see for instance Deutsche Bundesbank, 1995, p. 80 and pp. 88-89). In that respect it is quite interesting that a number of recent studies about German monetary policy conclude that despite the Bundesbank rhetoric about money growth targeting, German monetary policy is best described as an interest rate policy, setting short-term interest rates to minimize deviations from rational expectations equilibrium values of inflation and real growth (see e.g. Clarida and Gertler, 1996 and Bernanke and Mihov, 1997).

There is another drawback to using monetary aggregates: suppose, for in-

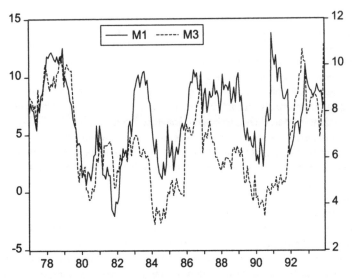

Figure 2.2 Comparison of growth rates of M1 and M3

stance, that fiscal policy turns expansionary before elections. If the monetary authorities would passively accommodate the resulting budget deficits, one could detect an electoral cycle in the growth rate of the money stock (for example, Berger and Woitek (2001) examine monetary policy in Germany and conclude that political business cycles can be found in monetary aggregates, because money demand reacts to upcoming elections, as the Bundesbank 'only' tolerates the cycles). This cycle is, however, not due to deliberate policy actions of the central bank.

If one nevertheless wants to use a monetary aggregate, a choice has to be made of which one to use. Several monetary aggregates have been used in previous studies: M1, M3 and central bank money stock. Vaubel (1997) used M1, arguing that this aggregate is best controlled by the central bank and its changes have the biggest impact on German business cycles. Still, we believe that if monetary aggregates are used to proxy what the Bundesbank is doing, one should stick to what they claim they target: in our opinion the proper monetary aggregate to use is M3 or the central bank money stock.

Figure 2.2 shows that the choice between M1 and M3 may be crucial since they have developed quite differently.[19] The differences between M3 and the central bank money stock are small, as both have largely developed in a parallel way.

d) Short-term interest rates

Next, there is the possibility of using short-term interest rates. They are located somewhere between instruments and aggregates: the use of monetary instruments changes interest rates, which in turn has an impact on monetary aggregates. As all instruments either directly or indirectly influence interest rates they could be viewed as capturing the 'net effect' or the 'sum' of all monetary instruments. Indeed, the Bundesbank also considered the day-to-day rate as 'key indicator' (Deutsche Bundesbank, 1995).[20]

Following Johnson and Siklos (1994), there is a second argument why the choice of an interest rate might be appropriate: if politicians try to influence a central bank before elections, the demand will in most cases not be formulated in terms of a monetary aggregate ('Increase the growth rate of M1'), but in terms of interest rates ('Lower the interest rate'). Eijffinger et al. (1996), in a panel data approach, use the money market rate to estimate a reaction function for ten industrial countries. They find country-specific effects which are interpreted as signs of actual central bank independence.

Goodhart (1994) provides additional support why researchers should focus on interest rates and claims that interest rates are indeed manipulated by politicians:

> ... those in charge of CBs generally regard monetary base control as a non-starter. The instrument which they can, and do, control is the short-term money market rate. Politicians ... suggest that an electorally inconvenient interest rate increase should be deferred, or a cut 'safely' accelerated. This political manipulation of interest rates ... leads to a loss of credibility...[21]

For these reasons we prefer short-term interest rates as measure of what the central bank does over the alternative choices of monetary instruments or aggregates.

e) Monetary policy indices

How we can measure what the central bank tells the public (or wants the public to believe) remains an open question. Here monetary policy indices are useful: they were developed to overcome the impossibility to fully characterize the policy stance with just one single instrument. Constructing such an index, the researcher not only looks at the combined use of all monetary instruments to assess the policy stance, but also takes statements from official central bank bulletins into account. Therefore, these indices try to give a more accurate picture of the overall policy stance than can be derived from just tracking one instrument. Therefore they can be used to measure the rhetoric of a central bank.

These indices exist for Germany, Japan and the US.[22] They assign monetary policy a value and run from 'very restrictive policy' (index value -2) to very expansive (index value +2). Monetary policy indices are explained in more detail in section 4.2.

Figure 2.3 compares the discount rate, an instrument which has frequently been used in previous empirical studies, and the monetary policy index of Dominguez (1997). Differences exist for instance in the early 90s, where the index of Dominguez quickly switches to restrictive policy, whereas the discount rate only gradually increased.

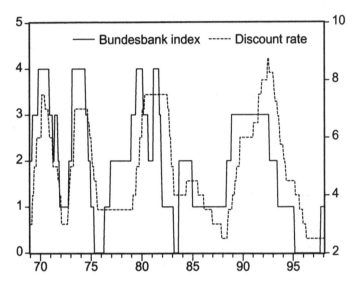

Figure 2.3 Comparison of the discount rate and the monetary policy index for Germany ('Bundesbank index')

Monetary indices may provide additional information, which cannot be derived from just one single instrument. A drawback of these indices, however, is that (a) their distribution are truncated on both sides and (b) it is implicitly assumed that linear relationship exists, that is the change from -2 to -1 is considered being comparable from switching from +1 to +2. This is a drawback that interest rates, for example, do not have, as (a) at least theoretically their distribution are not truncated and (b) interest rates – even if they are hardly used this way – can theoretically vary in infinitively small steps from contractionary to expansive monetary policy. Both points are econometrically important, as most econometric models assume a continuous, non-truncated distribution. This makes the use of monetary policy indices econometrically more difficult. See also section 4.3.

f) Summary: how monetary policy should be measured

To summarize the preceding discussion, we believe that to measure a central bank's monetary policy the following variables should be used:

- The *rhetoric* of a central bank should be measured using a monetary policy index. Today this is the only way to assess what the central bank wants the public to believe what it is doing.

- To measure the *actions* of a central bank, that is to measure the monetary policy that is actually implemented, a short-term interest rate should be used. The day-to-day rate is a good choice, as it captures the central bank's actions and is considered as important indicator.

- Alternatively, if monetary aggregates are used, we believe one should use those aggregates that have served as monetary targets. As in the German case only seasonally adjusted data is available for the central bank money stock, we propose using M3.

2.4   DIRECT POLITICAL INFLUENCE ON THE DEUTSCHE BUNDESBANK

In what follows we critically review existing studies on political influence in the German monetary policy. To gain reliable estimates and at the same time account for country-specific institutions two basic methods have to be distinguished: cross-country approaches and country-specific tests.

Cross-country approaches use data of various countries to test a common hypothesis. This makes results for different countries easily comparable. For some investigations only a cross-country approach can be used, for example, to test for effects of varying institutional settings in different countries. Drawbacks result from the need to gather comparable data for all countries. Moreover, not all countries fit in one mould, as in this 'one model fits all'-approach institutional, country-specific differences are difficult to take into account.

Country-specific tests focus on one country only. National peculiarities, such as choosing the right economic variables or instruments, can be taken into account more easily. Besides, some tests cannot be run as cross-country tests as certain indicators are only available for only one country. However, results of different country-specific tests are less comparable, the more adjustments for national institutions and differences are made.

In the literature both approaches have been used: to test hypotheses of political influence on central banks large samples are used to test electoral effects in different countries. On the other hand, concentrating on country-specific tests enables researchers to use more sophisticated models and to analyse what was really going on in each country.

First, we report results for Germany of studies focusing on various countries; we then continue with studies dealing exclusively with Germany. This distinction is useful as multi-country studies appear to be less reliable since (a) less care has been taken to account for peculiarities of Germany's institutional setting, and (b) internationally applicable economic variables must be used. Data availability and compatibility of indicators tend to limit the evidence of some studies. Unless noted otherwise, 'statistically significant' implies the 5 per cent level of significance.

2.4.1 Cross-country studies

Cowart (1978) examined partisan effects on monetary policy in several European countries, focusing on the discount rate. His formulation of the (then unknown) partisan model differs from the one described in section 2.2, as this author argues that under socialist governments the discount rate would be higher than under conservative governments. Cowart's sample covers the period 1951-75 (quarterly data). Indeed, his results show that under left-wing governments the discount rate is significantly higher than under conservative governments. Moreover, leftist governments tend to respond to changes in unemployment and inflation more dramatically than conservative governments. It is unclear how the author handles the period of the 'grand coalition'. Moreover, Cowart focuses only on one instrument which does not thoroughly characterize monetary policy. Besides, one might question whether the higher discount rates are due to the Social Democratic government, or whether they are due to external influences such as the first oil price shock, undervalued currency and labor shortage, which are not included in the model.[23] Frey and Schneider (1981) re-estimated Cowart's model, concluding that none of the political dummies is significant for the sample period 1957-77.

Soh (1986) looked for PBCs in twenty industrialized countries. He used three indicators to measure economic performance: the growth rate of real income, inflation and unemployment. Economic policy was measured by the growth rate of money supply and the rates of change of government expenditures. This author compared the election year averages to non-election year averages of his indicators and interprets a 'far greater' percentage of election year acceleration as evidence for a PBC. Soh reports evidence for a PBC in German money growth rates and inflation. He used the growth rate of M1, which is not the best indicator for monetary policy, as shown above. Critique came from Neumann and Lohmann (1987) who argued that Soh does not provide any statistical test for his results. All in all, we conclude that Soh's results are not very reliable.

Alesina and Roubini (1990; 1992)[24] covered all democratic OECD countries over the period 1960-87, using output growth, the change in the inflation rate, and the unemployment rate as dependent variables. They tested for PBC, PT and RPT. Their results show that Germany has significant post-electoral upward jumps in the inflation rate indicating PBC; the PT dummy is significant too, indicating that leftist governments have higher inflation rates. However, one has to notice several serious drawbacks of this study. Apart from the misspecification of the political dummy variable outlined in appendix 10.3, these authors focus on one policy outcome (the inflation rate) only and do not cover any monetary aggregate nor any policy instrument.

Alesina et al. (1997) overcome some of the drawbacks of the previous study as they focus on the yearly rate of change of M1. This study concentrates on PBC, but also examines whether governments of different parties have different monetary growth rates at the end of their terms in office. The explanation is that leftist governments try to fight inflation as the election date comes nearer, whereas conservative governments accelerate monetary growth to stimulate economic growth. Both would increase the government's popularity for the medium voter. This hypothesis is another variation of the PT hypothesis, which we call PT*. The estimated coefficient has the correct sign, but is only significant for right-wing governments. Evidence for a PBC in M1 is found at the 10 per cent significance level only. As M1 never was the monetary target and the coefficient for PT* is only significant for conservative governments, we have to conclude that the evidence for Germany is rather weak.

Johnson and Siklos (1994) cover 16 OECD countries (sample period: 1960-90, monthly data). They focus on a market-determined interest rate (the yield on a three-month financial instrument such as a Treasury bill). The electoral dummy is constructed following Alesina and Roubini (1992), which means that it is inaccurate. They find no evidence for PBC in Germany during the Bretton Woods period. The hypothesis that during the post-Bretton Woods area the Bundesbank responds to governmental pressure cannot be rejected. There is no evidence for PT. Unfortunately, these authors do not further specify which German interest rate has been used.

2.4.2 Studies on Germany

We next turn to studies that focus exclusively on Germany. Basler (1978) uses a loss function to assess whether the preferences of the Bundesbank match with those of the federal government, and if not, whether government's preferences influenced the bank's policy. Although this is not exactly a conflict model,

Basler's approach goes in the same direction. The possible goals are the inflation rate, the growth rate, the unemployment rate and the balance of payments. Basler confirms that the Bundesbank mostly concentrated on price stability, but at the beginning of the 1970s the Bundesbank's preferences were biased towards growth. At this time, Germany had a Social Democratic government, which – according to Basler – ranked growth as the second most important goal (after the unemployment rate). Hence, Basler concludes that the Bundesbank preferences were 'not independent' from those of the government, indicating significant governmental influence on the Bundesbank. Two objections have been put forward to this study. Baum (1983) argues that no conclusions can be drawn about the Bundesbank's ranking of the unemployment goal, and the government's preferences were not derived from empirical estimates. Missong and Herrault (1990) note that the central bank's preferences cannot be deducted from reaction functions as long as the central bank's structural model of the economy is unknown.

Frey and Schneider (1981) give empirical evidence for their conflict model. They focus on 'economic conflicts': the Bundesbank's policy is measured by the change in free liquidity reserves, the government's policy by the difference between a 'business cycle neutral' budget and the actual budget volume. If those policies diverge, a conflict between the government and the Bundesbank is assumed. They run regressions for various monetary policy instruments, with the conflict dummy as additional independent variable. They show that for each single instrument the coefficients have the expected sign and are significant, so that the Bundesbank gives in during conflicts and supports the government's policy. Vaubel (1997) argues, however, that the free liquidity reserves might not be a proper monetary policy indicator. Still, Frey and Schneider's selection might be justified by the fact that free liquidity reserves have been used as monetary indicator during the period covered. As pointed out before, the main drawback of this study is the measurement of fiscal policy.

Baum (1983) re-defined a state of conflict as a situation when at the same time the unemployment rate and the inflation rate are higher than desired, thereby avoiding the measurement problems of the 'business cycle neutral' budget. He ran similar regressions as Frey and Schneider, using the discount rate as dependent variable. Baum argues that the conclusion of Frey and Schneider does not hold.

Berger and Schneider (2000) have picked up the Frey/Schneider model again and extended it to a longer sample period (1951-94). The direction of fiscal policy is measured as the change of the federal full employment budget balance in percentage of GDP, the direction of monetary policy is derived from the growth rates of M3. They estimate reaction functions for various Bundesbank instruments, and apply a HP-filter to the conflict dummy to get a continuous series. As additional independent variable besides the conflict dummy they included real growth, the inflation rate and a dummy to capture German monetary unification. The conflict dummy is mostly significant, especially in the models for the day-to-day rate and the discount rate.

Lang and Welzel (1992) look for support for PBC and RPT. They use an electoral dummy that splits the four-year election term in pre-election and post-election and a political dummy specified as in Alesina and Roubini (1992) – which means that it is misspecified.[25] Their results clearly reject the PBC hypothesis. However, the coefficient for testing RPT is significant for M3. Including the federal budget deficit as additional independent variable shows similar results. The authors conclude that there is not only evidence for RPT, but the Bundesbank is also likely to accommodate budget deficits. However, these results can only be interpreted as weak evidence, as the outcomes are sensitive to changes in the monetary aggregate: if the central bank money stock is used the coefficient has the correct sign but is not significant.

Vaubel (1997) uses a rather simple method to test for PT, RPT and PPT: he compares the growth rate of M1 with the political majority in the Bundesbank council. Then he counts the cases in favor of and against the hypothesis and computes the ratio. Comparing this ratio to a standard binominal distribution, Vaubel tests for PT and RPT, which both have to be rejected. Two more hypotheses are tested: (1) If the majority in the Bundesbank council changes in favor of the government, the monetary expansion rate will grow and vice versa. This hypothesis has to be rejected. (2) If the government has the majority in the Bundesbank council at the beginning of the pre-election period, or if the majority changes in favor of the government during the pre-election period, the monetary policy is expansive (PPT). This hypothesis cannot be rejected at the 1 per cent significance level.

However, this study has been subject to severe criticism. Neumann (1993) shows that certain elections should not be included in the sample, which leads to a rejection of the PPT hypothesis. Moreover Vaubel's data set for M1 is only partly seasonally adjusted. Berger and Woitek (1997*a*) employed a regression analysis to examine Vaubel's PPT approach. They used the annual growth rate of M1 and the discount rate as dependent variables, a dummy variable covers the effect of a supportive or reluctant Bundesbank council before the election. They reject Vaubel's PPT hypothesis for M1, the discount rate and the HP-filtered annual growth rates of M1, M2 and M3. In addition, Berger and Woitek followed Vaubel's own test, using seasonally adjusted data instead, which still rejects the PPT hypothesis. Therefore, Vaubel's result in favor of PPT may be mainly due to the fact that his data is not thoroughly seasonally adjusted.[26]

Additionally, Berger and Woitek (1997*a*) and Neumann (1998) provide information from the Bundesbank minutes and show that the voting behavior of the members of the Bundesbank council on discount rate decisions was not consistent with the voting behavior assumed by Vaubel. As the voting behavior does not follow Vaubel's assumptions, the support for the model can only be called very weak. However, the study of Berger and Woitek (1998b) shows that the political composition of the Bundesbank council still might be important: they use generalized impulse response functions to test whether the degree of 'conservatism' of central bankers (as measured by the color of the government that appointed them) has a significant impact on monetary policy. They conclude that the Bundesbank's response to expansionary shocks was significantly stronger when the median voter on the Bundesbank council was conservative.

Berger and Woitek (1997b) use a VAR model; the discount rate is used to proxy the Bundesbank's policy stance. They conclude that the inflation rate goes down (instead of up) before elections, clearly rejecting the PBC hypothesis, and as there is no significant impact of elections on the Bundesbank's discount rate, these authors also reject the RPBC hypothesis. Nevertheless, their results indicate that in the six months before elections, M1 expands on a fairly regular basis and contracts in the twelve months afterwards. The hypothesis of both a partisan effect or the rational partisan cycle in M1 or in the discount rate has to be rejected. Impressive as this study looks, it should be noted that M1 growth has never been the target of the Bundesbank.

Berger and Woitek (2001) considered money demand instead of money supply. They conclude that the Bundesbank follows an interest rate policy rule that sets short-term interest rate to minimize deviation from rational expectations equilibrium values of inflation and real growth.[27] According to their interpretation the Bundesbank just tolerates the enlargement of monetary aggregates before elections. This enlargement is due to the uncertainty of the outcome of the next election.

Lohmann (1998) conducts several regressions, using the growth rate of the central bank money stock (ZBG) as dependent variable and dummy variables to control for the Bretton Woods system and the EMS. In a first regression, a simple election dummy is significant and has the correct sign. However, two federal elections were called earlier; if the election dummy is adjusted accordingly, it becomes insignificant. PT also has to be rejected. Furthermore, Lohmann checks for Vaubel's PPT by creating a 'supportive Bundesbank majority' variable, taking the value 1 if the median voter in the Bundesbank council supports the government, and -1 otherwise.[28] When this dummy is multiplied with the election dummy for PBC the resulting coefficient is insignificant.

Finally, Lohmann assesses the question of whether the degree of independence (which is assumed to be varying with the support of the Federal government in the Bundesrat) affects monetary policy. Assuming partisan behavior, Lohmann takes a linear combination of the election dummy and the dummy variable reflecting central bank support in the Bundesrat.[29] This coefficient is significant. Then, Lohmann multiplies the election dummy with the proportion of Bundesrat members supporting the Federal government. This second variable is also significant and as it outperforms her other findings, Lohmann concludes that the Bundesbank council consists of partially independent technocrats.

Several major reservations have to be made: first, the specification of the Bundesbank's 'independence', i.e. the support that the federal government has in the Bundesrat, looks very much like an ad hoc specification. Lohmann claims that this measure outperformed other possible specifications, such as the popularity of the federal government in opinion polls or a binary dummy for unified party control of Bundestag and Bundesrat. Still, Lohmann's measure has little (if any) theoretical foundation. Second, as the proxy for independence is multiplied with the electoral dummy, this can basically be viewed as another confirmation of the PBC hypotheses for the central bank money stock (see also figure 4.5 in section 4.4.3). Third, Vaubel (2002) notes that Lohmann's Bundesrat support model is 'historically implausible', as during the periods under consideration the government would not have dared to touch the Bundesbank's independence:

> Probably most, if not all, observers of German monetary policy would agree that, in the period under consideration, no German government would have dared to abolish the legal independence of the Bundesbank if the latter had pursued a less expansionary monetary policy at election time... Moreover, even if anybody had doubts on this point, it is highly improbable that such a government could have been hindered by the Bundesrat.[30]

Table 2.1 summarizes all studies reviewed. Studies focusing on various countries are marked with an asterisk.[31]

2.5   INDIRECT INFLUENCE ON THE DEUTSCHE BUNDESBANK

If government uses fiscal policy in line with some version of the political business cycle theory and the central bank accommodates the subsequent increases in the budget deficit, an election cycle may show up in some monetary variables. Indeed, in a study often cited, Alesina (1988) found some evidence of a political business cycle in German fiscal policy. However, others fail to find such evidence; see e.g. Kirchgässner and Pommerehne (1997). To examine this indirect influence of government on monetary policy, various authors have tested whether the budget deficit has a significant impact on central bank behavior.

One important issue here is which deficit indicator should be used: The federal budget, the federal budget plus the sum of the state budgets, or should even

Study	Model	Variables	Result
Basler (1978)	CM	Inflation	Bundesbank's preferences biased during 70s
* Cowart (1978)	PT	Discount rate	Leftist governments have higher discount rates.
Frey and Schneider (1981)	CM	Discount rate	During conflicts Bundesbank yields in to the government
Baum (1983)	CM	Discount rate, Lombard rate	No evidence for Bundesbank adopting government's policy
Berger and Schneider (2000)	CM	Various instruments	During conflicts Bundesbank yields in to the government
* Soh (1986)	PBC	Various outcomes	Money growth and inflation higher in election years
* Alesina and Roubini	PBC, PT	Inflation	Post-electoral upward jump in inflation, inflation higher under leftist governments
* Alesina et al. (1992)	PBC, PT*	M1	PBC in M1, rightist governments have higher M1 growth
Lang and Welzel (1992)	PBC, RPT	M1, M3, ZBG	No evidence for PBC, RPT in M3, but not in M1 or ZBG
Vaubel (1997)	(R)PT PTT	M1	No evidence for PT or RPT, evidence for PPT
Berger and Woitek (1997a)	PPT	M1, Discount rate	Rejection of PPT and its basic assumptions
* Johnson and Siklos (1994)	PBC PT	Interest Rate	PBC after Bretton Woods, PT significant, but wrong sign
Berger (1997a)	PBC, PPT	Discount rate	Rejection of PBC and PPT
Berger and Woitek (1997b)	(R)PBC (R)PT	VAR model	No support for PBC, weak evidence for RPBC
Lohmann (1998)	PBC, PT, PPT CM	Central bank money stock	Bundesbank only partially independent, influence of the Bundesrat significant

Table 2.1   Direct influence on the Deutsche Bundesbank

the social security funds be included? Except for Lang and Welzel (1992), all empirical studies we are aware of have used IMF data, which refer to consolidated central government (that is, operations of budgetary central government, extra budgetary units, and social security funds).

Demopoulos et al. (1987) have estimated two sets of reaction functions, one for the fixed exchange rates period and one for the period with flexible exchange rates. The money base, divided by the trend value of the national income, is used as dependent variable. In the regressions for both periods, the coefficient for the budget deficit is greater than one and significant at the 10 per cent level. This would mean that government deficits are accommodated by the Bundesbank. However, the monetary base is not the best choice for a monetary aggregate. Moreover, this method requires the estimation of the trend value for real income, leading to measurement problems.

Giannaros and Kolluri (1985) estimate various reaction functions for the monetary authorities on the basis of annual time series from 1950 to 1981. The results reveal no significant influence of fiscal policy on the growth rate of M1 for Germany. However, as mentioned above, M1 has never been the official target of the Bundesbank. Still, this finding is important, since various studies summarized in the previous section found some evidence in favor of an electoral cycle in the growth rate of M1. So the results of Giannaros and Kolluri suggest that this result is not due to the accommodation of electorally driven budget deficits.

Burdekin (1987) conducts analyses for Canada, France, Germany and the UK, using quarterly data covering the period of 1961-83 and employing the monetary base as dependent variable. He uses a rather complicated method of multiplying the deficit with other variables and shows that the multiplicative terms (multiplication of the deficit and some other explanatory variable) are significant. He finds a significant impact on the monetary base, but if, for example, the variable (*governmental deficit * balance of payments*) is significant this may also result from the fact that the balance of payments itself is highly significant, for which other studies have indeed found evidence. Therefore, it may be doubted whether the government deficit itself is of major influence.

Missong and Herrault (1990) ran regressions for Germany and France. Their sample covers the period of 1974-87 (quarterly data). As dependent variable they choose the money market interest rate. The estimated value for the budget deficit coefficient for the large sample (1974-87) is significant, but it has a negative sign, which would indicate that if the budget deficit increases, the interest rate drops. Missong and Herrault's explanation, according to which inflationary pressures from an increase in the budget deficit are less feared by the Bundesbank than the crowding-out effect, is not really convincing. For the shorter period 1980-87 the budget deficit coefficient is not significant.

Lang and Welzel (1992) estimate a money supply function for the Bundes-

Study	Variables	Result
Demopoulos et al. (1987)	Monetary base	Accommodation of budget deficits
Giannaros and Kolluri (1985)	M1	No significant impact
Burdekin (1987)	Monetary base	Weak evidence for accommodation.
Missong and Herrault (1990)	Interest rate	If budget deficit raises interest rate drops
Lang and Welzel (1992)	M1, M3, ZBG	Significant impact of budget deficit

Table 2.2   Indirect influence on the Deutsche Bundesbank

bank for the monetary aggregates M1, M3 and the central bank money stock in the years 1962-89. The coefficient for the budget deficit has the correct sign for all monetary aggregates and budget deficit measures. The inflation rate has the strongest impact on the monetary growth rate, followed by the budget deficit. The GDP growth rate has the least influence.

Finally, table 2.2 summarizes the preceding evidence on direct influence.

2.6   INTERPRETATION OF THE EMPIRICAL STUDIES

In the preceding sections we have reviewed empirical evidence on political influence on monetary policy of the Bundesbank. We have seen that political influence may be due to electoral or partisan effects or due to conflicts between governments and central banks.

We have shown that monetary policy should be measured in two ways: the rhetoric is captured in a monetary policy index, the actual Bundesbank policy should be examined using a short-term interest rate (i.e. the day-to-day rate). While the first part has not been examined in the empirical literature so far, economists have tested the actual policy by employing monetary aggregates and instruments. Both are probably not the best available indicators for the monetary policy stance.

The evidence as presented is far from being convincing (see table 2.3): studies that used single monetary instruments tend to reject an impact of elections or partisan behavior. However, they are difficult to judge, as the required 'key instrument' does not exist. Therefore, we can say that the only part of monetary policy that has been examined carefully is that of monetary aggregates.

So what can be said about political influence in monetary aggregates? We conclude that studies that include more countries than just Germany do not

Impact of political pressure on monetary policy	Results of previous studies
Impact on monetary aggregates	Mixed evidence: Possible electoral cycles in M1 Little evidence for cycles in M3
Impact on monetary instruments	Mixed evidence: Political pressure likely ('Lower interest rates!') Measurement problems as the monetary 'key instrument' does not exist Evidence for certain instruments (notably discount rate) is rather unclear
Impact on short-term interest rate	No reliable study available
Impact on Bundesbank's rhetoric	No study available
Indirect influence: Accommodation of fiscal deficits	Very weak evidence.

Table 2.3   Summary: Impact of political pressure on the Deutsche Bundesbank

yield solid evidence that the Bundesbank was very much under the spell of government. Although some studies find indications for this view, most of these studies do not take German institutional and policy features correctly into account. Glancing at the results of the studies focusing exclusively on Germany, one might conclude that the Bundesbank is under constant pressure and often yields to politicians, not only being partisan, but also actively creating political business cycles. However, a closer look reveals that in several cases, those studies that indicate political influence on the Bundesbank have not used the optimal choice for monetary indicators, that the data set is not properly transformed or that the political dummy is wrongly specified.

More specifically, the results for the PBC and RPBC are not very convincing, as monetary policy has not properly been measured. Support for the PPT has only come from Vaubel (1997) so far, and his study is not very reliable. Favorable results for (R)PT may suffer from the wrongly specified political dummy. Berger and Woitek (1997b) showed that the evidence for (R)PT is not robust, ultimately leading to rejection of the two partisan hypotheses.

Thus, only one type of models remains, the conflict model. This model is not only preferable as its underlying assumptions seem more realistic than those of the other models, but we also have to conclude that there exists some evidence pointing out that the Bundesbank might – under pressure – yield to the federal government. Still, it is also clear that much can be improved upon in this line of research.

With respect to studies on the impact of fiscal policy on monetary policy, one has to notice that except for Lang and Welzel (1992), generally wrong monetary aggregates have been used. Lang and Welzel show that there is only very weak evidence for accommodation of budgetary deficits by the Bundesbank. All in all, we conclude that the view that budget deficits are accommodated by the Bundesbank is not well supported by the data.

Based on our assessment of monetary policy, there are several directions deserving further research worth pursuing, before we start to augment or change the models: (a) we must find better ways to measure what the central bank actually does and (b) we must improve the indicators for political pressure.

(a) With respect to indicators for monetary policy, two possibilities seem worth investigating: First, the use of short-term interest rates, second, to examine the central bank's rhetoric, using the monetary policy index approach of Dominguez (1997). So far, both have not been used to test for political influences on German monetary policy. This line of research is followed in the chapters 3 and 4.

(b) With respect to indicators for a conflict between the government and the central bank, the methodology of Havrilesky (1993) seems promising: his approach is based on the idea that conflicts between important policy makers can be traced back by using reports on pressure on the central bank. Based on information from the

(c) Wall Street Journal Havrilesky constructed a conflict index, which turned out to have a highly significant impact on the US Federal Funds rate. This construction of a conflict indicator is all the more interesting, as it can be extended to allow for pressure not only from the government, but also from organized groups such as trade unions. We pursue this direction in chapter 5.

As we have seen testing the original version of the partisan theory for Germany is not very useful, as not enough political shifts have occurred for a meaningful interpretation of the results. In what follows we have therefore decided to largely skip the partisan theory.

3. Political Pressure in OECD Countries Before Elections

3.1 OVERVIEW

In this chapter we use short-term interest rates as indicator for monetary policy. This allows us to check whether central banks are influenced by electoral deadlines. This question is examined in a cross-country setting to make results from different countries comparable.

Surprisingly, the empirical literature has little to say about the exact role of governments and central banks when it comes to PBCs. Worse, in most previous studies important institutional features have largely been neglected: in many economies the scope for electorally motivated monetary policies is reduced, since national or international restrictions bind central bankers. In a regime of fixed exchange rates, for example, opportunistic policies are less likely to occur than in a flexible exchange rate system. Similarly, independent central banks are less likely to be involved in electorally motivated policies than central banks that are under the spell of the government. The restricting effects of these institutional features are recognized in economic theory, yet many empirical papers on political business cycles do not explicitly control for them.

Indeed, Clark et al. (1998) argue that common cross-country studies of PBC models may be seriously flawed since they do not account for institutional differences that constrain national policymakers (Clark and Hallerberg, 2000, formulate this idea in terms of a theoretical model). However, these authors only examine economic outcomes (output growth and unemployment). Although these variables are likely to be influenced by monetary policy, there are a number of other influences that may offset or reinforce the impact of monetary policy. Furthermore, the rational political business cycle predicts that policymakers manipulate instruments, while the effects on outcomes are less certain. We want to focus on policy outcomes for which the central bank can be held responsible, namely the short-term interest rate. Thereby we also wish to answer the question of whether the central bank can be blamed for active opportunistic behavior. Our sample runs from the 1960s until 1997 and consists of monthly data for 14 OECD countries. The results are simple and strikingly robust. The short-term interest rate shows hardly any sign of a political business cycle, thus we reject the hypothesis that central banks actively engage in opportunistic behavior.

The outline of this chapter is as follows. In the next section, we explain our choice for the new monetary policy indicator in more detail and show why internal or external constraints can prevent politicians from using monetary policy for short-sighted purposes. Our estimation results are presented in section 3.3. In section 3.4 we summarize our findings.

3.2   WHEN DO POLITICAL BUSINESS CYCLES OCCUR?

A test for the existence of political business cycles requires the following: first, we need a theoretical basis to explain why such short-sighted behavior should be pursued by the government or the central bank. This basis has been provided in section 2.2. Second, one has to account for restricting institutional features that limit the possibility to implement such a policy. And finally, we need an appropriate measure for the central bank's policy stance.

3.2.1   Restricting institutional features

The PBC model as we have presented it in section 2.2 makes the simplifying assumptions that (a) the central bank and the government pursue similar policies, and (b) policymakers have sufficient national autonomy to implement their policies. Especially in a cross-country study these assumptions need not hold.

The following two types of constraints may prevent governments from implementing an opportunistic policy:

National constraint If we assume that the central bank enjoys a low degree of statutory independence, then it is likely that pressure is applied in such a way that monetary policy follows the opportunistic pattern set by fiscal policy. In this case, electoral cycles may be observed in monetary instruments. However, central banks are increasingly made independent. If we abstract from the idea that central banks have their own interests, due to which they prefer one government to another, then one should not expect them to engage in opportunistic behavior. After all, one of the main arguments for making them independent is that this enables their optimization to be based on a longer time-horizon, which rules out short-sighted behavior. Still, even for central banks with a high degree of statutory independence it might be rational to comply with the government's wishes, as its independence might

Austria	Belgium	Canada	Denmark	Finland
+	-	+	+	-
France	Germany	Italy	Japan	Norway
-	+	-	-	-
Spain	Sweden	UK	US	
-	-	(-)	+	

Table 3.1   National constraints

be threatened by a change in the central bank law. If this is realized by the central bank, then independent as well as dependent central banks have an incentive to engage in PBC behavior.[32]

International constraint From economic theory we know that under a regime of fixed exchange rates and high capital mobility, the scope for autonomous monetary policies is reduced. Since the worldwide increase in capital mobility in the 1970s we can thus assume that the possibility to implement a national monetary policy has declined for those countries that have either been member of a fixed exchange rate regime (such as the Bretton Woods system or the European Monetary System), or that have pegged their currency unilaterally. Participation in a fixed exchange rate regime, however, restricts national economic policies and lowers the possibility of PBCs.

a)   National constraints

To account for internal constraints, we first need to classify the degree of statutory central bank independence (CBI) in the various countries. Usually this is done by setting up criteria to measure the degree of independence and assigning scores to the various countries. Both require subjective judgment and it comes as no surprise that different authors have come up with different rankings (Eijffinger and de Haan, 1996). Forder (1999) argues that ... 'the difficulties in measuring independence have not been sufficiently overcome to allow persuasive or meaningful tests...'.[33] Here, we use the index developed by Cukierman et al. (CWN, 1992).[34] We divide the countries into two groups, those having scores above the median which we consider as 'independent central banks' and those with scores below the median ('dependent central banks'). This classification is reported in table 3.1. Countries ranked above the median value are marked with '+' (i.e., internal constraints are present) and countries ranked below the median value with '-' (i.e. absence of internal constraints).

We expect this classification to give a reliable overall ranking of the degree of statutory independence: in the '+' countries PBCs are not likely to occur in monetary policy, as these countries have an independent central bank. Countries with a '-' have a central bank with a low degree of statutory independence and if PBCs are to be found, we expect them there.

Country	Snake	EMS	Pegged
Austria	-	1995:01-97:12	1973:04-94:12
Belgium	1973:04-78:12	1979:01-97:12	-
Canada	-	-	-
Denmark	1973:04-78:12	1979:01-97:12	-
Finland	-	1996:01-97:12	1977:01-95:12
France	Intermittent	1979:01-97:12	-
Germany	1973:04-78:12	1979:01-97:12	-
Italy	-	1979:01-92:08	-
Japan	-	-	-
Norway	1973:04-78:12	-	1979:01-97:12
Spain	-	1989:01-97:12	-
Sweden	1973:04-76:12	-	1977:01-97:12
UK	-	1990:10-92:08	-
US	-	-	-

Table 3.2   Participation in Fixed Exchange Rate Systems

b) International constraints

To classify for each country in our sample those periods, where it could determine its monetary policy in an entirely autonomous way, we check its participation in fixed exchange rate regimes.

From an economist's view, the 1970s marked a turning point in at least two respects: since the 1970s international capital mobility increased sharply, and the Bretton Woods system of fixed exchange rates collapsed in 1973. Clark et al. (1998) have assumed that during the Bretton Woods period capital mobility was low, so this fixed exchange rate system did not pose a constraint on monetary policy. While we generally follow the methodology of Clark et al. in deriving the institutional constraints we believe that capital mobility was sufficiently high before 1973 to effectively constraint monetary policy. Therefore, we count the Bretton Woods system as a constraint for all countries but the US, that dominated the system.

Table 3.2 shows when countries were part of a fixed exchange rate system (source: Clark et al., 1998). The first and the second column show the participation in the Snake (the predecessor of the European Monetary System) and in the European Monetary System (EMS), respectively. Note that Italy and the UK left the EMS after the turmoil in 1992. In the third column we show when countries pegged their currencies.

As Germany has been the anchor currency in the EMS we do not count the EMS as a binding restraint for German monetary policy (see also Lohmann, 1998). We also do not consider the snake to be a binding constraint for France as its participation has been highly unstable.[35]

Country	Fixed Exchange Rates ($FEX = 1$)	No international constraint ($FEX = 0$)
Austria	1960:01-97:12	-
Belgium	1960:01-97:12	-
Canada	1960:01-73:03	1973:04-97:12
Denmark	1960:01-97:12	-
Finland	1960:01-73:03, 1977:01-97:12	1973:04-76:12
France	1960:01-73:03, 1979:01-97:12	1973:04-78:12
Germany	1960:01-78:12	1979:01-97:12
Italy	1960:01-73:03, 1979:01-92:08	1973:04-78:12, 1992:09-97:12
Japan	1960:01-73:03	1973:04-97:12
Norway	1960:01-97:12	-
Spain	1960:01-73:03, 1989:01-97:12	1973:04-88:12
Sweden	1960:01-97:12	-
UK	1960:01-73:03, 1990:10-92:08	1973:04-90:09, 1992:09-97:12
US	-	1960:01-97:12

Table 3.3   International constraints

	Fixed Exchange Rates		
CBI	*No autonomy*	*For part of period*	*Full autonomy*
Above Median	Austria, Denmark	Canada, Germany, UK (1960-71)	US
Below Median	Belgium, Norway, Sweden	Finland, France, Italy, Japan, Spain, UK (1972-98)	-

Table 3.4   Summary: National and international constraints

In table 3.3 we have defined the dummy FEX: the first column shows those periods where the countries maintained fixed exchange rates, that is monetary policy autonomy was absent ($FEX = 1$). The second columns shows when an autonomous monetary policy could have been pursued ($FEX = 0$).

c)   What to expect in a regression analysis

Summarizing the above, table 3.4 shows for each country the combination of both constraints. Note that only the US experienced monetary policy autonomy for the entire period (the right column of table 3.4); this, however, does not pose a problem as we find a lot of variation in the left part of the table. This should give us reliable estimates for the influence of fixed exchange rate systems.

3.2.2 Possible interest rate patterns before elections

As we have explained in section 2.3 we think the proper way to measure monetary policy is by employing short-term interest rates, the main argument being that short-term interest rates capture the 'net effect' of the use of all monetary instruments. What interest rate pattern can be expected before elections?

Assume a standard IS/LM model. Three possibilities arise: first, only expansionary monetary policy is used and the LM-curve shifts to the right. Then we would expect that the interest rate goes down before elections and (correctly) indicates that the central bank caused the PBC. Second, if only expansionary fiscal policy is used, the IS-curve shifts to the right and we would expect an increase in the interest rate before elections. Both cases can easily be interpreted. The third case is more difficult: imagine a situation where monetary policy accommodates expansionary fiscal policy. Both curves shift to the right. If accommodation is perfect, then the interest rate could remain unchanged. A similar pattern could be observed if both the government and the central bank try to create a PBC in such a way that the combination of both effects on the interest rate 'cancels out', or if the central bank followed an interest rate rule (vertical LM-curve). In these cases we have an identification problem.

These considerations show that the use of interest rates is not without caveats. In practice, however, these problems are less serious: the evidence presented in section 2.5 indicates that the third case is highly unlikely. To show up in a pooled regression it would require a PBC in fiscal policy in *all* countries in our sample. Such a cycle has for most countries been rejected by Alesina et al. (1997) in a more recent study Andrikopoulos et al. (2002) show that there is no empirical evidence for political business cycles in fiscal policy for EU member states. An alternative would be that all central banks in our sample follow an interest rate rule. Again, such a behavior is highly unlikely, so that we have the following expectations: if interest rates remain unchanged (or go up) prior to elections central banks refrain from opportunistic manipulation. Only if the interest rate decreases before election we conclude that central banks actively create political business cycles.

We use short-term interest rates which are tightly controlled by the central banks and reflect their intentions. Should political business cycles exist and should they be actively created by central banks, they should be visible in these interest rates.

In a regression analysis, we would therefore not expect to find PBCs in countries that are constrained in either way. Clark et al. (1998) have shown this hypothesis to hold for policy outcomes, such as inflation or unemployment rates. However, this test cannot reveal the precise role of central banks, since these policy outcomes are influenced by many additional factors (e.g. supply and demand shocks). To get comparable figures, we use monthly IFS data on the short-term interest rate for 14 OECD countries. The sample period starts for most countries in the 1960s and goes until 1997. Further details on the data can be found in appendix C.1.

3.3 EMPIRICAL EVIDENCE

3.3.1 Country-specific results

For all country-specific tests, the models include lagged dependent variables, the order of which is determined by examining the (partial) autocorrelation function. With respect to the stationarity of the interest rate, we adopt the approach of Bierens (1997) and take the short-term interest rates to be nonlinear trend stationary processes. To see whether the inclusion of lagged disturbances is necessary, we perform a Breusch-Godfrey serial correlation LM test and find no evidence of serial correlation. We use the White test to check for heteroskedasticity. When necessary, a heteroskedasticity-consistent covariance matrix is used to calculate standard errors. The model coefficients are estimated using OLS techniques.[36]

The country-specific tests we apply seek to examine whether a significant degree of covariation exists between elections and the short-term interest rate if we control for institutional restrictions. We start with a general model description incorporating changes in the internal and external constraint. Following Alesina et al. (1997), we start with the following model specification:

$$
\begin{aligned}
r_{it} = & \ \beta_{0i} + \beta_1 E_{it} + \beta_2 FEX_{it} + \beta_3 E_{it} * FEX_{it} \\
& + \sum_j \beta_{j+3} r_{i,t-j} + \delta_1 IP_{it} + \delta_2 \pi_{it} + \delta_3 OC_t + \varepsilon_{it},
\end{aligned}
\tag{3.1}
$$

where r_{it} is the log of the nominal short-term interest rate.[37] E_{it} is the election dummy, defined as $+1$ in the month containing a general election and the eleven preceding months, and 0 otherwise. FEX_{it} is the coefficient for participation in fixed exchange rate systems as defined in table 3.3. The variable $E_{it} * FEX_{it}$ is included as interaction term, equaling $+1$ during electoral periods in countries lacking monetary policy autonomy. Finally, as additional economic variables we have added industrial production IP_{it} as proxy for GDP growth, the inflation rate π_{it} and a dummy covering the impact of the oil crisis (OC_t). Further details on the variables can be found in the appendix.

The interpretation of equation 3.1 is as follows: if a country does not participate in a fixed exchange rate regime and determines its monetary policy

Country	E_{it}	FEX_{it}	$E_{it}*FEX_{it}$	IP_{it}	π_{it}	j
Austria	−0.319***	−	−	0.182	0.496	3
Belgium	0.004	−	−	0.182	0.500	2
Canada	0.005	−	−	−0.023	0.370	2
Denmark	0.025	−	−	0.878*	2.382**	4
Finland	−0.004	0.003	0.014	−0.151	0.786***	3
France	0.000	0.009	0.008	−0.020	0.606**	2
Germany	0.001	−0.046**	−0.008	−0.428	2.310*	3
Italy	0.016	0.022**	−0.028*	0.003	0.267*	2
Japan	0.025***	0.016	−0.028**	0.552**	0.142	4
Norway	−0.024	−	−	0.279	0.813	2
Spain	0.054	−0.037	−0.001	0.142	0.289	6
Sweden	0.012	−	−	0.080	0.628*	3
US	−0.006	−	−	2.479***	0.698**	4

Table 3.5   Country-specific tests

autonomously, then $FEX_{it} = 0$. In this case the model is reduced to a standard PBC model:

$$r_{it} = \beta_{0i} + \beta_1 E_{it} + \sum_j \beta_{j+1} r_{i,t-j} + \delta_1 IP_{it} + \delta_2 \pi_{it} + \delta_3 OC_t + \varepsilon_{it}. \quad (3.2)$$

If, however, $FEX_{it} = 1$ and an international constraint is present, then the sum $E_{it} + E_{it}FEX_{it}$ becomes important: if our argument is correct that the absence of monetary policy autonomy decreases the probability that politicians will manipulate the macroeconomy for electoral purposes, we should expect this sum not to be significantly different from zero. This is checked performing a Wald test to test for $\beta_1 + \beta_3 = 0$. Note, however, that this only makes sense if the election coefficient E_{it} is significantly different from zero, otherwise political business cycles cannot be found in our sample.

Our results are strikingly simple:[38]: table 3.5 shows that for most countries we cannot find any evidence of an electoral cycle (the significance of the estimates is marked with the superindex ***/**/* if $p < 0.01/0.05/0.1$). In the last row of table 3.5 j we show the number of lags. We observe that the coefficients for inflation and industrial production are not significant in a number of cases. The FEX_{it} coefficients are only significant for Germany and Italy which means that interest rates are not significantly higher or lower under a fixed exchange rate regime for all other countries. The FEX_{it} coefficients are significant for Germany and Italy: the negative coefficient for Germany is probably due to the reunification, the positive coefficient for Italy shows that leaving the EMS after the turmoil in 1992 led to lower interest rates.

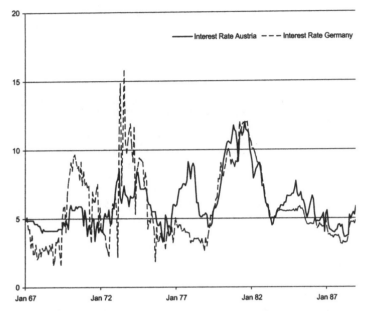

Figure 3.1   Comparison of short-term interest rates in Austria and Germany

The PBC coefficient is insignificant for most countries, which indicates that PBCs are not visible in the short-term interest rate in most OECD countries. Note, however, two exceptions: Austria and Japan.

Austria yields a negative, highly significant coefficient, which means that the interest rate decreases before elections. This would mean that Austria, despite its relatively independent central bank, experiences a PBC. This is rather puzzling, as officially Austria has closely been following the German interest rate policy since the late 1970s (see also figure 3.1). Only very little differences between the Austrian and the German interest rate existed, which we consider to be too small to be used for systematic opportunistic monetary policy (Hochreiter and Winckler, 1995, provide details about Austrian exchange rate policy). An explanation could be that the significant coefficient is more a statistical coincidence than clear opportunistic evidence.

This idea can quite easily be verified: if we find a PBC in Austria even when we use the German short-term interest rate as dependent variable, this would mean that the German central bank creates it, that is the German Bundesbank systematically misuses its monetary policy to influence Austrian election outcomes. This seems, at the very least, highly unlikely. And indeed, as can be seen in the upper part table 3.6, the election coefficient for Austria is no longer significant if we use the German interest rate as dependent variable. It therefore

(a) Results for Austria, using a German interest rate			
Country	E_{it}	IP_{it}	π_{it}
Austria	-0.011	0.068	0.160

(b) Wald-test for Japan:	
$E_{it} + E_{it} * FEX_{it}$:	-0.003
F-statistic:	0.051

(c) Results for Japan with a 18 month pre-election dummy:					
Country	E_{it}	FEX_{it}	$E_{it} * FEX_{it}$	IP_{it}	π_{it}
Japan	0.008	0.016	-0.018	0.571***	0.124

Table 3.6   Additional results for Austria and Japan

seems that indeed there were differences between the German and the Austrian interest rate, and that they were big enough to allow for opportunistic policies. This result could be explained by the fact that Austria is a very corporatistic country, which could result in a relatively close cooperation between the (on the surface relatively independent) central bank and the government. Following this reasoning a PBC in Austria does not necessarily come as a surprise, but rather shows the weakness of common CBI indicators. Yet, to some extent the results for Austria remain a puzzle.

Japan deserves a closer look as both the election coefficient and the FEX-election interaction term are significant. Do we have a binding constraint here in the sense that the Bretton Woods system prevented electoral cycles in Japan's monetary policy? This would be the case if the sum of the two coefficients E_{it} and $E_{it} * FEX_{it}$ was zero. To test this we use a Wald-test. The results in the second part of table 3.6 show that the constraint is binding and that the Bretton Woods system indeed was a restriction. This, however, does not mean that the Bank of Japan used monetary policy in an opportunistic sense: first, note that the sign of the election coefficient is positive, which indicates that before elections the short-term interest rate was higher instead of lower (contrary to what the PBC model predicts). Thus the Bank of Japan rather used monetary brakes before elections instead of stimulating the economy. Second, the coefficient is not robust. In fact only for a pre-election period of 12 months (as we have assumed in table 3.5) the coefficient is significant. A pre-election dummy covering a 18 months periods is insignificant, as table 3.6 (c) shows.[39]

Finally we take a look at the country-specific results for the UK. They are of particular interest as of the fourteen countries in our sample the UK is the only one whose score of CBI changed over time: Great Britain experienced a change in central bank independence sufficiently large for the CWN index to place it below the median for one part of the period and above the median for the other part. In 1971 the Bank of England became less independent, which means that our CBI dummy for Great Britain is 0 from 1971 to 1997. This is

UK	Coefficient
E_{it}	−0.043
FEX_{it}	0.011
$E_{it} * FEX_{it}$	0.056
CBI_{it}	−0.034
$E_{it} * CBI_{it}$	−0.017
IP_{it}	0.959
π_{it}	−0.974**

Table 3.7   Results for the UK

captured in our second country-specific regression:

$$r_{it} = \beta_0 + \beta_1 E_{it} + \beta_2 FEX_{it} + \beta_3 E_{it} * FEX_{it} + \beta_4 CBI_{it} + \beta_5 E_{it} CBI_{it}$$
$$+ \sum_j \beta_{j+5} r_{i,t-j} + \delta_1 IP_{it} + \delta_2 \pi_{it} + \delta_3 OC_t + \varepsilon_{it}. \tag{3.3}$$

The CBI_{it} coefficient is +1 during the time that the level of central bank independence in the UK is above-median, and 0 otherwise. Again we have added an interaction term for elections and CBI, as we did for FEX and elections before. For the period that the Bank of England enjoyed a low degree of CBI the model reduces to equation 3.1.

The results are presented in table 3.7. None of the reported coefficients is significant.[40] This indicates that the Bank of England was not involved in PBCs. The results are in line with the literature: similar findings for the UK are reported in the study by Clark et al. (1998).

Robustness Checks   A series of robustness checks can be done. First, we have replaced the economic variables by the real interest rate (proxied by subtracting inflation from the nominal interest rate). This did not qualitatively change our results. Second, we have experimented with different lag lengths. Economic theory can give no clear recommendation how long we should expect the pre-election period to be. In the literature, lags with the lengths of 12, 18 and 24 months are commonly used. We found that in most cases our results do not depend on the length of the pre-election lag.

To summarize, the country-specific tests show little evidence of a political business cycle in monetary policy for the countries in our sample.

Variable	Coefficient	S.E.
E_{it}	0.021	0.015
FEX_{it}	0.019***	0.007
CBI_{it}	0.033	0.022
$E_{it} * FEX_{it}$	−0.020	0.016
$E_{it} * CBI_{it}$	−0.024	0.016
$FEX_{it} * CBI_{it}$	−0.037*	0.019
$E_{it} * FEX_{it} * CBI_{it}$	0.017	0.022
OC_t	0.007	0.010
IP_{it}	0.113**	0.057
π_{it}	0.411***	0.155

Table 3.8　Results for the panel regression

3.3.2　Panel data estimation

By pooling the data, we can examine the effects of cross-national differences in the internal and external constraint. We use an autoregressive panel data model with fixed effects,[41] in which the relevant parameters are estimated using the Least Squares Dummy Variable (LSDV) estimator. This is the standard estimator in a panel with fixed effects. In Judson and Owen (1999) is shown that for an unbalanced panel with a very large time dimension, the LSDV estimator is recommended. Our total number of unbalanced observations is 5105. As before, White heteroskedasticity-consistent standard errors are computed. The lag length used in this model is $j = 4$. Only estimates of the relevant dummy variables are reported in the tables.

The constraint on PBC behavior for the pooled sample can be modeled as follows:

$$
\begin{aligned}
r_{it} = & \ \beta_1 + \beta_2 E_{it} + \beta_3 FEX_{it} + \beta_4 CBI_{it} \\
& + \beta_5 E_{it} FEX_{it} + \beta_7 E_{it} CBI_{it} + \beta_8 FEX_{it} CBI_{it} + \beta_9 E_{it} CBI_{it} FEX_{it} \\
& + \sum_j \beta_{j+9} r_{i,t-j} + \delta_1 IP_{it} + \delta_2 \pi_{it} + \delta_3 OC_t + \varepsilon_{it}.
\end{aligned} \tag{3.4}
$$

In this model we have thus included all possible combinations of central bank independence, fixed exchange rates and elections. The results for this model are reported in table 3.8.

As in our previous regressions, the estimated coefficient for elections remains insignificant. This confirms our findings of the country-specific model: as before, we cannot detect any pattern compatible with the PBC model. The influence of the exchange rate systems is quite strong: the FEX_{it} is significant at the 1 per cent level; its positive sign shows that countries abandoning their monetary policy autonomy by participating in a fixed exchange rate regime have a tendency for higher interest rates.

To summarize, these panel regressions confirm our previous findings. The main result is that the E_{it} dummy remains insignificant, which implies that elections do not influence the short-term interest rate. As we do not find any evidence for an electoral pattern, neither the degree of central bank independence, nor participation in fixed exchange rates influences our findings. Given these results, we have to reject the whole PBC theory, as far as central banks are concerned. We do not find evidence that central banks actively engage in short-sighted behavior before elections. Indeed, we have to conclude that if cycles occur in monetary aggregates (as has been reported in previous studies), they are probably fiscally induced, but central banks should not be held responsible for them. The results are not sufficiently significant to conclude that national or international constraints effectively reduce the scope for electoral manipulations. Our estimation results suggest that central banks are quite unimpressed by upcoming elections and do not engage in political business cycles at all.

3.4 SUMMARY

Making central banks independent is often justified by the fear that monetary policy might give in to opportunistic behavior:

> The major argument for FED independence is that monetary policy is politically neutral and technical. If the FED is caught with its hand in the electoral cookie jar, then it can hardly claim to be apolitical in any sense of that word.[42]

Using a short-term interest rate we have tested whether central banks in OECD countries indeed create political business cycles – and whether the degree of CBI is crucial to prevent that.

We derived two pieces of evidence. First, our results for the country-specific tests, based on the short-term interest rate for 14 OECD countries, are encouraging with respect to central banks. Overall, we find hardly any support for the PBC hypothesis. Two possible explanations arise. First, we could simply conclude that central banks do not manipulate interest rates before elections. This suggests that either governments do not have possibilities to influence central banks, or central banks have effectively resisted government's wishes. Our results do not suggest that the degree of statutory central bank independence matters in this respect. Second, our results could be due to the fact that the short-term interest rate is not as tightly controlled by the central banks as we have assumed. If financial markets have a strong impact on the short-term interest rate, under rational expectations manipulations are useless. This, however, would have the following implication: if (as the theory suggests) central banks use interest rate to manipulate monetary growth (and finally the inflation rate), and if their actions before elections have no effect on the short-term interest rate, then PBCs – if they exist in macroeconomic data, such as GNP growth or unemployment – cannot be due to central bank action, as their actions have no effect.

The second piece of evidence stems from our panel data regressions. We get more or less the same picture, that is, no evidence for central banks actively creating political business cycles.

Overall, the implications are clear. If political business cycles in macroeconomic variables such as unemployment show up, then the central banks should not be blamed. Either their actions have no effect, or they simply do not engage in short-sighted behavior.

4.   The Rhetoric of Central Banks

4.1   OVERVIEW

In this chapter we examine public rhetoric of central banks, testing various hypotheses about political pressure. Some models require a deeper knowledge of the institutional setting than could be applied in the multi-country study of the last chapter. Therefore, a large part of the chapter focuses on the German case. Moreover, we differentiate between what the central bank tells the public it does, and what it actually does, by presenting a possibility to measure central bank rhetoric. Where possible, we extend this type of research to the Bank of Japan and the Federal Reserve of the United States.

While we can reject the impact of conflicts with the government on the Bundesbank's policy, we find a significant impact of elections on the announced Bundesbank policy. Our conclusion is that the Bundesbank rhetoric seems to respond to pressure, although the aim is merely to calm down politicians before elections. The German central bank does not change the policy stance substantially enough to allow political interference to have an impact on the day-to-day rate. The results for Japan and for the US show no difference between the central banks' rhetoric and their effectively implemented monetary policies.

This chapter is organized as follows: in the next section, we explain the idea behind monetary policy indices in some detail. In section 4.4.1 the standard PBC model is tested for the Bundesbank. Also, additional conflict hypotheses are investigated, before we examine Japan in section 4.5 and the US in section 4.6. The final section summarizes the main findings.

4.2   MONETARY POLICY INDICES AS INDICATORS FOR A CENTRAL BANK'S RHETORIC

We claim that monetary policy indices can measure the rhetoric of a central bank. Therefore, we first have to explain how these indices are constructed and why they measure a central bank's rhetoric.

4.2.1 How monetary policy indices are constructed

The general idea is simple: if there is no 'key instrument', but we nevertheless want to use the information from the use of monetary instruments, one has to construct a new variable. This new variable should then contain all the information from the use of *all* monetary instruments. Romer and Romer (1989) call this the 'narrative approach'.

One has to build a variable with different categories, distinguishing between states such as 'very expansive policy', 'expansive policy', 'neutral policy' etc. Having defined these categories one needs to classify each period.

In the German case this classification was done as follows: the development of all monetary instruments and official statements of the Bundesbank in the 'Monthly Reports' are closely monitored. Then, if, for instance, the lombard rate or minimum reserve requirements are increased, the index switches to more contractionary policy. In cases of doubt the 'Monthly Reports' usually allow a fairly accurate assessment of the intentions of the Bundesbank.[43] The resulting variable is called 'Bundesbank Index'.

Why do we say that this variable measures a central bank's rhetoric? Because a change in a monetary instrument need not be effective. One could imagine a situation where a central bank wants to send a signal to trade unions before wage negotiations by pretending to tighten monetary policy (e.g. by raising the lombard rate – usually the ceiling for short-term interest rates, thus having a limited impact). Such a signal could be accompanied by a somewhat 'conservative' description of the situation in the monthly bulletin, while in fact knowing that the policy measures taken are not sufficient for a fundamental change.

To see whether this rhetoric also translates into economic outcomes, one needs to check its effectiveness. This can be done by examining a short-term interest rate that quickly reacts to changes of the monetary policy stance.

In this chapter we have therefore decided to use a two-step procedure:

Central bank rhetoric We capture the rhetoric of the central bank by monetary policy indices. These indices characterize the intended or publicly announced policy stance, since variations of the instruments are closely measured.

Effective central bank policy In a second step we examine whether the rhetoric translates into lower (market) interest rates. We will measure the actual or effective monetary policy by the day-to-day rate. This variable shows how the sum of policy measures becomes effective and – as pointed out in section 2.3 – is considered as an important indicator for monetary policy.

This allows us to check whether (a) the central bank's rhetoric reacts to political pressure and (b) whether a possible effect in public statements also leaves traces in the central bank's effective conduct of monetary policy. We run the same regressions for the rhetoric of the central bank (the monetary policy index) and the effective policy stance (the day-to-day rate).

What do we gain by using the monetary policy index? As we have explained before, we would like to investigate not only how monetary policy becomes effective, but also what exactly the central bank is doing. Normally, one would examine monetary instruments, but lacking a 'key instrument' (which fully characterizes the policy stance), this possibility does not exist. Yet, one would still like to measure directly what the central bank does, as interest rates can only show the effect of monetary policy in combination with the reaction of the financial markets, but not the use of instruments alone. The monetary policy index covers the variation of all monetary instruments, which is why we get an additional insight in what the central bank does. Again, from examining the behavior of these announcements we cannot conclude that they have economic effects, this can only be verified using a short-term interest rate, but we can check whether announcements (e.g. variation of instruments) and impact on economic outcomes (e.g. variation of the day-to-day rate) fully match.

Obviously, to a certain extent monetary policy indices also mirror the behavior of other economic variables. Therefore, we first look at the relationship between the announced and effective monetary policy and variables that have been used in previous studies. This also gives additional information about monetary policy indices. As before we use the example of the Bundesbank.

4.2.2 Properties of the German monetary policy index

The monetary policy index for Germany, originally developed by Dominguez (1997), is available on a monthly basis for the period 01:1969 until 02:1998.[44] The Bundesbank index is coded between the values 0 (very expansive) and 4 (very contractional), such that the higher the value of the index, the more contractionary the monetary policy. This enables direct comparison with interest rates.[45]

A plot of the Bundesbank index (dotted line) and the day-to-day rate (solid line) shows that the latter fluctuates much more (see figure 4.1, pre-election periods are marked as gray). This is no surprise, since the index measures the intended policy stance, and intentions of a central bank will not change very frequently between expansive and contractionary monetary policy. The day-to-day rate, on the other hand, is closely controlled and smoothed by the Bundesbank, but still inhibits many external influences.

We also see that neutral monetary policy (the Bundesbank index has the value +2) is compatible with very different levels of the day-to-day rate. In the early 1980s and 1990s, the Bundesbank index seems to precede the reduction of the day-to-day rate, while in the early 1970s the rhetoric of the Bundesbank

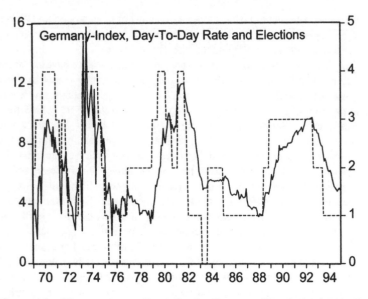

*Figure 4.1   The monetary policy index for Germany ('Bundesbank index')
and the day-to-day rate*

is more restrictive than the actual policy. This is due to the external constraint
of the Bretton Woods system, when the Bundesbank tried to fight imported
inflation, but could not effectively use its instruments in the fixed exchange
rate system.

We did a Granger causality test to check whether past values of the day-to-
day rate can explain the Bundesbank index or vice versa. As we are working
with monthly data, we use a Granger causality test with 12 lags. Tests with
other lag specifications confirmed our results. The impression that the Bundesbank index seems to precede the day-to-day rate is indeed confirmed by
the Granger test, since the causality runs from the Bundesbank index to the
day-to-day rate (see table 4.1).

Null Hypothesis	Obs.	F-Stat.	Prob.
Day-to-day does not Granger Cause Buba Index	338	1.25	0.25
Buba Index does not Granger Cause day-to-day		4.49	0.00
CPI does not Granger Cause Buba Index	338	0.92	0.53
Buba Index does not Granger Cause CPI		3.26	0.00
M3 does not Granger Cause Buba Index	338	1.66	0.07
Buba Index does not Granger Cause M3		1.20	0.28

Table 4.1   Properties of the Bundesbank index: Granger causality tests

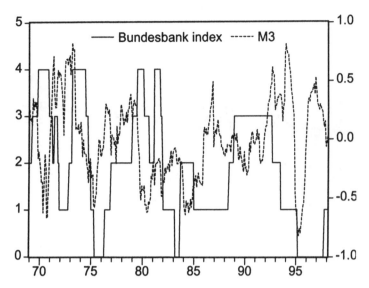

*Figure 4.2   The monetary policy index for Germany ('Bundesbank index')
and the growth rate of M3*

Previously we have seen that the rhetoric of the Bundesbank need not always
translate into changes of the actual use of policy instruments. Figure 4.2 compares the Bundesbank index to the detrended growth rate of M3.[46] Apparently,
changes in the announced policy stance translate slowly into changes in M3 (for
instance in the early 1970s). The second half of the 1980s show that constant
Bundesbank rhetoric does not lead to constant monetary growth rates, which
may indicate external influences or may be a sign of differences between announced and implemented policy. The Granger causality test reveals that while
the Bundesbank index does not Granger cause M3, M3 has explanatory power
for the Bundesbank index. Thus the Bundesbank rhetoric reacts to changes
in M3, which seems plausible, as M3 is one of the variables the Bundesbank
monitored very closely.

Finally, we compare the Bundesbank index to the detrended growth rate
of the consumer price index (figure 4.3) to verify that the Bundesbank index
indeed translates into changes of the inflation rate. We see that over a large
part of the sample the CPI seems to follow the Bundesbank's rhetoric with a
considerable lag. This is also confirmed by the Granger causality test, which
shows that causality runs from the index to the inflation rate.

We have seen in this section that the rhetoric or announced monetary policy
and the actually implemented or effective monetary policy may differ. This

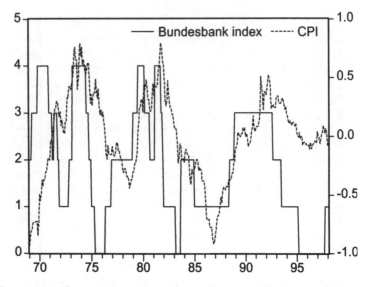

Figure 4.3   The monetary policy index for Germany ('Bundesbank index') and the consumer price index

means that potentially there is some 'scope' for central banks for additional rhetoric not backed by similar changes in the monetary policy. This scope may be the result of economic constraints, but it could also be due to external pressure on the central bank. In the latter case the central bank could use this difference between rhetoric and monetary policy measures e.g. to calm down politicians during periods of conflicts.

4.3   THE BASIC MODEL

We start with the assumption that a central bank not only cares about inflation, but also about GDP growth (proxied by industrial production, as GDP data is not available on a monthly basis) and – perhaps to a lesser extent – about unemployment. This is true for the central bank's rhetoric, but of course also for the actually implemented policy stance. We estimate the following equation:

$$Index_t = \alpha + \beta_1 Index_{t-1} + \beta_2 \pi_{t-3} + \beta_3 IP_{t-3} + \beta_4 u_{t-3} + \beta_5 OC_t + \beta_6 Dum_t + \varepsilon_t \tag{4.1}$$

The dependent variable is the monetary policy index $Index_t$. π_{t-3} is the annual growth rate of the consumer price index, IP_{t-3} is the annual growth rate of the production index and u_{t-3} is the annual growth rate of the unemployment rate. Since the data on the inflation rate, the production index and the unemployment rate are only available with a certain lag, we use a three-month lag in our estimates (Berger, 1997b applies a similar procedure). OC_t is a dummy to cover the impact of the oil crisis, defined as +1 during 01:1974-12:1975 and 01:1978-12:1981. This formulation of the OC_t dummy assumes that during the oil crisis monetary policy was on average more contractionary. We have also run regressions with a different formulation of the oil price dummy to control for a possible structural break. It turns out that this simple OC_t dummy covers the oil crisis impact quite well. Dum_t are the different political variables for the models, which will be explained when the models are estimated, and ε_t is a random variable.

Estimation by OLS is not feasible for this model since we have a limited dependent variable on the left-hand side. Therefore, an ordered logit model is estimated (see Greene (1997) for a detailed description of ordered logit models).

A similar basic model is also used to explain the level of the day-to-day rate r_t. Since the day-to-day rate fluctuates more and has a strong AR-part, we add a second lag. We estimate the following equation by OLS:

$$
\begin{aligned}
r_t = {} & \alpha + \beta_1 r_{t-1} + \beta_2 r_{t-2} + \beta_3 \pi_{t-3} + \beta_4 IP_{t-3} + \beta_5 u_{t-3} + \\
& \beta_6 OC_t + \beta_7 Dum_t + \varepsilon_t.
\end{aligned} \tag{4.2}
$$

This model differs only moderately from regression models used by other authors, such as Berger (1997b), Lohmann (1998) or Lang and Welzel (1992). All time series have been detrended if necessary to ensure stationarity. Where the results are sensitive to the inclusion of the Bretton Woods period, we estimated for the entire sample period and separately for the post-Bretton Woods period (05:1973-12:1994). Separate results for the Bretton Woods period were not estimated as the sample period was considered too short.

To perform a test of the basic model, we use the dummy $PBCN_t$ that takes the value +1 before elections and 0 otherwise. Following Alesina and Roubini (1990), we have chosen the pre-election period N to be 12, 18 or 24 months preceding an election. A further implication of the PBC model is that after elections monetary policy is tightened to fight inflation. This prediction is tested by using the dummies $PostN_t$, where we have chosen N again to be +1 for the 12, 18 or 24 months after an election and 0 otherwise.

However, in some cases it is useful to run additional PBC tests. For this

Quarters after an election	1	2	3	4	5	6	7	8
$AltPBC - 1_t$	16	15	14	13	12	11	10	9
$AltPBC - 2_t$	1	2	3	4	5	6	7	8
Quarters after an election	9	10	11	12	13	14	15	16
$AltPBC - 1_t$	8	7	6	5	4	3	2	1
$AltPBC - 2_t$	9	10	11	12	9	6	3	0

Table 4.2   Additional political variables

purpose Allen (1986) proposed a whole series of political pressure variables, two of which we will use (see table 4.2).

The first variable, $AltPBC - 1_t$, focuses on political costs: as governments prefer to have a booming economy before elections, tight monetary policy is politically costly for the central bank as Election Day approaches. Therefore, if monetary policy has to be tightened, it is least costly early in an incumbent's term and the central bank might even 'overtighten' early to avoid a political conflict towards the end of the term (Beck, 1991).

The second variable $AltPBC - 2_t$ captures the idea of a sudden boost before elections: during non-election times priority is given to fight inflation, whereas just before elections the central bank tries to stimulate the economy. Those are additional constructions of the political variable to test central bank behavior. Neither are covered by the standard formulation of PBC models, but it is apparent that their significance in a regression would indicate some form of electoral manipulation of monetary policy. As we have already tested the PBC model for effective monetary policy (the short-term interest rate) in those two countries (using the short-term interest rate) in section 3.3.1, we only report results for the rhetoric, thus the intended policy stance.

It is interesting to see how other central banks perform in comparison to the Bundesbank. Therefore, we apply a similar methodology to analyse the rhetoric of the Bank of Japan and the American Federal Reserve, as for these two countries monetary policy indices are available. Those two are quite interesting cases, as both central banks are quite different: the FED enjoys a high degree of independence, whereas the Bank of Japan is considered to be less independent. The results for the Deutsche Bundesbank should be viewed in light of results for those central banks.

What can be expected for these countries? We have seen in chapter 3 that neither for Japan nor for the US we have found signs of a political business cycle in the short-term interest rate. As the FED is ranked as an independent central bank, whereas the Bank of Japan is considered to be less independent, we expect political cycles in Japan, but less in the US – if these cycles exist at all.

Pre-election	$N = PBC12_t$	$N = PBC18_t$	$N = PBC24_t$
$Index_{t-1}$	2.67***	2.70***	2.73***
π_{t-3}	0.34	0.39	0.24
IP_{t-3}	0.21**	0.200**	0.18**
u_{t-3}	−0.01***	−0.01***	−0.01***
OC_t	0.40*	0.42*	0.45*
N	−0.50**	−0.56***	−0.47**
LR-Index	0.72	0.73	0.72
Post-election	$N = Post12$	$N = Post18$	$N = Post24$
π_{t-3}	0.14	0.12	0.20
IP_{t-3}	0.18**	0.18**	0.17**
u_{t-3}	−0.01**	−0.01***	−0.01***
OC_t	0.43*	0.43*	0.47*
N	0.53***	0.41**	0.34*
LR-Index	0.72	0.72	0.72

Table 4.3   Pre- and post-electoral behavior of the Bundesbank index

4.4   RHETORIC OF THE BUNDESBANK

4.4.1   Estimating the basic model

We start the analysis with the Bundesbank. For Germany we also examine conflict models, but we start by estimating the political business cycle model. Our regressions are based on monthly data for the period 01:1969-12:1994.[47]

Figure 4.1 reveals that the gray-marked pre-election periods are characterized as well by relatively contractionary rhetoric (for instance in 1991) and high day-to-day rates, but there are also elections, such as the election in 1972, when mildly expansive rhetoric goes along with expansive effective monetary policy.

In the upper half of table 4.3 we report the results for the pre-electoral effects. Our results show that the $PBCN_t$ dummies all have the expected sign and are mostly highly significant. We find no significant impact of the consumer price index, but the Bundesbank responds to higher unemployment by switching to more expansive rhetoric. The impact of the dummies is negative, thus before elections the intended policy stance becomes more expansive. This is in line with the predictions of the PBC model.[48] Changing the lag structure or using M3 instead of the consumer price index delivered qualitatively similar results.[49]

Next, we check whether the rhetoric of the Bundesbank changed to more contractionary policy after elections. This is tested with the dummies $PostN_t$. Our estimates for the Bundesbank index are shown in the lower half of table

Pre-election	$N = PBC12_t$	$N = PBC18_t$	$N = PBC24_t$
r_{t-1}	0.64 ***	0.64 ***	0.64 ***
r_{t-2}	0.19 ***	0.19 ***	0.20 ***
π_{t-3}	0.97 ***	0.96 ***	0.92 ***
IP_{t-3}	0.10	0.09	0.09
u_{t-3}	−0.01 ***	−0.09 ***	−0.01 ***
OC_t	0.20	0.22	0.23
N	−0.21	−0.15	−0.12
R^2 adj.	0.81	0.81	0.81
SSR	363.97	365.09	365.74
$F - Stat.$	188.74	188.03	187.62
	$N = Post12_t$	$N = Post18_t$	$N = Post24_t$
r_{t-1}	0.63 ***	0.64 ***	0.64 ***
r_{t-2}	0.19 ***	0.19 ***	0.19 ***
π_{t-3}	0.95 ***	0.92 ***	0.93 ***
IP_{t-3}	0.09	0.09	0.09
u_{t-3}	−0.01 ***	−0.01 ***	−0.01 ***
OC_t	0.25	0.24	0.25
N	0.25 *	0.13	0.12
R^2 adj.	0.81	0.81	0.81
SSR	362.90	365.54	365.67
$F - Stat.$	189.42	187.75	187.66

Table 4.4   Pre- and post-electoral behavior of the day-to-day rate

4.3: the dummies are mostly significant, at least at the 10 per cent level.[50] These results indicate that a complete political business cycle can be observed in the Bundesbank rhetoric, with announced monetary ease prior to elections and announced contractionary monetary policy once elections are over.

We proceed by examining what the Bundesbank actually did, thus the effective Bundesbank policy. We start by estimating equation (4.2) for the $PBCN_t$ dummies. Our results are given in the upper half of table 4.4. We find that although all dummies have the right sign, they are far from being significantly different from zero. Given the results in chapter 3 this does not come as a surprise, but it follows that while the rhetoric of the Bundesbank shows a political business cycle, the effective policy stance does not.

Thus one can argue that the Bundesbank does not support the pre-election talk by adjusting monetary instruments in a way such that expansive announcements also show up in the actual conduct of monetary policy. Cautiously formulated, they would try to 'mislead' the public (or the politicians) by their rhetoric. This would imply a weak position of the Bundesbank on the surface, but a strong independent position when it comes down to actions.

	$N = AltPBC - 1$	$N = AltPBC - 2$
$Index_{t-1}$	2.72***	2.72***
π_{t-3}	0.22	0.13
IP_{t-3}	0.21**	0.16*
u_{t-3}	−0.01***	−0.01**
OC_t	0.49**	0.38
N	0.06***	−0.03
$LR - Index$	0.73	0.72

Table 4.5   The impact of additional PBC variables on the Bundesbank index

Next, we look at post-electoral effects (lower half of table 4.4): positive values of the $PostN_t$ coefficients indicate that after elections the day-to-day rate is higher than its normal level. This could be due to contractionary Bundesbank policy. However, in most cases the coefficients are insignificant, which may either be explained by the theoretical prediction of irregular cycles or 'blips' – or supports our argument that the Bundesbank acts independently. In this case, post-electoral cycles must not show up, since there is no pre-electoral inflationary potential, which has to be fought after elections.

4.4.2   Additional tests for PBCs

The preceding results are quite surprising: the Deutsche Bundesbank, which has been considered to be the most independent central bank in the world, shows signs of a political business cycle in its intended policy stance. To get a deeper insight of what exactly happens we ran additional tests for the Bundesbank's rhetoric, using additional political pressure variables by Allen (1986) (table 4.2).

First we look at the results for the $AltPBC - 1_t$ variable (table 4.5): this variable is significant for the Bundesbank index, which indicates that monetary policy, as measured by the index, constantly becomes more expansive, as elections approach. This also explains why the tests for the simple political business cycle performs so well: before elections, announced monetary policy becomes more and more expansive, while after elections monetary policy is suddenly tightened. Re-examining figure 4.1 again, one seems to observe such a cycle for instance between the elections in 1972 and 1976.

The second political dummy $AltPBC - 2_t$ is insignificant in both regressions. Apparently, the behavior of the Bundesbank cannot be characterized by a constant increase in monetary tightening and then a sudden switch to expansive policies just before elections. This does not come as a surprise, since it would be a clear contradiction to the previous hypothesis.

As a final test we have run regressions with these alternative PBC variables

	$N = AltPBC - 1$	$N = AltPBC - 2$
r_{t-1}	0.63***	0.64***
r_{t-2}	0.19***	0.20***
CPI_{t-3}	0.97***	0.90***
IP_{t-3}	0.10*	0.09
u_{t-3}	−0.01***	−0.01***
OC_t	0.26	0.24
N	0.03*	−0.01
R^2 adj.	0.81	0.81
SSR	362.46	366.09
$F - Stat.$	189.70	187.40

Table 4.6   The impact of additional PBC variables on the day-to-day rate

and the short-term interest rate. Given the previous results we did not expect a significant impact. These expectations are confirmed: the $AltPBC - 1_t$ dummy is significant at the 10 per cent level in the regression for the whole sample, but if we restrict the estimation to the post-Bretton Woods periods, none of the dummies is significant. Given a very low level of significance for the $AltPBC - 1_t$ dummy in the shorter sample period, we conclude that we do not find any evidence for PBC in the effective policy stance.

As noted before the index was constructed by Dominguez (1997), but was later extended to a longer sample period (Maier, 1999). To exclude the possibility that this extension was not properly done, we have also tested the standard PBC hypothesis with electoral dummies on the original index, that is for the shorter sample period 1977-1993. Again we found a highly significant impact of elections (results not reported). This shows that there is no 'author effect', which means that the significant impact of elections does not show up because we have 'constructed' the index accordingly, but already the original index (which was not even aimed at investigating PBC models) features electoral cycles.

To summarize, we conclude that a political business cycle can be observed in the Bundesbank rhetoric, but not in the actual use of monetary policy. This outcome certainly reflects the political pressure faced by the Bundesbank before elections. Although the distinction between rhetoric and ex-post policy is certainly less clear-cut in reality, it is nevertheless surprising that the Bundesbank announcements exhibit such a clear pattern.

4.4.3   Additional econometric tests for Germany: conflict models

As we have explained in section 2.2 conflict models have a number of advantages over simple election dummies. Therefore we also test three conflict

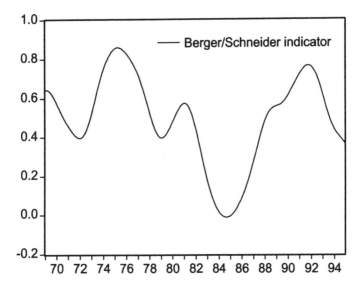

Figure 4.4   The Berger/Schneider conflict indicator

models, first focusing on conflicts between the Bundesbank and the federal government, then examining the credibility of threats in pre-election periods, and finally testing whether the composition of the Bundesbank council leads to different monetary policies.

a)   The Frey/Schneider conflict model

As stated in section 2.2.3 the main issue of the Frey and Schneider (1981) model is how different policy stances are measured. As a start, we use data from Berger and Schneider (2000) who employed the change of the federal full employment budget balance in percent of GDP as a proxy for fiscal policy and detrended annual growth rates of M3 to measure monetary policy. If those policy stances point in different directions a conflict is assumed. A plot of this indicator can be found in figure 4.4 (this indicator will be discussed in more detail in section 5.5). Berger and Schneider (2000) find a highly significant impact of their conflict indicator on various monetary instruments (such as the discount rate or minimum reserve requirements).

To perform a test of this hypothesis we estimate:

$$
\begin{aligned}
Index_t = {}& \alpha + \beta_1 Index_{t-1} + \beta_2(1-\zeta_t)\pi_{t-3} + \beta_3(1-\zeta_t)IP_{t-3} + \\
& \beta_4(1-\zeta_t)u_{t-3} + \beta_5 OC_t + \beta_6\zeta_t POLGOV_t + \varepsilon_t
\end{aligned} \tag{4.3}
$$

Bundesbank index		Day-to-day rate	
$Index_{t-1}$	2.67 ***	r_{t-1}	0.65 ***
$(1-\zeta)\pi_{t-3}$	0.33	r_{t-2}	0.21 ***
$(1-\zeta)IP_{t-3}$	0.23	$(1-\zeta)\pi_{t-3}$	1.33 ***
$(1-\zeta)u_{t-3}$	−0.02 **	$(1-\zeta)IP_{t-3}$	0.10
OC_t	0.08	$(1-\zeta)u_{t-3}$	−0.02 ***
$\zeta POLGOV_t$	2.47	OC_t	0.05
		$\zeta POLGOV_t$	0.71
LR-Index	0.71	R^2 adj.	0.81
		SSR	372.93
		$F-Stat.$	183.17

Table 4.7   The Berger/Schneider conflict model for the Bundesbank index and the day-to-day rate

$$r_t = \alpha + \beta_1 r_{t-1} + \beta_2 r_{t-2} + \beta_3 (1-\zeta_t)\pi_{t-3} + \beta_4(1-\zeta_t)IP_{t-3} +$$
$$\beta_5(1-\zeta_t)u_{t-3} + \beta_6 OC_t + \beta_7 \zeta POLGOV_t + \varepsilon_t \qquad (4.4)$$

where ζ_t is the conflict indicator, which continuously varies between +1 (states of conflict), and 0 (states of no conflict) and $POLGOV_t$ is the direction of fiscal policy. Thus the equations basically state that during non-conflicts ($\zeta_t = 0$) the Bundesbank pursues monetary policy as it did before according to the models 4.1 and 4.2, whereas during times of conflict ($\zeta_t = 1$) the Bundesbank adopts the government's policy stance, measured by the change of the full employment budget $POLGOV$.

First we examine whether the Bundesbank rhetoric changes during periods of conflicts (left part of table 4.7): the Berger and Schneider conflict indicator is never significant for the announced policy stance. This shows that during conflicts the rhetoric of the Bundesbank shows no sign of weakness. Moreover, in contrast to previous results, we have to conclude that fewer of the coefficients are significant, which indicates that premultiplying the economic variables with the conflict indicator explains the behavior of the Bundesbank rather poorly.[51]

Next, we ask whether the actual Bundesbank policy responds to conflicts. After all, it could be that the rhetoric of the Bundesbank cultivates the image of an independent central bank, resisting governmental pressure, while the actual policy still yields to the government.

This idea is not confirmed by the data (see the right part of table 4.7). Instead, we find that the relevant coefficients are far from being significant. The poor performance could be explained by the fact that the model was originally conceived for monetary instruments and it might be a wrong application to test this model for a monetary outcome. On the other hand, we believe the day-to-day rate reflects the use of all instruments, therefore the poor results come as a surprise.

So, to conclude, the evidence for this model is weak: conflicts do not seem to influence the intended policy stance, since there is no significant impact on the Bundesbank index, and the effective monetary policy of the Bundesbank does not react to conflicts in our model neither. If the Berger/Schneider conflict indicator is indeed a reliable measure for conflicts between the government and the German central bank, the Bundesbank is not impressed by the potential threat of losing its autonomy.

b)   The Lohmann conflict model

Next, we turn to the model of Lohmann (1998): she claims that the support for the federal government in the second chamber, the Bundesrat, has a significant impact on monetary policy. She measures the Bundesrat support by the number of seats of the Bundesrat held by the same party as the federal government. Since Lohmann's model differs from our model only marginally, we will try to capture the influence of the Bundesrat in the following way: using her data set we form a variable, which captures the size of Bundesrat support for the federal government, $Bundesrat_t$. Lohmann's hypothesis suggests a negative sign of the dummy if it is premultiplied by an election dummy such as $PBC12_t$. Moreover, she controls for the political party that rules the federal government and multiplies a party-code dummy with the measure of Bundesrat support. By doing so, we get two new dummy variables:

- $BRPBC12_t = Bundesrat_t * PBC12_t$, which is a measure for the support of the government in the Bundesrat, and

- $BRPC_t = Bundesrat_t * PC_t$, which shows the Bundesrat support of the different ruling parties (Lohmann, 1998).

Since the total number of seats in the Bundesrat changed after 1990, we can test the model for the period 01:1969-12:1989.

Our findings for the Bundesbank index are summarized in table 4.8. While the $BRPC_t$ dummy is insignificant, the coefficient for $BRPBC12_t$ has the right sign, and is highly significant. At first glance, the results seem to indicate that the Bundesbank's intended monetary policy stance before elections seems to depend on the question of whether both chambers of parliament are under unified party control or not.

However, a closer inspection of the political variable reveals that Lohmann's variable is quite similar to the pre-election dummy $PBC12_t$ (see figure 4.5): the only difference is the amplitude, as the $PBC12_t$ dummy (right axis) just switches between +1 and 0 and the $BRPBC12_t$ variable (left axis) takes values between 0 and +41. Therefore, it is not really a surprise that the $BRPBC12_t$

$Index_{t-1}$	2.47 ***
π_{t-3}	0.09
IP_{t-3}	0.19*
u_{t-3}	−0.01 ***
OC_t	0.22
$BRPBC12_t$	−0.03 **
$BRPC_t$	−0.01
LR-Index	0.70

Table 4.8   The Lohmann conflict model of Bundesrat support for the Bundesbank index

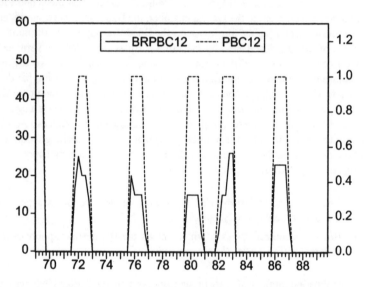

Figure 4.5   Comparison of the traditional PBC indicator and Lohmann's conflict variable

variable is significant, since the $PBC12_t$ dummy is highly significant itself. Given that, we would assume that there is no significant impact on the day-to-day rate, as we have just shown that the day-to-day rate does not react to forthcoming elections. Table 4.9 confirms this prior: the dummies are insignificant in regressions for the day-to-day rate for the large sample period.

Our confirmation of the Lohmann model is basically another confirmation of the political business cycle model: again we find electoral behavior in the rhetoric of the Bundesbank, but not in the effective monetary policy. A strong additional impact of the Bundesrat is not visible, and is – according to Vaubel (2002) – also not very plausible (see also section 2.4.2).

	01:1969-12:1989
r_{t-1}	0.64***
r_{t-2}	0.19***
π_{t-3}	0.93***
IP_{t-3}	0.10
u_{t-3}	−0.01***
OC_t	0.20
$BRPBC12_t$	−0.01
$BRPC_t$	0.0
R^2 adj.	0.81
SSR	364.35
$F-Stat.$	164.39

Table 4.9   The Lohmann conflict model of Bundesrat support for the day-to-day rate

c)   The Vaubel model of obstructionist central bankers

The last two models assumed that the Bundesbank remained politically neutral as governments were supported regardless of their political color. This view is not shared by Vaubel (1997) who claimed that the political composition of the Bundesbank council, the supreme policy-making body of the Bundesbank, has a significant impact on monetary policy.

There are three hypothesis following more or less directly from Vaubel's hypothesis of partisan central bankers.

Level effect   The composition of the council could have a significant 'level impact' on monetary policy, if rightist central bankers are more concerned about fighting inflation than leftist central bankers and under a rightist majority in the Bundesbank council the monetary policy stance is in general more contractionary. This hypothesis is tested by adding a *Council*$_t$ variable to our regressions (4.1) and (4.2), taking the value +1 if the central bank council is dominated by a rightist majority, −1 if the council is dominated by a leftist majority, and 0 otherwise. We would expect a positive sign of the dummy if conservative central bankers implement more contractionary policy.

'Hawks' and 'doves'   Next, we can test whether a conservative majority in the central bank council reacts differently to economic changes in rhetoric and effective monetary policy than a leftist majority. The political majority has already been captured in the variable *Council*$_t$, thus a test of this hypothesis is done by premultiplying our explanatory variables with the *Council*$_t$ variable and adding them to the regression:

$$
\begin{aligned}
Index_t = {} & \alpha + \beta_1 Index_{t-1} + \beta_2 \pi_{t-3} + \beta_3 IP_{t-3} + \beta_4 u_{t-3} + \\
& \beta_5 Council_t * \pi_{t-3} + \beta_6 Council_t * IP_{t-3} + \\
& \beta_7 Council_t * u_{t-3} + \beta_8 OC_t + \varepsilon_t \qquad\qquad (4.5) \\
r_t = {} & \alpha + \beta_1 r_{t-1} + \beta_2 r_{t-2} + \beta_3 \pi_{t-3} + \beta_4 IP_{t-3} + \beta_5 u_{t-3} \\
& + \beta_6 Council_t * \pi_{t-3} + \beta_7 Council_t * IP_{t-3} \\
& + \beta_8 Council_t * u_{t-3} + \beta_9 OC_t + \varepsilon_t. \qquad\qquad (4.6)
\end{aligned}
$$

The political view of the central bankers has to be rejected if the estimated coefficients β_5-β_7 of equation (4.5) and β_6-β_8 of equation (4.6) are insignificant. Otherwise, we may conclude that the political majority in the Bundesbank council does have an impact: if for instance β_5 in equation (4.5) is significant, then a conservative council ('hawks') reacts stronger to changes in the inflation rate than its social democratic counterpart ('doves').

Obstructionist view Finally, the more provocative part of the Vaubel hypothesis is that the Bundesbank might obstruct the re-election of a government if the political majority of the Bundesbank council does not share its political affiliation.

To test this hypothesis, we create a variable that takes the value +1 if the majority of the Bundesbank council and the federal government share the same political affiliation, and -1 otherwise. This dummy is then multiplied with the pre-election dummies $PBCN_t$ to form the variables $ObstructN_t$. They take the value +1 during the N quarters preceding an election if both policymaking bodies share the same political view, -1 if the political views are not shared and 0 during non-pre-election periods.[52] If the Vaubel hypothesis is correct, we would expect a positive sign on the coefficients for the dummy variables.

We first consider the hypotheses of a 'level effect' and the possibility that 'hawks' employ different rhetoric than 'doves'. Our results for the Bundesbank index are presented in the table 4.10: the columns (1) and (3) show the results for the level hypothesis, column (2) and (4) the results for the 'hawks and doves' test.

First, we look at the columns (1) and (3): the $Council_t$ dummy has the right sign and is significant at the 5 per cent level for the entire sample, but remains insignificant if we restrict our analysis to the post-Bretton Woods period (column 3). If we use M3 instead of the consumer price index, the dummy becomes insignificant. As the dummy lacks robustness the hypothesis of a level effect should be rejected.

	(1)	(2)	(3)	(4)
	01:1969-12:1989		05:1973-12:1989	
$Index_{t-1}$	2.43***	2.47***	0.26***	2.65***
π_{t-3}	0.70*	0.19	0.33	0.01
IP_{t-3}	0.14	0.10	0.09	0.04
u_{t-3}	−0.02***	−0.01***	−0.01**	−0.01**
OC_t	0.59**	0.47*	0.51	0.47
$Council_t$	0.33**		0.21	
$Council_t * \pi_{t-3}$		0.87*		0.83*
$Council_t * IP_{t-3}$		0.19*		0.09
$Council_t * u_{t-3}$		0.0		0.0
LR-Index	0.69	0.70	0.72	0.73

Table 4.10   Impact of political majority of the Bundesbank council on the Bundesbank index

Next we turn to the columns (2) and (4) to test the hypothesis that 'hawks' employ different rhetoric than 'doves'. Our results indicate that indeed such an effect is significant (see table 4.10) on the inflation rate for both sample periods (coefficient $Council_t * \pi_{t-3}$), and on the production index if we look at the entire sample ($Council_t * IP_{t-3}$). This indicates that a conservative majority of central bankers indeed reacts more strongly in their announced monetary policy to changes in the inflation rate than their social democratic counterparts, such that higher inflation leads to more contractionary rhetoric (this is in line with Berger and Woitek, 1998a). However, this result is not robust: if we use M3 instead of the consumer price index the estimated coefficient becomes insignificant. We therefore conclude that Vaubel's hypothesis cannot sufficiently explain the Bundesbank's announced policy stances.

Finally, we test Vaubel's 'obstructionist view'. Our results for the Bundesbank index are presented in the table 4.11. Our results for the $ObstN_t$ reject the 'obstructionist hypothesis': the coefficients are mainly insignificant. Negative values indicate that if the majority of the Bundesbank council shares the political view of the federal government in pre-election periods (thus the dummy has the value +1), then the Bundesbank's intended policy stance is expansive. This is not what the hypothesis suggests. Similar results are obtained if we exclude the 1972 and 1983 elections.

Next, we focus on the effective Bundesbank policy. We start with testing the hypothesis of a 'level effect': the results can be found in the left columns of table 4.12. Our results for the day-to-day rate are similar to those for the Bundesbank index: we do not find a 'level' impact of the political majority in the Bundesbank council on the effective policy stance, since the $Council_t$ dummies are far from being significant.

Second, we evaluate the possibility that conservative central bankers employ

	$N = Obst12_t$	$N = Obst18_t$	$N = Obst24_t$
$Index_{t-1}$	2.48***	2.47***	2.48***
π_{t-3}	0.33	0.42	0.32
IP_{t-3}	0.16*	0.17*	0.16*
u_{t-3}	−0.01***	−0.01***	−0.01***
OC_t	0.38	0.49*	0.34
N	−0.25	−0.40**	−0.11
LR-Index	0.69	0.70	0.69

Table 4.11   Vaubel's obstructionist hypothesis for the Bundesbank index

	01:1969-12:1989		05:1973-12:1989	
r_{t-1}	0.64***	0.61***	0.54***	0.50***
r_{t-2}	0.20***	0.18***	0.35***	0.32***
π_{t-3}	0.91***	1.43***	0.55**	1.13***
IP_{t-3}	0.09	0.09	0.05	0.04
u_{t-3}	−0.01***	−0.01***	−0.01***	−0.01***
OC_t	0.23	0.21	0.20	0.22
$Council_t$	0.0		−0.06	
$Council_t * \pi_{t-3}$		−0.54		−0.61*
$Council_t * IP_{t-3}$		0.09		−0.02
$Council_t * u_{t-3}$		0.0		0.01*
R^2 adj.	0.81	0.78	0.88	0.86
SSR	366.71	357.84	186.75	178.58
$F - Stat.$	187.01	99.55	278.49	140.62

Table 4.12   Impact of political majority of the Bundesbank council on the day-to-day rate

a different effective policy stance than their non-conservative counterparts. The results are presented in right-hand columns of table 4.12. We see that the relevant coefficients for the long sample period are all insignificant. If we restrict our analysis to the post-Bretton Woods period, 'hawks' react more strongly to an increase in the inflation rate, but also to higher unemployment.

However, the coefficients are only significant at the 10 per cent level. Again, they are not robust, e.g. the influence completely vanishes if we use M3 instead of the consumer price index. We therefore believe that 'hawks' do not implement substantially different policy stances than 'doves'.

Finally, the results of the obstructionist hypothesis for the day-to-day rate are presented in table 4.13. This hypothesis can be rejected easily, since none of the $ObstN_t$ dummies is significant.

To conclude, we find that all three Vaubel hypotheses have to be rejected. Apparently the political composition of the Bundesbank council has no sig-

	$N = Obst12_t$	$N = Obst18_t$	$N = Obst24_t$
r_{t-1}	0.64***	0.64***	0.64***
r_{t-2}	0.20***	0.20***	0.20***
π_{t-3}	0.90***	0.91***	0.89***
IP_{t-3}	0.09	0.09	0.10
u_{t-3}	−0.01***	−0.01***	−0.01***
OC_t	0.22	0.23	0.23
N	0.01	−0.03	0.05
$\overline{R}^2$ adj.	0.81	0.81	0.81
SSR	366.70	366.63	366.39
$F - Stat.$	187.02	187.06	187.21

Table 4.13   Vaubel's obstructionist hypothesis for the day-to-day rate

nificant impact on the Bundesbank's effective monetary policy: neither the Bundesbank's rhetoric nor the effective policy stance show a 'level effect' or can confirm the 'obstructionist model' according to Vaubel's predictions. There is weak evidence that conservative central bankers respond more strongly to inflationary pressure, but the results lack robustness.

In light of the results of other studies this result is not very surprising: as we have pointed out in section 2.4 Berger and Woitek (1997*a*) and Neumann (1998) have examined the assumption underlying Vaubel's hypotheses, namely differences in the voting behavior of conservative and non-conservative central bankers in the Bundesbank council. Both studies failed to find any evidence for the assumed voting behavior. All in all, Vaubel's hypothesis of partisan central bankers seems intuitively attractive, but is not confirmed by the empirical evidence.

4.4.4   Interpretation of the German evidence

After analysing several models for political pressure with our new indicators for the German monetary policy, we arrive at a twofold picture: while all models reject political influence on the day-to-day rate, thus on a proxy for the *actual* monetary policy, we do find robust evidence for electoral pressure on the Bundesbank index, thus on the measure for the *intended* monetary policy. It comes as quite a surprise that the simplest and least-sophisticated model of political pressure delivers such robust and clear results for the Bundesbank rhetoric. As we have stressed before, the Bundesbank is independent in legal status, therefore there seems to be little reason for giving in to governmental pressure before elections. However, recall that the actual conduct of monetary policy, thus the day-to-day rate, does not exhibit any sign of political influence.

Our findings suggest that the Bundesbank seems to respond to pressure by announcing relatively loose monetary policy, while at the same time knowing that the only effect this manipulation will have is the calming down of nervous politicians. This may be interpreted as a clear sign for the political pressure the Bundesbank faces before elections (see also Siklos and Bohl, 2002). However, we do not want to overstate the effect, it should be viewed as a clear sign of political pressure, but does not affect economic outcomes, as we fail to find an impact on interest rates. Instead, this behavior could offer a relatively 'cheap' way out of the dilemma that an independent central bank faces before elections: on the one hand politicians want a 'co-operative' central bank, on the other hand central bankers want to prevent economic damage.

4.5   RHETORIC OF THE BANK OF JAPAN

Dominguez (1997) has developed the monetary policy index for the Bank of Japan (hereafter called 'Japan index'). The time period for which this index is available is relatively short (01:1977 until 12:1993) and covers only five elections, two of which succeeded shortly after one another. This clearly limits the evidence.

Figure 4.6 compares the Japan index (dotted line), our measure for the effective monetary policy stance, with the Japanese short-term interest rate (solid line). As usual, 12 months pre-election periods are marked in gray.[53] A clear electoral pattern cannot be identified, neither for the Japan index which declines and rises before elections, nor for the Japanese short-term interest rate.

The literature on political business cycles has given relatively little attention to the case of Japan, also due to some particularities of the Japanese parliamentary system: the Liberal Democratic Party (LDP) has maintained a majority in the House of Representatives (Lower House) and ran the government from 1955 until July 1993. The LDP has almost been a sure winner, which usually provides little incentives for political business cycles (see also Cargill et al., 1997). Nevertheless, the LDP tried to maximize the winning margin. This is also reflected in the timing of elections: the Lower House has regularly been dissolved before the end of the four-year term. Moreover, researchers have found Japan's Philips curve steeper than those of other industrial countries, which increases the cost for short-term manipulation since small output gains lead to big increases in inflation (Hamada and Hayashi, 1985).

The empirical evidence on the Japanese political business cycle might be summarized as follows: since the timing of elections is endogenous, there is a relatively broad consensus that elections are more likely to be held when economic conditions are favorable for the incumbent (Ito and Park, 1988 and Cargill and Hutchison, 1991, who find that '... the path of GNP growth is correlated with the timing of Japanese elections'). As for whether the Japanese

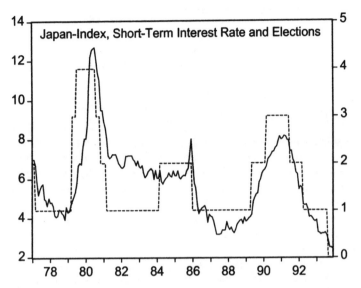

Figure 4.6 The monetary policy index for Japan ('Japan index') and Japan Overnight Call Money-Market Rate

government *actively* manipulates the economy: Johnson and Siklos (1994) conclude that the Bank of Japan exhibits electoral effects during the Bretton Woods period, but not after the collapse of the Bretton Woods system; Alesina et al. (1997) reject political business cycles in M1. Focusing only on Japan, Cargill and Hutchison (1991) cannot exclude the possibility of an active manipulation, a hypothesis Ito and Park (1988) rejected earlier.

Walsh (1997) and Cargill et al. (1997), however, argue that while the Bank of Japan is legally quite dependent, it should be seen as having achieved a certain 'reputational equilibrium'. This would mean that, despite its legal status, the Bank of Japan has little incentive to engage in political business cycles, otherwise its reputation would be seriously damaged.

The evidence for Japan in section 3.3.1 yielded mixed results. As before, estimates for Japan turned out to be quite tricky. Our results for the rhetoric of the Bank of Japan suffer from several drawbacks: first, the estimated period is relatively short due to the availability of the Japanese index. Secondly, we had to drop the lagged dependent variable and the dummy to cover the oil crisis. Moreover, we could not estimate results for the $PostN_t$ and the $AltPBC_t$ variables. All these restrictions were due to serious estimation problems, which were at least partly caused by the rapid succession of two elections in 1979 and 1980.

Our results for the PBC_t dummies are reported in table 4.14. The relatively

	$N = PBC12_t$	$N = PBC18_t$
π_t	162.49 ***	161.55 ***
IP_{t-3}	54.31 ***	50.68 ***
u_{t-1}	−4.46 ***	−4.72 ***
N	0.64 ***	0.43 **
LR-Index	0.27	0.25

Table 4.14   The PBC model for the Japan index

poor fit of the regression can be explained by the missing lag of the dependent variable. We experimented with different lag structures and various economic variables in order to present robust results. We see that the $PBC12_t$ is highly significant, the $PBC18_t$ is significant, too, but less robust. However, both co-efficients have positive instead of negative signs, which indicates that before elections the rhetoric becomes more contractionary. This is in contrast to our theoretical prediction and more a sign of independence than of a political business cycle.

As we have mentioned before, we cannot present useful estimations for the $PostN_t$ dummies or the $AltPBC_t$ variables, mainly due to the timing of the elections. This clearly limits our evidence. However, at least for the short sample period, based on the results we report, we must reject the political business cycle hypothesis for the intended policy stance of the Bank of Japan.

4.6   RHETORIC OF THE US FEDERAL RESERVE

The monetary policy index for the US has been developed by Boschen and Mills (1995). We will refer to the index as the 'FED index' or 'US index' and examine the period 01:1960-12:1993.

Figure 4.7 shows the US monetary policy index (dotted line) and the federal funds rate, a short-term interest rate, which we will use as proxy for the effective monetary stance (solid line).[54] As before, the gray areas mark 12 months before elections. We see immediately that – especially during the 60s – the two series do not match as closely as in Japan or Germany. Glancing at the US index, we see that only in two cases the monetary policy switches to more contractionary policy during the 12 months pre-election periods (in 1975/76 and in 1987/88), in all other cases the current policy stance is maintained or even becomes more expansive. The pattern for the federal funds rate is less clear: it is certainly striking that in 1979/80 the high interest rates suddenly fell before elections, but during other pre-election periods the federal funds rate was increased (such as in 1983/84).

So far, the literature has found little electoral impact on US monetary pol-

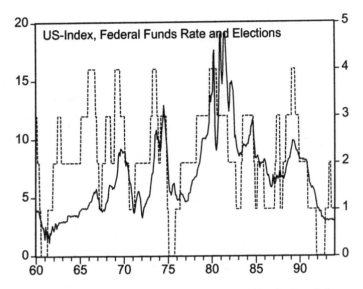

Figure 4.7 The monetary policy index for the US ('US index') and the Federal Funds Rate

icy. An overview has been provided by de Haan and Gormley (1997). In an extensive study Allen (1986) uses ten different electoral variables, but finds no evidence for a political business cycle in M1. Beck (1991) concludes that an electoral cycle in nominal M1 probably occurred only during the 1960s and 1970s, which the Federal Reserve did not actively create, but allowed. The absence of electoral pressure in M1 is confirmed by Alesina et al. (1997). Finally, a study by Johnson and Siklos (1994) found no electoral effect on the short-term interest rate.

Our results for the pre-electoral effects in the Federal Reserve's rhetoric are presented in table 4.15. All economic variables are significant (with the exception of the dummy to cover the oil price shock). The political dummies usually have the expected sign, but are in no case significant. Additionally, as a robustness check we also estimated the same model for the consumer price index instead of M3. This delivered qualitatively similar results for the political dummies, i.e. they remained insignificant. Our findings are quite in line with the literature, as mentioned above.

Since the Federal Reserve Board does not use expansionary rhetoric before elections, one would not expect that after elections tight monetary policy is announced. This expectation is confirmed by our results in table 4.16: we do not find a significant post-electoral effect on the FED's conduct of monetary policy.[55] Finding no sign of a political business cycle in the FED rhetoric, the

	$N = PBC12_t$	$N = PBC18_t$	$N = PBC24_t$
$Index_{t-1}$	2.66***	2.67***	2.67***
π_t	45.77*	44.48*	44.44*
IP_{t-3}	−25.31*	−25.91*	−25.93*
u_t	−3.84***	−3.80***	−3.80***
OC_t	−0.22	−0.21	−0.50
N	−0.10	0.0	−0.04
$LR - Index$	0.69	0.69	0.69

Table 4.15   The PBC model for the FED index

	$N = Post12_t$	$N = Post18_t$	$N = Post24_t$
$Index_{t-1}$	2.67***	2.67***	2.67***
π_t	45.26*	44.17*	44.48*
IP_{t-3}	−27.63**	−26.30*	−25.95*
u_t	−3.77***	−3.77***	3.80***
OC_t	−0.19	−0.20	−0.21
N	0.23	0.08	0.02
$LR - Index$	0.69	0.69	0.69

Table 4.16   Post-electoral behavior for the FED index

hypothesis for the announced monetary policy stance is clearly rejected.

4.7   SUMMARY

Monetary policy indices may not always measure 100 per cent accurately what central banks tell the public, but they are the closest measure economists have come up with so far. Based on the evidence presented in this chapter, we conclude that political business cycles can be observed in the rhetoric of the German Bundesbank, thus in the intended monetary policy stance. This outcome certainly reflects the political pressure faced by a central bank before elections. However, apparently the Bundesbank takes steps to prevent that the effective policy stance shows signs of political cycles, as it lacks evidence of electoral influences. The fact that the announced policy stance exhibits such a strong pattern is clear evidence for the heavy pressure on one of the world's most independent central bank before elections.

Next we have extended the analysis to Japan and the US. Forder (1996) argued that legal measures of central bank independence may not be useful in determining who actually sets monetary policy, as informal arrangements are difficult to quantify. Therefore, we conducted a number of regressions to verify whether differences in statutory independence also showed up in actual behavior. We find that, despite the tremendous differences in legal measures of central bank independence, all central banks are fully independent of political pressure in their effectively implemented monetary policy. However, it is helpful to distinguish between rhetoric and action, as the example of the Bundesbank shows.

Based on the indicators for statutory independence the Bank of Japan is most likely to be subject to political business cycles. This does not show up: the central bank rhetoric does not yield to pressure before elections. We found evidence for more contractionary monetary policy in the rhetoric and the short-term interest rate before elections, which indicates a behavior attributed to an independent central bank. This re-enforces the argument by Walsh (1997) and Cargill et al. (1997) that the Bank of Japan may have reached a reputational equilibrium. However, we recommend a careful analysis of these results, given (a) the relatively short sample period and (b) the timing of the Japanese elections, which posed serious difficulties in testing the model.

The Federal Reserve Board was ranked as independent central bank quite closely behind the German Bundesbank. In contrast to its German counterpart, the rhetoric of the US monetary policy does not exhibit any sign of political influence. The effective monetary policy shows that shortly before elections monetary policy is tightened. This might indicate that before elections inflationary pressures are fought, or it may be due to external influences, which bias our finding. In any case, the legally independent status of the FED is confirmed.

Our results show that the only measure of the degree of (in-)dependence of a central bank should be the effectively implemented policy. If we use this criterion, all three central banks pass the independence test.

5.   A New Indicator for (Political) Pressure

5.1   OVERVIEW

In the last two chapters we have introduced two new indicators for monetary policy. We have seen that the simple political business cycle theory performs quite poorly. Given the rather 'mechanistic' definition of political pressure, namely a 12, 18 or 24 months pre-election period, this does not really come as a surprise: first, it seems quite unlikely that *all* elections have the same business cycle effect. If, for instance, a government need not stimulate the economy as it is sure of winning the elections, PBC models will fail to detect an effect – strictly speaking, there is no political business cycle, even though politics might play an important role for the formation of monetary policy. It could also be that the length of the pre-election period (during which the stimulation takes place) differs across elections. These considerations show that the standard PBC model is intuitively appealing, but not necessarily the best way to analyse how political pressure affects monetary policy. We need a more general indicator for external pressure.

So far, we have only examined political pressure resulting from (potential) governmental threats. In this chapter we gradually shift our focus away from purely economic or electoral conflicts to political conflicts in general. We relax the assumption that the government is the only source of pressure and also examine the role of different interest groups. Like any other central bank, the Bundesbank was confronted with pressure from quite different sources and the question we try to answer now is how the German monetary authorities reacted to this pressure.

In doing so, we employ the approach as developed by Havrilesky (1993). To examine to which extent politicians influenced policies of the Federal Reserve, Havrilesky developed an indicator for political pressure on the central bank, based on reports in the *Wall Street Journal*. He found that the FED's policies respond to this index. As explained in the next section, the Havrilesky approach has a number of advantages in comparison to other ways to analyse to which extent a central bank responds to political pressures. Not only do we employ this approach to a country for which this has never been done before, we also extent the approach by including pressure arising from interest groups. We conclude that the Bundesbank did not respond to political pressure. However, its policies were in line with the wishes of the banking sector.

This chapter is organized as follows. Section 5.3 outlines the Havrilesky approach. Section 5.4 gives an overview over the data, section 5.5 compares the new pressure index to other conflict indicators. In section 5.6 we outline the estimation procedure, before presenting the results in section 5.7. The final section offers some concluding comments.

5.2   POTENTIAL SOURCES OF EXTERNAL PRESSURE ON MONETARY POLICY

In this section we extend the focus beyond governments by also focusing on interest groups. First, however, we have to explain the rationale for that, i.e. why would a central bank potentially give in to pressure for interest groups, especially an independent central bank such as the Bundesbank?

We have seen that even central banks with a high degree of legal independence might (at least partly) comply with the wishes of politicians, as they fear that otherwise their legal independence might be threatened. After all, the independence of a central bank is always relative, as the parliament always has the possibility to change the central bank act and (partially) remove the statutory independence. To some extent the ECB is an exception to that, as changes to its legal status require the unanimous consent of all EMU member states (see also chapter 8). Pressure groups do not have the chance to cut the level of independence.

Central banks might nevertheless listen to wishes and demands from governments or organized groups, as they might fear following a certain monetary policy 'against the wishes of the population'. Assume the following: a pressure group demands a certain monetary policy. If it is well organized and represents a significant share of the population, the government might listen to its demands. If the government concludes that they need the support of this group for their policy, they might be inclined to signal to the central bank that a change in the policy stance would be desirable. If the influence of the pressure group is strong enough, the government might even signal that otherwise the central bank's independence might be in danger.

This indirect influence of interest groups (via the government) is depicted in figure 5.1. Note, however, that one interest group probably also has more direct means to influence central banks: the financial sector, namely commercial banks. This is because of two main links:

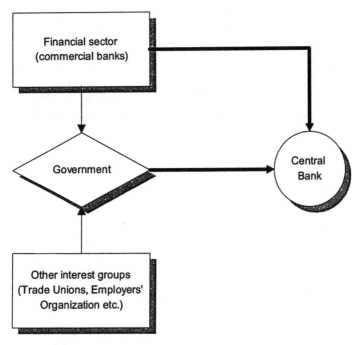

Figure 5.1   Potential sources of external pressure

1. Central bankers are maximizing agents, surrounded by the financial sector. One part of their individual utility function is 'popularity' or 'high reputation', which central bankers achieve by maximizing their reputation among commercial bankers. If this explanation holds, then central bankers have an incentive to listen to the signals of commercial banks.

2. At a more fundamental level, the major factor securing a central bank's independence is a high reputation. To a great extent such reputation is build up among other (commercial) bankers, stockbrokers etc. Constantly pursuing a monetary policy against their interests will leave them fed up, damaging the central bank's image in the financial world. This cannot be in a central bank's interest, which is why the financial sector probably has more chances to directly exert external pressure.

This relates to Posen (1993, 1995), who examined the impact of the financial sector. He argues that intermediaries such as commercial banks fear inflation as they are net creditors. Therefore they may seek to influence central banks. He concludes:

Rather than mustering votes directly, the financial sector gains access to elected officials by being their main outside source of information and advice about monetary policy.[56]

Overall, a central bank might fear to lose the support of public opinion as only a high degree of confidence of society as a whole can guarantee independence in the long run. This makes the Bundesbank not indifferent to pressure from organized groups, even though it is nominally independent.

5.3   THE HAVRILESKY APPROACH

5.3.1   Methodology

Researchers testing political business cycle models in monetary policy encounter a number of methodological problems. PBC models assume that policy turns expansionary before every election, while one can easily imagine a situation where a government does not need this type of policy, as it may have a high level of popularity. Moreover, it is assumed that the extent to which expansionary policies are used is the same before every election. The impact of regional elections has completely been neglected: if a whole series of regional elections occurs within one year, with general elections at the end of the year, the pre-election stimulation might occur much earlier. And finally, conflicts between the government and the central bank outside pre-election periods have been completely neglected in PBC models.

These criteria should be met by more sophisticated 'conflict indicators'. Political pressure on the central bank may also exist due to other reasons than elections and pressure on the central bank may also arise from interest groups. Trade unions, for instance, are notoriously known for demanding lower interest rates.

The approach as developed by Havrilesky (1993) does not suffer from these drawbacks. He has constructed an indicator for political pressure on the FED, based on the number of newspaper reports in which politicians argue in favor of a more or less restrictive monetary policy: he assumes that all monetary policy information from exchanges between the government and the central bank

> ... that is of value to market participants will systematically appear in the financial press. Specifically, we assume that the policy content of formal and informal communications from the Administration to the Federal Reserve ... is reliably and consistently reported in the press.[57]

In particular, this holds for conflicts between government and the central bank: those are reported in the newspapers (possibly with a certain lag), and more severe struggles lead to more articles. Havrilesky has therefore counted the number of articles in the *Wall Street Journal*, in which government officials demanded a change in monetary policy. Reports calling for monetary ease were counted as +1 and reports in favor of more restrictive monetary policy were counted as -1. The sum of pluses and minuses constitutes the SAFER index. Havrilesky (1993) reports that in regressions for the Federal Funds rate this indicator is highly significant. Froyen et al. (1997) have shown that if economic control variables are included in the model for the interest rate the SAFER index remains significant.

This indicator has the following desirable properties: first, it does not exclusively focus on elections, but on conflicts at any time. Second, it indicates the strength of a conflict. The criteria for a good 'pressure indicator' ('conflict indicator') we have set up in the beginning of this section are met.

5.3.2 Constructing a 'pressure indicator' for Germany

In the following sections we apply the Havrilesky methodology to Germany. We also extend it, as we take pressure on the central bank from other sources into account. The first step is that we have to select a newspaper. To give a reliable picture of the relationship between the central bank, the government and interest groups, a newspaper has to fulfill the following criteria:

- Independence: the more independent and politically neutral the newspaper is, the more accurate the description of political conflicts will be.

- Availability: to get a meaningful sample, the newspaper should cover economic affairs for quite a long period.

- Circulation: the wider the circulation of the newspaper the higher the effect on the public opinion and also (presumably) on the Bundesbank.

It is difficult, if not impossible, to find a newspaper that fulfills all criteria. Therefore, we have decided to gather all articles on the Bundesbank from three German newspapers: *Frankfurter Allgemeine Zeitung* (FAZ), *Handelsblatt* (HB) and *Die Welt*. This also allows a test to determine whether these newspapers report the same issues and whether selection of a particular newspaper influences the results.

Articles expressing a desire for monetary ease (lower interest rates) are counted as -1, whereas articles calling for a tighter monetary policy are counted as +1. We do not only focus on signals from the government (i.e. the executive branch and the ruling party), but also take signals from the following interest groups into account (a detailed description of the data can be found in the appendix C.3):[58]

- Financial sector: commercial banks, bank organizations, savings banks and credit cooperatives.

- Employers: here we distinguish two types of employers organizations, one representing export-oriented firms, the other representing firms that mainly produce for the domestic market.

- Unions: this category contains all statements from trade unions.

- Other: here we count statements from economic researchers and supranational organizations (IMF) as well as comments from journalists and consumer organizations.

A number of potential drawbacks with the approach should also be pointed out. A conflict will most probably be covered much more extensively during 'dull season' (no other news available) than during a period with much news. Furthermore, it is assumed that two articles means twice as much pressure than one article, which may, but need not, be correct.[59] Obviously, these limitations not only apply to this paper, but also to the original work by Havrilesky (1993).

The next section describes the pressure data in more detail.

5.4 PROPERTIES OF THE NEW 'PRESSURE INDICATOR'

Figure 5.2 shows our index for pressure from the government on the Bundesbank. This index is constructed counting all reports in the three selected newspapers for the sample period 01:1960-12:1998. A comparison with the SAFER index of Havrilesky (figure 5.3) shows that political pressure on the central bank is much more prevalent in the US than in Germany. (To make Havrilesky's data comparable to ours, we show minus SAFER in figure 5.3.) Unlike Havrilesky, we count articles demanding higher interest rates as +1 and articles calling for monetary ease as -1. This is done to facilitate the interpretation of the regression results. Despite the fact that we have gathered data from three newspapers (whereas Havrilesky focused only on the *Wall Street Journal*) the number of observations of pressure from the government is far higher in the American case than for Germany.

There are at least two possible explanations: first, German newspapers may simply report less on monetary issues. This, however, is probably not very convincing, as at least one newspaper (the *Handelsblatt*) is known to focus on financial and economic matters. Second, there may be less pressure on the Bundesbank, either because the government appreciates the Bundesbank's policies, or because the German public holds it in high esteem.

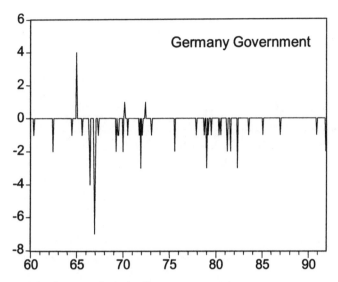

Figure 5.2   Pressure from the German government

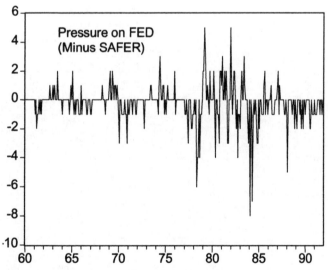

Figure 5.3   Political pressure on US monetary policy (Havrilesky)

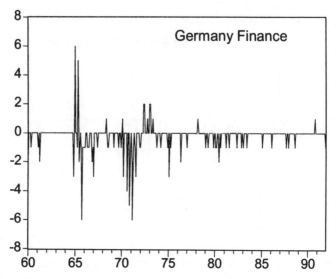

Figure 5.4   Pressure from the German financial sector

A second major difference between German and US data is that the US government frequently pushed for monetary contraction, whereas governmental pressure in Germany generally seeks for monetary ease. This is possibly due to the fact that inflation on average was lower in Germany than in the US, especially during the periods of high US inflation after the oil shocks. Also the impact of the Reagan administration, which fought to reduce inflation rates in the early 1980s, is clearly visible in the conflict indicator for the US.

Figure 5.4 presents our index for pressure from the financial sector, while figure 5.5 shows pressure from all sources on the Bundesbank (this is also called 'total pressure', as pressure from all sources is aggregated). Again, it is clearly visible that there has been much more pressure on the Bundesbank for monetary ease than for monetary tightness. As in figure 5.2, spikes occur especially in the mid 60s under the office of Chancellor Erhard. Apparently, the governmental pressure was echoed by pressure from other social groups. Also in the early 1980s (fighting the consequences of the oil price shock) and after the reunification in the early 1990s there was pressure on the Bundesbank, although in the latter case pressure did not come from the financial sector.

Table 5.1 summarizes the pressure data, focusing on the differences between the various newspapers.[60] For each sector we report the number of observations (that is the number of articles found in this category), the sum of all observations (that is the value of all '+1's and '-1's for this category), and the 'ratio' (i.e. the percentage of articles demanding tighter monetary policy over

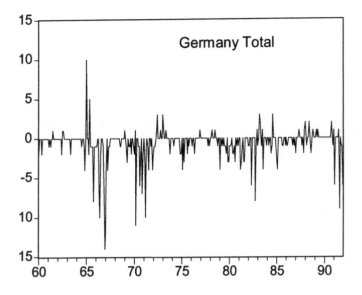

Figure 5.5   Total pressure on the Bundesbank

the total number of articles). The last line ('total pressure') shows the values if we aggregate over all observations. It follows that the *Handelsblatt* features far more articles on the Bundesbank than the *FAZ* or the *Welt*.

The table confirms some prior expectations regarding the attitude of different pressure groups with respect to monetary policy: export-oriented employers opt far more often for monetary ease than their domestic-oriented counterparts. As they can profit from lower exchange rates they are more likely to tolerate higher inflation rates than the domestic-oriented employers. Indeed, domestic-oriented employers are the only pressure group with a positive ratio, thus more often demanding higher interest rates than interest rate cuts.

There are a number of cases where the sum of observations is not equal to the total number of observations (for example 'Pressure from the Financial Sector' reported in the *FAZ* is -29, whereas the number of observations is 39). This means that several articles demanding more expansive monetary policy 'canceled out' against some articles demanding a tighter policy stance. This does not hold for the trade unions: they always want monetary ease.

Pressure from...	FAZ	HB	Welt	Total
# obs. 'Government'	36	30	19	85
Sum of 'Government'	-32	-26	-13	-42
Ratio	-89%	-87%	-69%	-49%
# obs. 'Financial Sector'	39	58	43	140
Sum of 'Financial Sector'	-29	-26	-23	-58
Ratio	-74%	-45%	-43%	-41%
# obs. 'Employers Organization (export-oriented)'	9	14	9	32
Sum of 'Employers Organization (export-oriented)'	-9	-12	-9	-30
Ratio	-100%	-86%	-100%	-94%
# obs. 'Employers Organization (domestic-oriented)'	7	13	3	23
Sum of 'Employers Organization (domestic-oriented)'	-1	3	-1	1
Ratio	-14%	23%	-33%	4%
# obs. 'Trade Unions'	16	42	11	69
Sum of 'Trade Unions'	-16	-42	-11	-69
Ratio	-100%	-100%	-100%	-100%
# obs. 'Other sources'	25	67	18	110
Sum of 'Other sources'	-17	-47	-8	-72
Ratio	-68%	-70%	-44%	-65%
Total # obs. ('total pressure')	153	254	120	527
Sum of all observations	-111	-158	-70	-339
Ratio	-73%	-62%	-58%	-64%

Table 5.1   Pressure on the Bundesbank as reported in the newspapers

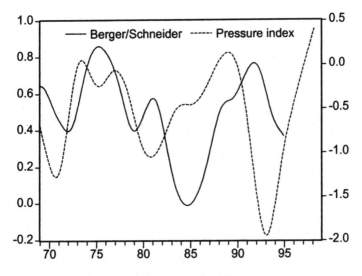

Figure 5.6 Comparison of different conflict indicators

5.5 COMPARISON OF DIFFERENT INDICATORS FOR 'PRESSURE' AND 'CONFLICTS'

Having presented our new pressure indicator we can compare this new indicator and indicators used in previous studies. These indicators are (a) the standard electoral dummies (PBC dummies) and (b) the Berger and Schneider (2000) indicator we have presented in section 4.4.3. Their indicator focuses on 'economic conflicts'; it varies between 0 and 1 with high values indicating that government and central bank pursue different policy stances, whereas low values indicate a low 'conflict potential' as both institutions have adopted similar policies.

In figure 5.6 we have plotted the Berger/Schneider conflict indicator, our 'total' pressure variable, and an electoral dummy by marking the 12-month pre-election periods as gray. As the Berger/Schneider indicator as we have used it was smoothed using a HP-filter, we have also applied a HP-filter to generate the variable Pressure*, a HP-filtered variant of the 'Total Pressure' indicator. This was done to facilitate the comparison between these indicators. Correlation coefficients between different sources of pressure and the electoral variable (PBC12) and the Berger/Schneider indicator are given in table 5.2.

	Total	Pressure*	Government	PBC12	BS indicator
Total	1.00	0.40	0.32	0.04	−0.01
Pressure*	0.40	1.00	0.12	−0.04	0.00
Government	0.32	0.12	1.00	−0.02	−0.02
PBC12	0.04	−0.04	−0.02	1.00	−0.03
BS indicator	−0.01	0.00	−0.02	−0.03	1.00

Table 5.2   Correlation of pressure indicators

a)   The new pressure index and the impact of elections

First, we focus on the comparison of the new pressure indicator with the electoral dummy. Figure 5.6 shows that there were elections before which pressure on the Bundesbank, as measured by the pressure index, was relatively high (e.g. in the 1970s). However, a clear electoral pattern cannot be detected in the pressure index and the correlation between 'Total Pressure' and the PBC12 dummy as reported in table 5.2 is very low.

One of the reasons for the low correlation could be that 'Total Pressure' is the wrong variable: if political pressure is applied before elections, the government will be the major source, not interest groups. Therefore we also report the correlation between 'Pressure from the government' and elections – yet, the relationship becomes even weaker. In other words, pressure occurs irrespective of whether elections are approaching or not, which means that we cannot say that pressure on the Bundesbank is high before elections, as implied by the PBC model.[61]

b)   The new pressure indicator and the Berger/Schneider index

Next, we compare the Berger/Schneider conflict indicator and the new pressure indicator. Clearly, the interpretation of both indicators differs: unlike the Berger/Schneider indicator our new pressure indicator aims at showing political, not economic conflicts, and it does not distinguish between two states (conflict or non-conflict), but rather shows how various pressure groups want monetary policy to change.

Therefore is does not come as a surprise that both indicators are quite different: a quick look at figure 5.6 reveals that until the early 1980s the conflict indicator by Berger and Schneider and our new pressure indicator seem to behave similarly. Since the early 1980s, however, they differ considerably. Especially the period after the reunification is noteworthy: apparently, economic policies differed (as the Berger/Schneider indicator detects a conflict), a finding that our pressure indicator cannot confirm.

The correlation between the Berger/Schneider indicator and the pressure indicator is very weak, regardless of whether we pick HP-filtered values or take the 'Total Pressure' variable. This indicates that economic conflicts (as measured by Berger/Schneider) need not result in high pressure.

5.6 ESTIMATION PROCEDURE

Now that we have presented a new conflict indicator, we examine whether it has a significant impact on Germany's monetary policy. To test this hypothesis, we perform Granger-causality analysis: pressure is said to 'Granger cause' a rise in the day-to-day interest rate, if the time-series prediction of the day-to-day interest rate from its own past improves when lagged values of the pressure indicator are added to the equation. This interpretation of causality is, of course, intuitively attractive. It has therefore become widely accepted, although some of its implications are still under debate.

We tackle two main questions: first, is there any significant influence of the government and pressure groups on the Bundesbank's policy? Second, is there a 'newspaper effect', i.e. does the selection of the newspaper influence our results? If so, then Havrilesky's earlier results for the US could also be biased.

Apart from the day-to-day interest rate (r) and the (several versions of our) pressure indicator (n), we have included the inflation rate (i) and the detrended and seasonally adjusted unemployment rate (u) as explanatory variables in the model (we seasonally detrended the monthly unemployment rate). The reason for this approach is obvious: inflation or changes in the unemployment rate might force the Bundesbank to act (see also Froyen et al., 1997).

This gives the following model:

$$r_t = c + \sum_{j=1}^{k} (\alpha_j r_{t-j} + \beta_j i_{t-j} + \delta_j u_{t-j} + \gamma_j n_{t-j}) + \varepsilon_t,$$

where k is the number of lags included in the specification and ε_t is an independent and identically distributed disturbance term.

Our monthly data cover the period January 1960 until March 1998. To capture possible structural changes we include dummies for the Bretton Woods period (01:1960-04:1973), the EMS period (06:1979-03:1998), the German unification (06:1990-03:1998) and both oil crises (01:1974-12:1975 and 01:1978-12:1981, respectively) in all regressions (the results are not sensitive to the inclusion of these dummies).

A practical disadvantage of this model is that the number of parameters to be estimated can easily become large. In our case – with four explanatory variables – each additional lag brings in four extra parameters. This quickly reduces the degrees of freedom. Often, however, a substantial number of coefficients hardly differ from zero. Moreover, Ahking and Miller (1985) and Thornton and Batten

(1985) have shown that imposing common lag lengths has no basis in theory and may lead to misleading inferences concerning causality. To overcome this problem Hsiao (1981) suggests to use Akaike's (1969, 1970) Final Prediction Error (FPE) criterion to determine the lag structure. Therefore, we will use the FPE criterion to select the appropriate lag specification for the individual variables in the above equation (see also Canova, 1995 and Sturm et al., 1999 for a description and application of the procedure that we followed). Hence, the equation becomes

$$r_t = c + \sum_{j=1}^{k_r} \alpha_j r_{t-j} + \sum_{j=1}^{k_i} \beta_j i_{t-j} + \sum_{j=1}^{k_u} \delta_j u_{t-j} + \sum_{j=1}^{k_n} \gamma_j n_{t-j}) + \varepsilon_t,$$

where k_r, k_i, k_u and k_n are the number of lags included according to the FPE criterion. In the empirical implementation we start with a maximum number of lags equal to 12.

Hsiao (1981) has shown that under fairly general conditions the inclusion of a variable based on the FPE criterion is evidence for a weak Granger-causal ordering. If the lagged values of the explanatory variable further exert a statistically significant effect, then the Granger-causal impact can be identified as a strong form (Kawai, 1980).

The Granger-causality testing procedure generally does not give us an estimate of the sign of the overall effect. In order to test whether there exists a positive or negative effect of one variable on another, we apply the neutrality test in which we calculate the sum of the lagged values of an explanatory variable and test whether it significantly differs from zero (Zarnowitz, 1992).

In this setting, the analysis of a Granger-causal relation from pressure on the day-to-day rate boils down to testing whether each of the γ_j-elements in the previous equation differs from zero. If furthermore the sum of these γ-elements is significantly positive, we know that pressure positively influences the day-to-day rate. Following Geweke et al. (1983), who indicate that the Granger procedure conducted using a Wald χ^2-test statistic outperforms other causality tests in a series of Monte-Carlo experiments, we apply Wald tests. As simple Granger-causality analysis may be obstructed by simultaneity effects: pressure may Granger cause monetary policy, while at the same time monetary policy causes pressure. To avoid this problem, we also analysed Granger causality in a Vector Auto Regression (VAR) model. The results hardly change (results available on request).

A common econometric problem with time-series modeling is the existence of a unit root in the variables used. In standard inference procedures it is assumed that the variables concerned are stationary, i.e. they do not have a unit root. Non-stationary series invalidate many standard results. To determine whether the series are stationary, we follow the testing strategy of Dolado et al.

(1990) and use the augmented Dickey-Fuller (ADF) test (Dickey and Fuller; 1979, 1981). The number of lags used in the estimated equations have been determined similar to Perron (1989). We start with a maximum of 12 lags. If the last lag is insignificant at a 10 per cent level it is omitted. Then we include one lag less. Again it is tested whether the last lag is significant or not. This procedure is repeated until the last lag is significant (results available on request).

5.7 EMPIRICAL EVIDENCE

5.7.1 The aggregated 'pressure index'

Table 5.3 presents the estimation results. The first column reports the number of lags selected according to the FPE-criterion, the second column shows the sum of the estimated coefficients (neutrality test) and in the third we report the F-statistic whether each of the estimated coefficients equals zero (Granger-causality test).

We find that lagged interest rates explain the largest part of the actual interest rate (nine lags are included, which are highly significant). The other two variables included by the FPE criterion are the detrended and seasonally adjusted unemployment rate and the annual inflation rate. Both enter the equation with two lags and have the expected sign. The coefficients of the EMS dummy and the German unification dummy are also significant. The pressure indicator we have added is total pressure, i.e. pressure from government and pressure groups. According to the FPE criterion, this variable has to be included (with two lags) in explaining the interest rate: at a 10 per cent level the aggregated indicator is significantly positive.

5.7.2 Disaggregating the 'pressure index'

Next, we have used disaggregated data. This allows to test (a) for the impact of pressure from organized groups or the government and (b) whether the selection of newspapers matters for the construction of the pressure index.

The results for the influence of organized groups are very clear: pressure stemming from the banking sector is driving all results for the 'total pressure' indicator. Table 5.4 reports the results for 'pressure from the banking sector', while the right set of columns summarizes pressure from all other sources. The FPE criterion selects the pressure indicator of the financial sector with two lags and its coefficient is significant at the 1 per cent level. Accounting for particularities in the German banking sector we have also differentiated between pressure reports from commercial banks and those from savings banks

Variable	Lags	Sum	F-Each
Constant		0.193	0.639
Bretton Woods		0.120	0.539
EMS		0.689∗∗∗	14.637∗∗∗
Unification		−0.342∗	3.387∗
First oil crises		−0.144	0.332
Second oil crisis		−0.011	0.004
Lagged interest rate	9	0.835∗∗∗	94.704∗∗∗
Unemployment	2	−0.163∗∗	7.925∗∗∗
Inflation	2	0.137∗∗∗	6.702∗∗∗
Total Pressure	2	0.053∗	2.858∗
R^2 adj.		0.892	
#. of obs.		451	

Table 5.3   The influence of the 'Total Pressure' variable

(Sparkassen). This gave similar results for both categories (not shown). The indicator for all other pressure categories (expressed here as sum of all other pressure) is not selected by the FPE criterion, which means that it is not significant. Of particular interest is the impact of the government: again the results are clear, the variable 'Pressure from the government' has no significant impact.

In other words, pressure from politicians did not affect German monetary policy. This is an additional confirmation that political pressure did not have clear effects on Germany's monetary policy. However, the Bundesbank's policies were in line with the wishes of the banking sector.

This strong influence of the banking sector does not necessarily come as a surprise. Posen (1993, 1995) has emphasized the importance of the financial sector for reducing inflation rates.[62] Havrilesky (1993) analyses directives of the Federal Advisory Council (FAC) to detect influence of the banking sector on US monetary policy. His results suggest that the monetary authority was responsive to banking industry views as reflected by the directives of the FAC. The FAC Council is composed of members of 12 large banks. The conventional views is that the Council's opinions are relatively unimportant, yet if the banking industry is viewed as an interest group, the FAC might serve as a signal as to what monetary policy stance the banking industry prefers (Havrilesky (1993), pp. 254-256).

Finally, we have investigated to what extent the selection of the newspaper as source for our indicator influences our results. The indicator used for this purpose is aggregated pressure from all sources. The tables 5.5–5.7 show our findings: the results for the *FAZ* and the *Handelsblatt* indicators are quite similar, both being highly significant at the 1 per cent level. The indicator

		$n = $ financial sector	
Variable	Lags	Sum	F-Each
Constant		0.163	0.469
Bretton Woods		0.137	0.731
EMS		0.674***	14.465***
Unification		−0.378**	4.290*
First oil crises		−0.147	0.359
Second oil crisis		−0.010	0.004
Interest rate	9	0.845***	101.400***
Unemployment	2	−0.160**	9.265***
Inflation	2	0.136***	7.074***
Pressure from n	2	0.282***	10.533***
R^2 adj.		0.896	
# of obs.		451	

		$n = $ all other pressure	
Variable	Lags	Sum	F-Each
Constant		0.186	0.589
Bretton Woods		0.086	0.280
EMS		0.707***	15.32***
Unification		−0.336*	3.244*
First oil crises		−0.115	0.212
Second oil crisis		−0.034	0.041
Interest rate	9	0.821***	95.995***
Unemployment	2	−0.151**	8.514***
Inflation	2	0.153***	8.277***
Pressure from n			
R^2 adj.		0.891	
# of obs.		451	

Table 5.4   Disaggregating the 'Pressure index'

constructed on pressure reported in *Die Welt*, however, is not selected by the FPE criterion.[63]

So apparently, the selection of newspapers indeed influences the results. This means that the original work of Havrilesky might also suffer from this problem. Selection of more than one newspaper could help to give a more reliable picture. (Careful readers will notice that some of the newspaper coefficients in the tables 5.5–5.7 are relatively high. This is merely a statistical result, based on the difficulty that some newspapers only feature a relatively limited amount of articles, compared to the long sample period. This result should not be overinterpreted, it just underlines the point that more newspapers provide better and clearer indicators.)

Variable	Lags	Sum	F-Each
Constant		0.230	0.947
Bretton Woods		0.116	0.525
EMS		0.965***	15.367**
Unification		−0.382***	4.271***
First oil crisis		0.110	0.201
Second oil crisis		−0.063	0.141
Lagged Interest Rate	9	0.827***	100.080***
Unemployment	2	−0.171***	8.969***
Inflation	2	0.128***	7.915***
Pressure reported in the *FAZ*	2	0.420**	6.621***
R^2 adj.		0.895	
# of obs.		451	

Table 5.5   The influence of the newspapers: pressure from the financial sector reported in the Frankfurter Allgemeine Zeitung

Variable	Lags	Sum	F-Each
Constant		0.111	0.226
Bretton Woods		0.149	0.881
EMS		0.790***	19.642***
Unification		−0.435***	5.702**
First oil crisis		−0.190	0.624
Second oil crisis		0.080	0.230
Lagged Interest Rate	9	0.842***	94.497***
Unemployment	2	−0.182***	11.402**
Inflation	2	0.140***	10.353***
Pressure reported in the *Handelsblatt*	2	0.964***	5.443**
R^2 adj.		0.901	
# of obs.		449	

Table 5.6   The influence of the newspapers: pressure from the financial sector reported in the Handelsblatt

Variable	Lags	Sum	F-Each
Constant		0.186	0.589
Bretton Woods		0.086	0.280
EMS		0.707***	15.320***
Unification		−0.336*	3.244*
First oil crisis		−0.115	0.212
Second oil crisis		−0.034	0.041
Lagged Interest Rate	9	0.821***	95.995***
Unemployment	2	−0.151***	8.514***
Inflation	2	0.153***	8.277***
Pressure reported in the *Welt*			
R^2 adj.		0.891	
# of obs.		449	

Table 5.7   The influence of the newspapers: pressure from the financial sector reported in the Die Welt

5.7.3   Interpretation and policy implications

So far, we have found evidence that only pressure from the financial sector has affected monetary policy by the Bundesbank. Pressure from other organized groups or from the government did not have a significant influence on German monetary policy. This raises two questions: (1) How should the findings for the financial sector be explained? (2) If other organized groups do not have a significant impact, why did they nevertheless try to apply pressure?

How should the findings for the financial sector be explained?   Although the institutional setting is somewhat different in the US, our findings for the financial sector can be related to evidence presented by Havrilesky (1993):

> The evidence ... supports the symbiotic view that the Federal Reserve monetary policy has responded to the signal from the banking industry as reflected in the directives of the Federal Advisory Council over the 1969-1988 period.[64]

Our results for the banking sector may be interpreted in two ways. First, economic data used as the basis for the Bundesbank's decisions, is also available for commercial banks. If banks have large research departments and thus large information sets, they may signal on the basis of this information. The Bundesbank may act on the basis of the same information. We have therefore added some additional economic state variables (industrial production, the Dollar-Deutschmark exchange rate) to check whether bank signaling simply picks up the effects of omitted variables. The results are reported in table 5.8.

Results according to the FPE criterion			
Variable	Lags	Sum	F-Each
Constant		0.142	0.341
Bretton Woods		0.099	0.371
EMS		0.695***	14.770***
Unification		−0.440**	5.186*
First oil crises		−0.108	0.191
Second oil crisis		−0.009	0.003
Interest rate	9	0.847***	88.670***
Unemployment	2	−0.186**	6.577***
Exchange Rate			
Ind. Output	1	0.026*	3.729*
Inflation	2	0.150***	8.769***
Pressure from *Financial sector*	2	0.272***	9.916***
R^2 adj.		0.896	
# of obs.		451	

Results if at least one lag of all explanatory variables is taken up.			
Variable	Lags	Sum	F-Each
Constant		0.270	1.041
Bretton Woods		0.031	0.033
EMS		0.645***	12.140***
Unification		−0.498	6.280*
First oil crises		−0.105	0.180
Second oil crisis		−0.024	0.020
Interest rate	9	0.850***	88.936***
Unemployment	2	−0.209**	7.240***
Exchange Rate	1	−0.005	1.486
Ind. Output	1	0.023*	3.034*
Inflation	2	0.128***	6.194***
Pressure from *Financial sector*	2	0.277***	10.221***
R^2 adj.		0.891	
# of obs.		451	

Table 5.8   Robustness checks with additional economic variables

It follows that our financial sector pressure variable remains highly significant. These outcomes suggest that a second explanation, related to the introductory considerations put forward in section 5.2, is more likely: central bankers have incentives to listen to the financial sector, be it because their utility increases from higher 'popularity' among colleagues, or be it to build up reputation for the central bank and thus ensure independence in the long run.

If other organized groups do not have a significant impact, why did they nevertheless try to apply pressure? Despite the fact that other organized groups apart from the financial sector did not have any significant impact on the Bundesbank's policy at all, attempts to apply external pressure, in particular from interest groups, have never ceased. At some point it may seem not worthwhile to continue demand changes in monetary policy, while effectively these statements do not lead to changes in the policy stance. Why did the attempts to influence the Bundesbank never stop?

The answer is relatively straightforward: it is in the interest of the leaders of the organized group. Its members simply expect these sorts of statements, so these requests are issued to send a message to its own interest group members, not primarily to the central bank. For instance, nearly every time trade unions talk about unemployment it seems part of the 'ritual' to demand lower interest rates to foster economic activity. To some extent this is simply what trade unions members expect their leaders to do, but these requests to the central bank may possibly also be used as a vehicle to distract the attention from other mistakes that could have occurred e.g. in the wage-bargaining process.

Finally, if – as we assume – these messages are more intended to calm down own supporters than to 'force' monetary policy to take some action, this also explains why the German central bank largely remained unimpressed.

5.8 SUMMARY

In this chapter we have applied a new indicator for (political) pressure, which extended the PBC model into a conflict model. We did this by presenting a new conflict indicator, based on Havrilesky's approach, but extending it to allow for pressure from various sources. As we have shown in section 5.3, this approach has several advantages in comparison to standard PBC-type of models.

Interpreting our results and comparing them with the evidence reported by Havrilesky (1993) leads to two main conclusions. First, the selection of the newspaper can have an important influence on the results. Second, our results point to some interesting differences between Germany and the US. In comparison to the US, relatively little government pressure is put on the

German central bank. In contrast to Havrilesky's findings for the FED, the Bundesbank does not respond to governmental pressure, nor to pressure from trade associations or unions. We do find, however, a clear and very robust impact of pressure from the financial sector on the Bundesbank's policy.

One potential drawback of the approach followed in this chapter is that our study could be biased against finding a significant impact of the signal variable as interest groups are most likely to be 'signaling' when they are dissatisfied with the course of policy. This is an issue we examine in the next chapter (section 6.5) when we introduce variables that measure public support of the Bundesbank.

6. The Role of Public Support

6.1 OVERVIEW

After a long debate the European Economic and Monetary Union finally started on January 1st, 1999. The slide of the euro exchange rate against the US dollar has again sparked the fears of Eurocritics: a weak currency, which translates into high inflation. So, to become a success in the long run, inflation in the euro area must remain low. The prerequisites for that to happen are unclear: as we have noted in the first chapter there is some evidence that a high degree of central bank independence lowers inflation. Probably more important than institutional arrangements, however, is the public attitude with regard to sound monetary policy: the Germans are often considered to be especially inflation averse due to the traumatic experience of two hyperinflations within a relatively short period of time.

Different societies tolerate different levels of inflation, but we do not know which factors determine a society's 'preferred' level of inflation. The Bundesbank has never hesitated to stress the differences in 'stability culture', i.e. relative inflation aversion, among euro member countries: Italians, for instance, are said to be less inflation averse than Germans. While these differences among countries certainly exist, they are hard to quantify.[65]

Before the EMU started inflation had declined in all member countries, which indicates that stability culture can be built up. This possibility has also been stressed by the Bundesbank; yet, it remains unclear how stability culture develops. Certainly a key aspect in that respect is the ability to maintain tight monetary policy during 'rough times', that is, when the central bank is under pressure from politicians or pressure groups to change the policy stance. This ability hinges at least partially on the degree of popular support, as high support for the central bank makes it easier to resist threats from pressure groups.

The question we want to tackle in this chapter is the following: when the Bundesbank was under pressure, did anyone support current monetary policies? And if so, how did the Bundesbank react to public support? Is there a certain pattern?

These questions cannot be answered within the traditional macroeconomic framework. We try to give an answer to these questions by estimating a model

for Bundesbank policies, which incorporates not only economic, but also political factors. We outline the methodological approach of this chapter in the
next section, before we estimate a purely economic model (section 6.3). In
section 6.4 the model is transformed into a public choice model by adding data
on political pressure, in section 6.5 we extend the model by including public
support. In the final section we summarize the main findings of this chapter.

6.2 METHODOLOGY

The classical literature on central banking assumes that monetary policy is
determined by economic variables, e.g. if inflation is high, then the central
bank will respond by raising interest rates. The timing of, say, elections, has no
influence on the central bank's policy. While the economic situation undoubtedly has the biggest impact on the current policy stance, the public choice
literature has pointed out that other factors should also be considered. As we
have shown in the last chapter, pressure is frequently applied from certain parts
of the population, while other groups with different interests may defend the
current monetary policy.

So far, we have extensively considered pressure on the Bundesbank, but have
neglected the possibility that the German central bank could also enjoy support
from the population (for historical evidence on Bundesbank support see Berger
and de Haan, 1999). Yet a central bank can only be strong if it enjoys broad
support. We extend the existing public choice framework of monetary policy by
adding public support as a factor influencing the central bank's decisions. Our
framework for monetary policy thus consists of three components: economics,
pressure and support (see figure 6.1). We explain each factor in turn.

Economics is a term for the economic situation, characterized by GDP growth,
    inflation etc. Traditional macroeconomics assumes that each economic situ-
    ation has an 'optimal' monetary policy, that is, a policy that fits the economic
    needs of the current situation. Such a behavior is for instance the basis of the
    type of policies reflected in the Taylor-rule (Taylor, 1992).

Pressure means that some parts of the population demand a change in mone-
    tary policy. In our view pressure might result from various parts of society
    (politicians, employer's organizations, trade unions or commercial banks),
    but also from public opinion, as expressed e.g. in comments in newspapers
    etc. If the pressure is strong enough, it might result in deviations from the
    optimal monetary policy, that is, it might force the central bank to pursue a
    policy not compatible with the current economic situation.

Support strengthens the central bank: if the central bank enjoys a high degree
    of confidence or support from the population, then it has a better position in

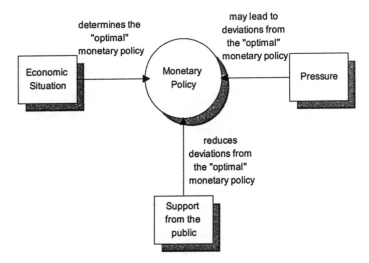

Figure 6.1   Economic and political determinants of monetary policy

public discussions about monetary policy. Thus support might (partly) offset the pressure of pressure groups. The higher the support, the 'stronger' the central bank and the more it can focus on economic variables. We assume that any group of the population can offer support to the central bank.

Most components of our model are well known: if we completely abstract from pressure and support, we only look at the economic situation. This is an approach e.g. followed by Clarida and Gertler (1996): they estimate a reaction function and include only economic variables as regressors to analyse the Bundesbank's behavior. Adding the pressure component to this basic model yields the public choice perspective, which has been examined in the last chapter. Finally, augmenting the public choice model by adding a support variable allows examination of supportive actions. As the literature has developed along these lines, we start with the simplest case and then extend the model.

6.3   TRADITIONAL MACROECONOMIC MODEL

In the world of traditional macroeconomics a central bank concentrates only on economic variables; political pressure on a central bank is neglected. Econometrically, this can be expressed as follows: the central bank would like to set monetary policy such that

$$i_{CB,t} = \Gamma(\text{Economic variables}) + \varepsilon_t, \tag{6.1}$$

where monetary policy is measured by $i_{CB,t}$ and the relevant economic variables are aggregated by a function Γ. As dependent variable we have again chosen the day-to-day rate i_t.

The interest rate may deviate from the predicted level by an error ε_t, which is caused by (1) our less-than-perfect knowledge of Γ, (2) by the fact that even the central bank does not fully control the market rate, and (3) possibly also by political factors which we have chosen to neglect in this early setup.

In practice, we encounter a few problems when we try to estimate the function Γ: some of the economic variables used by the bank are known, like the unemployment rate and the rate of inflation, but a number of other potentially relevant variables such as 'the mood on the stock market' (irrational exuberance, for instance) cannot so easily be quantified. Making matters worse, the number and kind of these unknown variables are probably subject to shifts over time. So while the function Γ is an interesting theoretical construct, there are major obstacles in its practical use by observers outside the Bank.

However, we do have an indicator that shows what the intentions inside the Bank led in the previous period, namely to the interest rate of that period. This rate is a perfect (up to ε_t) indicator of Γ. So, we can use lagged values of i_t as explanatory variables to increase our understanding of the current level of i_t.

This leads to a new formulation of equation (6.1):

$$i_t = \Delta(L(i)) + \Gamma(\text{Economic variables}) + \varepsilon_t', \tag{6.2}$$

where $L(.)$ is the lag function. Now, prediction errors ε_t' are caused by three things: imperfect knowledge of Δ and Γ, market fluctuations and, thirdly, unobserved circumstances inside the Bank that led to innovations in i.

To make the model econometrically feasible, we start with the standard assumption that the Bundesbank cares about inflation and, perhaps to a lesser extent, about unemployment. We estimate the following basic regression:

$$i_t = \alpha + \sum_j \beta_j i_{t-j} + \sum_k \gamma_k \pi_{t-k} + \sum_l \delta_l U_{t-k} + \varepsilon_t, \tag{6.3}$$

where π_t denotes the rate of inflation and U_t is the unemployment rate. We use growth rates, variables have been detrended if necessary to ensure stationarity (see the appendix for details). The number of lags is determined using Akaikes Information Criterion (AIC). Admittedly, this is a very simple reaction function, but this regression serves to illustrate the traditional macroeconomic approach – and more sophisticated specifications basically deliver similar results.

The results for this model are presented in table 6.1. The first column reports

Variable	Lags	Sum	F-Each
Interest Rate	9	0.95***	316.71***
Inflation	2	0.10***	9.28***
Unemployment	4	−0.22***	5.03***
R^2 adj.		0.89	
AIC		2.58	

Table 6.1   Traditional Macroeconomic model

the number of lags according to the AIC criterion, the second the sum of the estimated coefficients (neutrality tests) and the third the F-statistic testing whether each of the estimated coefficients equals zero. We see that both the coefficient of the inflation rate and unemployment are highly significant: higher inflation leads to higher interest rates, while rising unemployment leads to lower interest rates. This is the typical behavior we might expect from a central bank.

6.4   TRADITIONAL PUBLIC CHOICE MODEL

The traditional macroeconomic approach is useful as a starting point, but as we have seen in the previous chapters it is far from giving a complete picture of how monetary policy is determined. It might be desirable that monetary policy is only influenced by economic factors, but this is not very realistic. In the previous chapter we have shown that the Bundesbank has often been exposed to external influences, which may cause deviations from the 'pure economically determined' policy stance. We can deal with political pressure by augmenting our reaction function. In this case we write

$$i_t = \Delta(L(i)) + \Gamma(\text{Economic variables}) + \Phi(\text{Political variables}) + \varepsilon_t''. \quad (6.4)$$

With this formulation, it is still possible for researchers to predict the Bank's preferred interest rate, taking into account the political pressure. We assume that, like Γ, the function Φ can be estimated from the data. Errors in the prediction, denoted by ε_t' this time, are now caused by imperfect knowledge of Γ and Φ and by market fluctuations.

To estimate equation 6.4, we need data on pressure. Here we can use the pressure indicator we have presented in the previous chapter. It is relatively easy to incorporate this measure for pressure in our macroeconomic model: the impact of economic variables and pressure on the Bundesbanks policy is not fundamentally different – a cut in interest rates might be motivated by

Variable	Lags	Sum	F-Each
Interest Rate	9	0.96***	298.04***
Inflation	2	0.09***	8.11***
Unemployment	4	−0.20***	3.81***
Pressure	3	0.06*	1.93[66]
R^2 adj.		0.89	
AIC		2.57	

Table 6.2   Traditional Public Choice model

decreasing inflationary pressure, but could as well be the result of serious pressure from, say, the government. Thus we treat pressure like the economic variables and it enters the Bundesbank's reaction function in an analogous way. We estimate:

$$i_t = \alpha + \sum_j \beta_j i_{t-j} + \sum_k \gamma_k \pi_{t-k} + \sum_l \delta_l \pi_{t-l} + \sum_m \xi_m \text{Pressure}_{t-m} + \varepsilon_t, \quad (6.5)$$

where Pressure$_t$ denotes the pressure index discussed above. Similar equations are found in other empirical papers using the public choice approach: we use a different type of pressure indicator than most other studies, but the model as such is not very new.

Our estimates are presented in table 6.2. They basically confirm the results of the previous chapter: the pressure index has a significant impact; additional estimates (not reported) show that is highly significant with a lag of two months. The positive sign on the pressure variable means that pressure to lower interest rates indeed leads to interest rate cuts – again, this is what could have been expected. As pressure mostly occurred to lower interest rates (see figure 5.5), interest rates on average were lower than the economic variables would have required.

The estimated coefficients for inflation and unemployment hardly change. The AIC, Akaike information criterion, drops marginally, which indicates that this model performs slightly better than the previous one (using the Akaike information criterion as a model selection guide, one selects the model with the smallest information criterion). These results indicate that the type of regression we ran in the previous section (standard macroeconomic regression without political variables) can be improved upon when analysing the Bundesbank's behavior. Pressure is a significant variable, which means that if this variable is omitted in the estimation, the unexplained variance will be larger.[67] Therefore the public choice model gives a better picture of the factors that influenced the German monetary policy.

To summarize, the above result shows that the Bundesbank did not operate in a 'political vacuum': pressure from organized groups had a significant impact. Due to pressure interest rates were lower than they would have been if pressure had not been applied. So if we want to know what really influenced the Bundesbank's decisions we have to include political variables.

6.5 THE 'EXTENDED' PUBLIC CHOICE MODEL

The public choice model has a clear advantage over the traditional macroeconomic reaction function. The use of pressure data distinguished the public choice approach from the purely macroeconomic theory. This is, however, not the end of the story: reading through the newspapers one does not only find articles demanding changes in the monetary policy stance, but also supportive statements can be found. Indeed, they are quite frequent and basically say: 'Don't force the central bank to do anything, they know better how to apply monetary policy. Trust them, they will do the right thing.' Such a statement is fundamentally different from a pressure statement. How can such a supportive behavior be incorporated in our framework?

6.5.1 The support variable

Before we extend the estimates of the traditional public choice approach by adding support to the model, we first have a look at the support data. Again we have relied on Havrilesky's methodology: using the same newspapers we now have focused on supportive statements from the different sources distinguished above. Articles that expressed support of the current Bundesbank policy, regardless of the actual policy stance, were counted as +1, all other articles were counted as 0. This variable will be called 'support index'. As before, we have gathered data based on statements coming from the government and interest groups.[68]

Figure 6.2 plots the aggregated support index ('Total support'). Spikes in the mid-1960s, during the oil crisis, and in the early 1990s can easily be distinguished. In table 6.3 we summarize the main components of the support index. For each pressure group we report the number of supportive articles per newspaper and the ratio of the number of supportive articles over the total number of 'pressure' articles. As we can see, public support of the Bundesbank is relatively high across all categories; to some degree, even the trade unions supported the central bank.

Apparent is the degree of heterogeneity of the organized groups. Interest groups define themselves by members sharing a common interest (e.g. exporters profiting from lower exchange rates). Therefore, one would suspect that if such a group expresses wishes concerning monetary policy, most members

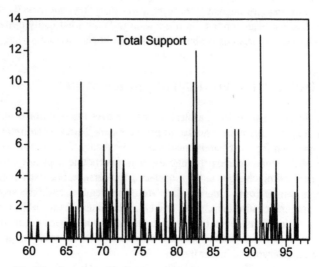

Figure 6.2   Total support for the Bundesbank

Support for the Bundesbank	FAZ	HB	Welt	Total
No. of obs. 'Government'	35	41	12	88
Ratio support/pressure	97%	137%	63%	104%
No. of obs. 'Financial sector'	29	64	18	111
Ratio support/pressure	74%	110%	42%	79%
No. of obs. 'Employers org. (export)'	12	17	6	35
Ratio support/pressure	133%	121%	67%	109%
No. of obs. 'Employers org. (domestic)'	9	12	3	24
Ratio support/pressure	129%	92%	100%	104%
No. of obs. 'Trade unions'	3	6	0	9
Ratio support/pressure	19%	14%	0%	13%
No. of obs. 'Public opinion'	1	12	1	14
Ratio support/pressure	4%	18%	6%	13%
Total no. of obs. ('total support')	104	163	47	314
Ratio total support/total pressure	68%	64%	39%	60%

Table 6.3   Support for the Bundesbank in different newspapers

would agree. Yet, clearly the expectation that the 'best' policy stance is debated only *between* interest groups is wrong, clearly the debate also occurs *within* groups. The high degree of heterogeneity can perhaps be explained by different preferences or discount factors of the individual members of an organized group.

To examine the relationship between pressure and support we use absolute values of the pressure index, denoted as *abs(Pressure)*. The correlation coefficient for *abs(Pressure)* and *Support* is 0.46, which is relatively low. Moreover, Granger causality test reported in table 6.4 show that correlation runs from *abs(Pressure)* to *Support*. This means that high pressure from certain parts of the population triggers off public support.

Of particular interest is the relationship between the government and the central bank. We see that the government more often supported the central bank than it applied pressure by demanding changes in the monetary policy stance (i.e. the ratio support/pressure for the government in table 6.3 is > 100 per cent). The common assumption that the relationship between these two institutions is characterized by frequent conflicts apparently does not hold, at least not for Germany.

To summarize, a first important finding is that interest groups are not homogeneous at all. The data reveals a high degree of heterogeneity among interest groups, that is while some members of a pressure group were demanding policy changes, other members of the same interest group supported the current monetary policy.

Using the support variable, we can also check the question we raised at the end of the previous chapter: it could be that our study is biased against finding a significant impact of the pressure variable, as interest groups are most likely to be 'signaling' when they are dissatisfied with the course of policy. If this argument was correct, we would expect that if government does not support the Bundesbank policies, pressure would occur. And similarly, if government puts pressure on the Bundesbank, there should not be support signals. Figure 6.3 shows the absolute value of the 'pressure from the government' variable on the negative axis, while our 'support from the government' index is shown on the positive axis. As follows from figure 6.3, both implications above are often refuted. So an important potential reason why our conclusions as reported in chapter 5 could be biased is not supported by these results.

Granger causality tests	*F-Stat.*	*Prob.*
abs(Pressure) does not Granger cause *Support*	2.07	0.02
Support does not Granger cause *abs(Pressure)*	1.11	0.35

Table 6.4   Relation between pressure and support

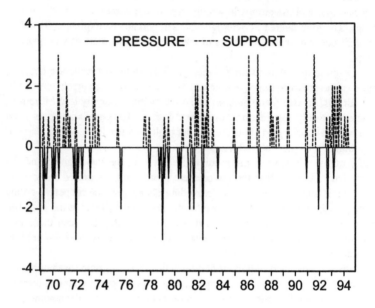

Figure 6.3   Pressure and support from the German government

6.5.2   Empirical evidence

So far, we have estimated simple reaction functions. Economic data and data on pressure easily entered our regressions, as both data have a simple interpretation, e.g. if inflation goes up, interest rates are raised. Our pressure variable was constructed in such a way that if pressure is positive, we expect a rise in the interest rate, whereas negative pressure leads to lower interest rates. That means that pressure has a *direction*, that is, we can distinguish between pressure for higher and for lower interest rates.

The support variable is different. Support can be high in periods with high interest rates as well as in periods with low interest rates. High support does not call for higher or lower interest rates, it is 'unconditional', which means that no matter what policy the Bundesbank is following, supporters back its actions. This makes estimation more tricky: we cannot simply add the support variable to our public choice model. Technically speaking, unlike the pressure variable, support has *no direction*.

It is at this point that we take an interest in the variance of the error term. Previously, it was an indicator of how well our model was doing in predicting the interest rate. However, you can also interpret the error term as a deviation from the 'optimal' monetary policy: if we go back to equation 6.1, ε_t is high if economic variables have less power in explaining variation of the interest rate. This means that other factors besides economic variables used in the regression might have influenced the central bank's decisions. One such factor has been identified in the last section: if political pressure is high, then the central bank deviates from the purely economic needs.

There are two reasons for this: first, high pressure means that people are complaining about the Bank's normal policy. This makes it more likely that the Bank will deviate from the optimal policy. Secondly, given that the bank is more likely to deviate, it will be more attractive for speculators to enter the debt market and try to manipulate r. Both factors should be expected to play up when the bank lacks public support.

We need to find a model to examine whether the central bank is led more by economic considerations when its support is high – and is more likely to deviate from the rules when support is low. In that case, our measure of policy (r_t) is not so well explained by the rule.

We will use a simple linear form to estimate Δ, Φ and Γ and use an ARCH model to explain the variance in the error term. ARCH, or Autoregressive Conditional Heteroskedasticity models, generally have the following form (see e.g. Gouriéroux (1997) and Harvey (1990) for details about ARCH models):

$$
\begin{aligned}
y_t &= x_t'\beta + \varepsilon_t \\
\varepsilon_t &\sim N(0, h_t) \\
h_t &= \alpha_0 + \alpha_1 \varepsilon_{t-1}^2
\end{aligned}
\tag{6.6}
$$

We see that the variance h_t of the error term ε_t varies over time, with a minimum of α_0 and increasing with the previous realization of the error term. We can amend (6.6) by allowing for exogenous variables:

$$
h_t = \alpha_0 + \alpha_1 \varepsilon_{t-1}^2 + z_t'\theta
\tag{6.7}
$$

Estimating these equations, now known as an XARCH model, can be done by maximum likelihood. The value of parameter θ tells us about the effect of the exogenous variable on the expected variance.

Our main estimation results are reported in table 6.5. We see that (a) the estimated coefficient for pressure is smaller, it becomes statistically less significant (still the Pressure$_{t-2}$ variable remains significant at the 10 per cent level) and the sum of the Pressure variable drops; and (b) the *Support$_{t-2}$* coefficient is highly significant with a two-period lag. The sum of the support variable has the expected negative sign and this model yields the lowest Akaike information

Variable	Lags	Sum	F-Each
Interest Rate	9	0.98***	346.38***
Inflation	2	0.05*	11.13***
Unemployment	4	−0.12**	1.79
Pressure	3	0.03	1.59
Arch (5 Arch terms)		Coefficient	
Support$_t$		0.01	
Support$_{t-1}$		0.00	
Support$_{t-2}$		−0.02***	
R^2 adj.		0.89	
AIC		1.77	

Table 6.5   'Extended' Public Choice model

criterion, which means that this model outperforms the previous ones and can therefore be considered as the preferred specification.

6.5.3   Interpretation and policy implications

How should these findings be interpreted? First, we have made the variance of the error term endogenous. The coefficient for public support is negative, which means that the variance of ε_t becomes smaller as support for the bank increases, larger when the Bundesbank lacks support.

Second, we look at the impact of public pressure: the pressure variable is less significant compared to earlier estimates and the estimated coefficient is smaller. This makes sense: we expect the effects of political pressure to surface when support for the economic rule is low – however, our model tells us that the variance of the error terms becomes large precisely when that happens. This makes it harder to detect the effects of the political variable as they are covered by a larger 'cloud of error'. Put in simple terms, we have shown that a high degree of support – at least partly – offsets pressure from interest groups.

We can illustrate this graphically: in figure 6.4 we have plotted two hypothetical distributions of the error term, with the dotted line representing a smaller variance. In the center of these distributions is our estimate of r_t. We know that the variance depends on the support of the Bundesbank with a negative sign. Translated into figure 6.4, the variance of the error term is larger (unbroken line) when support is low, and smaller when support is high. If we estimate the traditional public choice model and do not account for public support, the distribution will lie between the two figures. This means that adding support as an explanatory variable increases our understanding of the error term. It translates not only into a better understanding of the factors influencing the Bundesbank, but also – quite practically – allows us to make better forecasts.

Pierce and Rebeck (2001) have put forward a qualitative similar conclusion

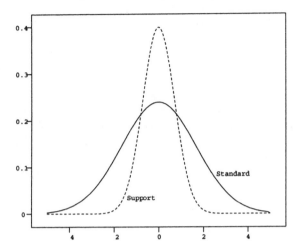

Figure 6.4 Effect of public support on forecast error ε_t

for the FED. They have examined the voting behavior in FOMC meetings: meetings at which voting was unanimous is viewed as a proxy for a less uncertain macroeconomic environment, meetings at which voting is non-unanimous as a proxy for a more uncertain environment. Their findings suggest that '... when the macroeconomic environment is less clear, there is greater scope for non-macroeconomic factors to influence monetary policy decisions'.[69]

The policy implications of these findings are clear: Public support helps the central bank to concentrate on economic needs and makes it easier to completely ignore political pressure. So in that sense from the point of view of a central bank the optimal response to a threat from politicians is not to respond at all, but let others defend the central bank's policy. If the population feels that a central bank is conducting sound monetary policy and generally doing a 'good job', threats to central banks become politically more costly and therefore less frequent. If a situation has been reached where public support is high, then this open support will discourage politicians in the long-run and establish not just legal, but also *de facto* central bank independence

The question remains: how did the German Bundesbank manage to reach such high esteem among the German population, resulting in such high levels of public support? The main explication focuses on the past: German history since World War II is probably the crucial factor. The argument goes as follows: Germany has to a large extent abandoned national symbols, in fact one of few things Germans were proud of (and was always welcomed abroad) was their currency. Moreover, the economic miracle (*'Wirtschaftswunder'*) was for many Germans closely associated with their currency. So one might say that the German mark has replaced other national symbols, which explains its high reputation. Moreover, having experienced two hyperinflations in one generation many Germans were relieved to finally have a stable currency. This is the main reason why the Bundesbank has enjoyed such high esteem and why its independence has only very rarely been in real danger.

At the same time such high esteem can turn out to be a somewhat risky burden to a central bank, if the public – resulting from a certain mistrust towards other state institutions or politicians – transfers other tasks to its central bank. The fact that the Bundesbank was asked to write a report about the possible consequences of the introduction of the euro might serve as an example. So from the point of view of a central bank to maintain such high reputation in the long-run it is essential to restrict itself to its core task, namely to guarantee low inflation rates, and not to engage in more general political discussion.

6.6 SUMMARY

In this chapter we have introduced a 'support variable', which measures public support for the Bundesbank across all major German pressure groups and the government. In the previous chapter we saw that the Bundesbank has been under severe pressure from different pressure groups. Now we have shown that, at the same time, it enjoyed broad support often from the same pressure groups. The first important finding of this chapter is thus that all pressure groups were heterogeneous. Furthermore, we have shown that pressure triggers supportive actions.

Traditional macroeconomics assumes that the Bundesbank prefers to focus on economic variables only. Section 6.4 has shown that this is not the case, as pressure from organized groups does plays an important role. In this chapter we have demonstrated that our understanding of the factors influencing monetary policy can be improved even more if we add public support to the traditional public choice model.

Our second finding results from regression analysis: we have shown that a high degree of public support for a central bank makes pressure from interest groups less important. This means that pressure of organized groups is (partly) offset by public support. In periods of high support, this means lower deviations from the optimal monetary policy, compared to the 'public choice'-type of reaction functions.

Third, the variance of the error is reduced compared to previous reaction functions, which means that we can make more accurate predictions about the Bundesbank's monetary policy. Neglecting public support does not give a complete picture of the factors influencing monetary policy.

Unfortunately, similar evidence is as yet not available for other central banks. It would be interesting to compare our findings for the Bundesbank with results for, for example, the US Federal Reserve. This issue clearly deserves further attention in the future.

This chapter concludes our treatment of the Deutsche Bundesbank. In what follows we investigate the European Central Bank, the successor of the Bundesbank and arguably the most important supra-national central bank. We examine to what extent our findings for the German central bank also allow us to improve our knowledge of the ECB.

7. The European Context: An Economic Analysis

7.1 OVERVIEW

In the preceding chapters we have analysed pressure on and support for the German Bundesbank. In the next two chapters we extend the analysis to the European Central Bank (ECB). Before we discuss the institutional side, we first focus on the economic side. As we will see, the results of this discussion has a strong impact on the political discussion in the next chapter. The main question we want to ask is: are there any additional, special issues that have the potential to make the ECB's task more complex than it previously was for the national central banks it replaced?

The fact that the euro area consists of heterogeneous member states indeed creates additional difficulties for European monetary policy. Moreover, fiscal policies remain under national responsibility, which potentially could create a situation of economic disparities caused by national policies, but for which the ECB is held accountable.

So the special construction of the European Monetary and Economic Union provides additional potential for conflicts. Moreover, the EMU member countries are quite heterogeneous in terms of their inflation and the years 1999-2001 additionally were marked by a surge in inflation in all European countries.

The variable we focus most on in this section is the inflation rate, as this is the variable the ECB is accountable for. In this chapter we examine the major reasons for inflation differentials and check to what extent the increase in European inflation during that period let to a higher dispersion of inflation rates. Our findings generally indicate that a fair part of inflation differentials can be explained by differences in relative productivities, as suggested by the Balassa-Samuelson hypothesis. Moreover, we present empirical evidence showing that present inflation dispersion in the euro area is not unusually high, compared to other monetary unions.

We start this chapter by giving a brief overview of what monetary policy can achieve in a monetary union (section 7.2). In section 7.3 we give a brief overview about the major causes for inflation differentials. In section 7.4 we

Data from 2000	Euro area	EU 15	US	Japan
Population in millions	303.0	377.0	278.1	126.8
GDP (in billion euro)	6 553	8 526	10 709	5 145
GDP per capita (in PPS)	22 360	22 530	34 880	25 030
GDP per capita (in euro)	21 520	22 530	38 900	40 600
Exports as share of GDP	37.2	36.0	11.2	10.8
Imports as share of GDP	36.3	35.3	14.9	9.4

Table 7.1   Key information on the euro area

examine the current state of EMU inflation differentials and compare them to evidence for other monetary unions, before we estimate one of the prime economic causes for inflation dispersion, the Balassa-Samuelson model, in section 7.5. Finally, we summarize our findings in section 7.6.

7.2   THE ROLE OF THE SINGLE MONETARY POLICY IN A MONETARY UNION

The euro area is one of the most important economic regions in the world, accounting for about 16 per cent of total world GDP, even though it comprises only 5 per cent of total world population. It is also one of the richest regions in the world with a GDP per capita of 21,520 PPS in 2000 (PPS or *Purchasing Power Standards* is an artificial currency that allows for variations between the national price levels not taken into account by exchange rates. It removes distortions due to price level differences). Some key figures about the euro area are summarized in table 7.1 (source: Eurostat. The EU 15 comprise the euro area plus Denmark, Sweden and the UK).

Comparing the situation of the ECB with the one previously faced by the national central banks from a public choice perspective highlights a fundamental difference between the potential pressure on the ECB and potential pressure on any European national central bank: pressure might not only result from politicians facing elections or dissatisfied interest groups, but also from individual countries, facing comparatively high inflation rates with respect to other member countries (the opposite case is, of course, also possible: that a member countries faces low inflation rates and wants to stimulate economic activity by lowering interest rates). This makes it necessary to first define what European monetary policy can achieve – and its limitations.

Any country can be viewed as a monetary union between several regions. Within these regions of a country economic dispersion such as inflation differentials are typically smaller than between countries, due to the lack of barriers to mobility such as different languages. In a monetary union, by definition one monetary policy applies to all member countries. However, in most cases not all countries will have the same inflation rate. To some extent national central banks face similar difficulties: for instance, in the United States the inflation rates in, say, Memphis and New York are quite likely to differ. However, policymakers in the US have a common fiscal instrument to compensate for these local differences, whereas coordination of economic policy in the EU is somewhat more difficult.

Moreover, European countries differ significantly in economic power and size. This means that inflation differentials within the euro area may trigger unequal responses:

> All else being equal, German inflation would only need to rise by 0.3 per cent to push up Euroland inflation by 0.1 per cent; Irish inflation on the other hand would need to rise by 11 per cent to have the same effect.[70]

What should be the role of monetary policy in such a situation? First and foremost, we talk about a single monetary policy, which is an economic instrument that cannot be used to fight regional or national developments. Just like US monetary policy cannot be used to give extra economic stimulus to New York and at the same time combat regional inflation in Washington, European monetary policy cannot and should not attempt to take into account national or regional differences. If Ireland has inflation rates above 5 per cent, whereas the euro area inflation is about 2 per cent, Irish fiscal or structural economic policy should react, not European monetary policy.

Even in a situation where, say, half of the euro area countries suffers from relatively high inflation rates and the other half from deflation, European monetary policy still must focus on the euro area aggregate. Strictly speaking, in such a case the single monetary policy does not fit the need of any member country! But there is no alternative, as this would imply to make the judgement whether high inflation is worse than low inflation or vice versa – and to define a whole set of 'rules' to deal with such a situation. This is not possible. National economic differences, be it inflation or growth differentials, thus are the target of national economic policy (e.g. fiscal policy, structural policy). This has also been made very clear by the ECB:

> Since the Eurosystem conducts its monetary policy for the euro area as a whole and hence cannot respond to the specific needs of individual economies, Member States have to take the euro area monetary policy stance as exogenously given.[71]

To conclude, the debate in the euro area to what extent monetary policy can take into account divergent developments in the euro area can be answered in a relatively simple way: Only in a very limited way, e.g. if a clear cyclical pattern emerges, inflation differentials might be an important signal (for instance one could imagine that increasing dispersion is a sign of an upcoming recession). Regional developments have to be targeted by appropriate regional policies, but should not influence the monetary policy of the European Central Bank.

This is not to say that high inflation differentials might not have consequences for European monetary policy. Indeed, public acceptance of monetary policy might suffer if regional economic differences persist or even grow. Inflation differentials might also influence the decision-making in the ECB. But from a purely economic point of view, monetary policy as such can do nothing against inflation or growth differentials.

7.3 ECONOMIC REASONS FOR INFLATION DIFFERENTIALS

We believe that inflation is especially in the medium or long run essentially a monetary phenomenon. Past inflation differentials in the euro area can be explained by diverging monetary policy. However, besides the influence of monetary policy other factors may play an important role, too. We will explain the main causes for inflation differentials and give a brief overview over the relevant empirical literature.

a) Purchasing power parity

The basic building block of both the literatures on purchasing power parity (PPP) and inflation differentials is the law of one price.[72] It states that '... absent natural or governmental barriers, a commodity should sell for the same price everywhere. The mechanism supposedly enforcing the law of one price is arbitrage' (Obstfeld and Rogoff, 1996). If the law of one price perfectly held and absent additional costs for transportation, tariffs etc., inflation differentials between countries should not exist.

However, as the law of one price is based on strong assumptions, it is no surprise that empirical support is rather weak (Froot and Rogoff, 1995 provide a survey on PPP). Possible explanations for the failure of the law of one price include: transportation costs, sticky prices in nominal currency in combination with highly variable exchange rates, different product regulations and market separation. With the exception of transportation costs, the influence of several of these factors should be fairly small in a common market with a common currency. At least the magnitude of inflation differentials should be considerably lower in monetary unions than between two countries having their own currencies.

There is some empirical evidence for the EMU available, for example for the car sector: car manufacturers tried to separate markets by demanding different prices for the same car in the various EMU countries, reflecting the different tax schemes or the relative income level. Since 1997 the European Commission

	Renault Clio	VW Golf	BMW 318i	Opel Vectra
1.5.2000	24,0	30,1	14,1	23,6
1.11.2000	23,0	32,9	13,9	25,2
1.5.2001	31,3	33,1	13,4	48,5

Table 7.2   Evolution of car prices in the EU (max. price differences in per cent)

is monitoring the prices for more than 70 cars and concludes that differences in car prices have been decreasing (European Commission, 1999; see also Goldberg and Verboven, 2001). Based on the evidence of table 7.2, that reports the development of price differences for car prices in the EU, we fail to find a major tendency towards car price convergence (source: *Frankfurter Allgemeine Zeitung*, 5.1.2001. In the same article, however, evidence from German car manufacturers was reported, indicating intended price convergence by Audi, BMW, Mercedes-Benz and Porsche).

The European Commission (2001*b*) uses bar code scanner data collected from supermarkets and provides evidence that 'price dispersion inside every Member State is always lower than price differences across countries for the same products. Generally, prices inside Member States vary 5 per cent round the national average; across the EU, prices vary 20 per cent or more.'[73] As a main explanation they put forward 'economic' factors such as industry or product-specific differences in manufacturer or distribution concentration or regulatory differences (as opposed to geographic factors such as transport costs, different consumption patterns or income differences). Rogers (2001) shows that prices in the euro area converged between 1990 and 1999. He constructed the indices of European price levels from actual prices of 168 goods and services in 26 cities in 18 countries. He concludes that for tradables, price dispersion in the euro area is now close to the US level, even though for some prices, deviations from the law of one price remain large (Rogers et al., 2002 reach similar conclusions with the same data set). Haskel and Wolf (2001) have examined violations of the law of one price for IKEA furniture. These goods are highly tradable and highly traded, as IKEA sources from 50 countries and sells in about 30 countries (Haskel and Wolf, 2001). They find that the ordering of prices displays no simple pattern, suggesting strategic pricing. Still, relative prices display a tendency towards convergence, with faster convergence for large divergences.

International evidence shows the following: the Penn World Table reveals that national price levels of identical, quality-adjusted output baskets might differ by a factor of about 20 (Summers and Heston, 1991). Wei and Parsley (1995) use a panel of 12 tradable sectors in 14 OECD countries to study deviations from PPP during the floating exchange rate period and find that deviations are related to volatility and transportation costs, but also find evidence for mean reversion towards PPP. Engel and Rogers (1996) and Parsley and Wei (2000) examine cross-border deviations of the law of one price. Both studies find that crossing national borders significantly increases price variability. Cechetti et al. (2000) studied the dynamics of price indices for major US cities. They estimate that the half-live of convergence of relative price levels is approximately nine years. Finally, Alberola and Marques (2000) examine regional inflation in Spain and conclude that regional inflation differentials are small (the range is less than half point per year in the long run), but very persistent.

b) Correlation of business cycles

Diverging business cycles can lead to inflation differentials: if business cycles diverge, one country might experience an economic boom with relatively high inflation rates, while other EMU member countries are in a recession with relatively low inflation rates. The higher the correlation between European business cycles the higher also the correlation between EMU members inflation rates. To check the correlation of business cycles between EMU member countries correlation analysis has been used.

Empirical evidence shows a mixed picture: Fatás (1997) uses annual employment growth rates to approximate business cycles. He analyses fluctuations at the regional, national and European level by employing a correlation analysis at two distinct periods of time. He finds that the correlation of economic indicators in different European regions even across borders has increased over time. Artis and Zhang (1999) cover 19 countries and use a non-parametric rank correlation approach to study whether business cycle affiliation is associated with relative exchange rate fixity. They find that the business cycle of the ERM countries have become more synchronized with the German cycle than with the US cycle (this view has been challenged by Inklaar and de Haan, 2001).

The European Central Bank (1999c) examines long-run variation in key economic indicators, such as industrial production, GNP growth or inflation rates. They find that the 1990s are marked by a reduction in the degree of synchronization, mainly due to the asymmetric effects of the German reunification. Yet, they conclude: 'Overall, while the degree of synchronization may vary over the period under review, it may be seen as being high in absolute terms...'.[74] De Haan et al. (2002) reach a similar conclusion.

Finally, Wynne and Koo (2000) check whether business cycles within Europe are as correlated as within the Federal Reserve districts in the US. They find that average volatility of output across the US is almost identical to the average volatility across the 15 EU members, but employment is much more volatile in the US.

c) Diverging tax policies

Diverging tax policies can lead to inflation differentials: if a member country increases, say, the value-added tax then the prices of most consumption goods will increase, having an upward effect on CPI inflation. However, this is a one-off shift in the price level, not an effect that alters inflation's trends. All else equal, that is if the tax increase is immediately and fully p̲a̲s̲s̲e̲d̲ ̲o̲n and unless secondary effects occur, 12 months later the rate of inflation will shift back to its earlier level.

Although this effect might be quite important, little empirical work is available and little guidance can be found in the literature about the impact of diverging tax policies on inflation differentials in the euro area.

d) The Balassa-Samuelson effect

A common explanation for inflation differentials is the Balassa-Samuelson effect (BS effect), which provides an explanation why inflation rates are higher in catching-up countries. This effect was first formulated in Balassa (1964) and Samuelson (1964): it has been observed that productivity increases faster in sectors that produce tradable goods than in the nontradables sectors, as capital intensity is higher in the tradables sector. If wages in both sectors rise uniformly, the costs for producing nontradables increase, which leads to rising relative prices (see also Asea and Corden, 1994).

Inflation rates are measured using a goods basket containing both tradable and nontradable goods, thus if the tradables price remains unchanged (due to PPP), inflation rises as the price for nontradables goes up. In the European context this means that a country in the catching-up process (which is typically associated with faster productivity growth) the costs in the nontradables sector rise faster than in other EMU countries.

International evidence on the BS effect is mixed: Gregorio et al. (1994) cover 14 countries, using correlation tests and regressions. They identify a demand shift towards nontradables and fast growth of total factor productivity in the tradable goods sector as the prime causes for inflation differentials. Strauss (1996) covers 7 countries and shows that productivity differentials affect the long-run proportional relationship between nominal exchange rates and relative prices. Canzoneri et al. (1999) use cointegration and panel data estimation for a pool of 13 OECD countries. They confirm the existence of a long run (or cointegrating) relationship between the relative price of nontradables and the ratio of average labor productivity, which confirms that the relative price of nontradables reflects the relative productivity of labor. However, they reject the PPP hypothesis to explain traded goods prices.

Hsieh (1982) tests the BS hypothesis for Germany (and Japan) against a weighted average of the most important trading partners and confirms the BS hypothesis. Alberola and Tyrväinen (1998) directly examine the BS model for 8 EMU countries. They consider two variants: the standard model and an extended model, which allows wages to differ between both sectors. They apply cointegration analysis and reject the standard BS model, but find that the extended BS model is endorsed by the data in every country. Canzoneri et al. (2000) find that the Balassa-Samuelson model cannot be rejected. Then they estimate the different parts of the model. These figures are used to calculate 'projections' of future inflation differentials, which could be as large as 2 or 3 percentage points. They also find that trends in relative prices of home goods can be attributed to trends in sectoral relative productivities. The study of Alberola and Marques (2000) rejects the Balassa-Samuelson hypothesis to explain inflation differentials in Spain. Finally, Sinn and Reutter (2001) estimate the minimum inflation rate that should prevail in the euro area, compatible with the requirement that no country faces a deflation. They conclude that minimum aggregate inflation should be 0.94 per cent, with inflation differentials mounting up to about 3 percentage points.

e) Differences in monetary transmission

Underlying structural differences among the euro area countries might also lead to inflation differentials. If, for example, monetary policy has asymmetric effects across countries, that is, if a change in interest rates has different effects on output, inflation and employment across the euro area, then monetary policy itself creates inflation differentials.

A large body of literature examines monetary transmission in the euro area. Both macroeconomic and microeconomic approaches are possible. We review a few selected studies (see also Angeloni et al., 2002): Clemens et al. (2001) show that monetary transmission mechanisms among European countries are quite diverse. Monetary policy exerts the most powerful effect on output in France and Finland, while the output responses of Portugal and the Netherlands are among the weakest. The timing and depth of the response to interest rate shocks varies markedly by country, suggesting that a common monetary policy could still further exacerbate divergences in cyclical positions. Suardi (2001) discusses the transmission mechanism in six EU countries (Belgium, Germany, France, Italy, the Netherlands, Spain). He also shows that the differences between these countries are smaller than between them and the UK or Sweden. Ciccarelli and Rebucci (2001) find that monetary transmission has changed in the EMU members in the run up to EMU, but that the degree of heterogeneity has not decreased.

Mihov (2001) compares monetary transmission in ten OECD countries, eight US regions and the regions of France, Germany and Italy. Based on VAR analysis he concludes that the diversity across European regions is not uniformly larger than across US regions. Finally, van Els et al. (2001) report the outcome of a simulation exercise done by the national central banks in the euro area. They conclude that the effect of an increase of interest rates leads to differences in the adjustment in the different member countries.

Table 7.3 summarizes the most recent empirical evidence. Studies reporting results for the euro area are marked with an asterix.

7.4 ANALYSING INFLATION DISPERSION IN EMU

7.4.1 Convergence of inflation rates – or price levels?

One of the main difficulties of the discussion about economic convergence is the difference between convergence of levels and growth rates. Inflation rate convergence, for instance, and price level convergence are two different issues. According to the Maastricht treaty, the aim of European monetary policy is not adjustment of price levels, but to guarantee price stability, that is to keep inflation low. Differences in price levels are only of interest for European monetary policy in as far as they translate into inflation differentials. Inflation convergence need thus not necessarily be accompanied by price level convergence. But from the law of one price we can expect at least a certain tendency for tradables' prices to convergence. This convergence, however, is not compatible with a convergence of inflation rates, as prices in countries with low initial price levels need to grow faster.

So price level convergence automatically leads to a certain divergence in inflation rates. In a sense, the part of a country's inflation rate attributable to price level convergence is an inevitable by-product of increased integration. If it was possible to measure this component of inflation accurately, it would make sense to categorize it differently, much in the same way that core inflation and headline inflation are two different concepts for central banks (Rogers, 2001).

Currently, price levels even for tradable goods are far from being uniform across Europe: table 7.4 compares euro prices for several consumption goods (source: *Frankfurter Allgemeine Zeitung*, 27.12.2001. The prices were collected in supermarkets in big cities in the respective countries). Big differences in prices for these tradable goods across countries are apparent.

The evidence on the law of one price of the previous section showed the following: no single country is expensive in every respect, simple pricing pattern cannot be found and prices differ per country and per sector. Still, all studies were quite clear that price level convergence – at least for tradables – was growing, and has for some goods reached levels found across US cities. Price levels for nontradables, however, still show a high degree of dispersion.

	Law of one price
Wei/Parsley (1995)	Deviations from PPP due to volatility and transportation costs, but mean reversion towards PPP.
Engel/Rogers (1996); Parsley/Wei (2000)	Crossing national borders significantly increases price variability.
Cechetti et al. (2000)	Convergence of relative price levels takes 9 years.
Alberola/Marques (2000)	Regional Spanish inflation differentials are small, but can be very persistent.
European Commission (2001b)*	Economic factors lead to higher price dispersion within EU members than across countries.
Rogers (2001)*	Tradables price dispersion in EMU comparable to US level.
Haskel/Wolf (2001)*	Relative prices tend to converge.
	Correlation of business cycles
Fatás (1997)*	Correlation of indicators in European regions has increased over time even across borders.
Artis/Zhang (1999)*	Business cycle of ERM countries has become more synchronized with Germany than with US.
European Central Bank (1999c)*	High degree of synchronization of key economic indicators in Europe.
Wynne/Koo (2000)*	Volatility of output in US almost identical to EU 15; employment more volatile in the US.
	Balassa-Samuelson Effect
Gregorio et al. (1994)	Higher demand for nontradables and productivity growth for tradables cause inflation differentials.
Strauss (1996)	Productivity differentials affect long-run relation between exchange rates and relative prices.
Alberola/Tyrväinen (1998)*	Rejection of the standard BS model, but confirmation of the BS model with wage differentials.
Canzoneri et al. (1999)	Cointegration between relative price of nontradables and ratio of average labor productivity, PPP hypothesis fails to explain traded goods prices.
Canzoneri et al. (2000)*	EMU inflation differentials could be up to 2-3 percentage points.
Sinn/Reutter (2001)*	Minimum EMU inflation is 0.94%, inflation differentials will be about 3 percentage points.

Table 7.3   Empirical evidence on inflation differentials

	Germany	France	Italy	Spain	Greece
Coca Cola 0.33l	0.30	0.37	0.77	0.32	0.39
Nivea 150ml	2.04	2.21	2.76	1.79	2.27
Levis 501 Jeans	97.95	73.00	79.53	61.11	67.2
McDonald's Big Mac	-	2.97	2.53	2.49	2.11
Kinder Surprise	0.55	-	0.59	0.63	0.46

Table 7.4   Price differentials for selected goods

7.4.2   Inflation differentials in the EMU and other monetary unions

The European Central Bank measures inflation in the euro area by increases in the Harmonized Index of Consumer Prices (HICP), so this is the variable we will examine.

There are several ways to measure economic dispersion. Among the most common are the (unweighted and weighted) standard deviation and the absolute spread between the lowest and the highest observation (for a more extensive discussion of these measures see the box entitled 'Inflation differentials within the euro area' in the December 2000 issue of the ECB Monthly Bulletin). When analysing inflation dispersion in the euro area three main issues are of interest: (1) What is the historical perspective, i.e. is the current level of dispersion high or low with regard to other monetary unions and (2) is inflation dispersion related to the level of inflation. Both questions are answered in turn.

The historical perspective   A statistical measure of dispersion alone gives little insight whether current inflation differentials should be viewed as a reason for concern or not – only when a 'benchmark' is available, to which EMU inflation dispersion can be compared to, is it possible to assess the importance of current economic dispersion.

Therefore, to get an idea about inflation dispersion in the euro area figure 7.1 shows the unweighted standard deviation for inflation in several monetary unions (Germany, Spain and the US) and compares this to evidence for the EMU.[75] We clearly see the sharp increase in inflation dispersion within Europe after the breakup of the Bretton Woods system. Until the early 1990s the unweighted standard deviation for the euro area was much larger than for the other monetary unions. However, it is also apparent that inflation dispersion in the euro area has declined considerably and is currently not higher than previously experienced in Spain or in the US. Analysis of other measures of inflation dispersion, such as the simple spread or the coefficient of variation (standard deviation scaled by the mean) confirmed this result.

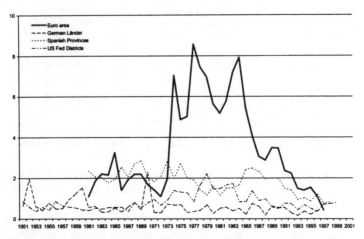

Figure 7.1   Spread of the inflation rate within different monetary unions

The relationship between inflation dispersion and the level of inflation   Next,
we check to what extent the recent hike in inflation has also contributed to
higher inflation dispersion. Here visual inspection gives very clear results: figure 7.2 is a scatter plot of inflation rates and the unweighted standard deviation
in the EU since 1996. A clear relationship between the level of inflation and
the unweighted standard deviation cannot be seen. To show the evolution over
time, figure 7.3 combines headline HICP and the unweighted standard deviation of inflation as a measure of inflation dispersion. HICP headline measures
overall inflation in the euro area, including all components. An upward trend
since 1999 is clearly observable, but it is also apparent that while inflation has
gone up sharply, inflation dispersion has not increased dramatically (a more
formal analysis (not reported) confirmed this result).

     To further investigate the hike in inflation rates in 2000 and the underly-
ing factors driving that increase, we examine HICP components. Figure 7.4
displays European inflation rates per HICP component. We clearly observe
that mainly the prices for energy and unprocessed food have gone up sharply,
whereas the other HICP components remained fairly stable. These increases in
energy and unprocessed food are due to (a) the strong increase in oil prices and
(b) BSE and foot-and-mouth diseases in some European countries.[76]

     Leaving out the two most volatile components of inflation rates, energy
and unprocessed food, reveals that the other inflation components remained
relatively unchanged: dispersion measures for HICP excluding energy and
unprocessed food have either declined or remained fairly stable since 1996
(see figure 7.5).

     All in all, simply looking at current inflation differentials one might con-

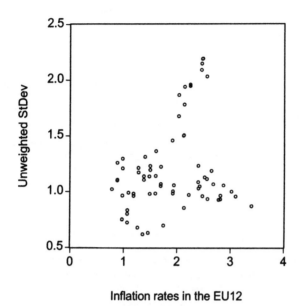

Inflation rates in the EU12

Figure 7.2   Inflation rates and unweighted StDev in the EU 12

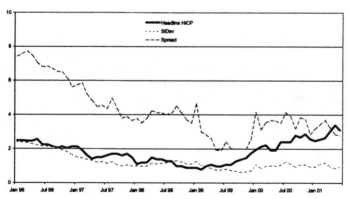

Figure 7.3   Inflation dispersion since 1996 in HICP headline (standard deviation)

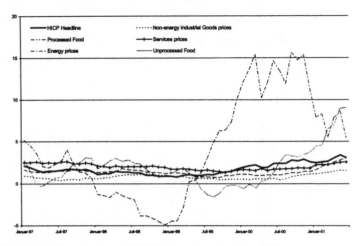

Figure 7.4   Development of HICP components since 1996

clude that they are of substantial magnitude. In comparison with historical benchmarks, i.e. data from previous monetary unions, it turns out that European inflation dispersion has decreased to levels fully compatible with a single monetary policy. In what follows we examine one of the prime causes for diverging inflation rates: differences in relative productivity.

7.5   SIMULATING NATIONAL INFLATION RATES IN THE EURO AREA

The effects discussed in the last sector can be divided into short-run effects (inflation differentials resulting from diverging business cycles or changes in indirect taxes) and long-run effects (the Balassa-Samuelson effect). As the BS effect, unlike the other effects, has a 'structural' impact, as it determines diverging inflation rates in the long-run, we have decided to further examine its impact. In this section we show estimates for the euro area countries, using the latest available data.

7.5.1   The model

In what follows we outline the necessary steps to estimate the BS model. A more comprehensive treatment can be found in Alberola and Tyrväinen (1998).

The standard BS model can be estimated using the following equation:

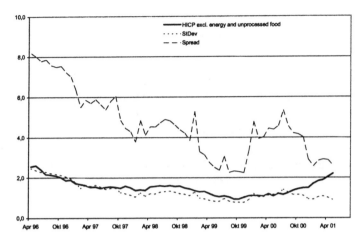

Figure 7.5   Inflation dispersion since 1996 in HICP excluding energy and unprocessed food (standard deviation)

$$p_{rel} = p^N - p^T = c + \frac{\sigma^N}{\sigma^T} q^T - q^N,$$

where p^T and p^N are the prices of tradables and nontradables, q^T and q^N are the sectoral productivities, and σ^T and σ^N are the labor intensities in the tradables and nontradables goods sector, respectively. This expression defines a relationship between sectoral price levels and sectoral productivities, which is expected to hold in the long run. Furthermore, this equation defines an *a priori* restriction, which implies that the long-run parameters associated with p^T, p^N and q^N are equal, which means that we can normalize with respect to $(p_{rel} + q^N)$. This gives an equation that can serve as a basis to test the BS model:

$$(p_{rel,t} + q_t^N) - \beta^T q_t^T + \varepsilon_t = 0. \tag{7.1}$$

Asuming that nontradables are more labor intensive than tradables we would expect β^T to be greater than one.

As we are interested in inflation differentials, we decompose real exchange rate movements. A national price index for country *i*, p_i, is a geometric average of the price of traded and nontraded goods, p^T and p^{NT}. Expressed in logarithms:

$$p_{i,t} = (1 - \gamma)p_{i,t}^T + \gamma p_{i,t}^{NT}, \tag{7.2}$$

where γ is the share of nontradables.

Our aim is to analyse inflation differentials. These differentials have to be estimated against a numméraire country. We have chosen France, the second largest EMU member country, as numméraire.[77]

The real exchange rate of country i, expressed in units of French national output per unit of country i's national output, is given by

$$z_{i,t} = e_{i,t} + p_{i,t} - p_{F,t}, \tag{7.3}$$

where $e_{i,t}$ denotes country i's exchange rate vis-à-vis France and $p_{F,t}$ is the French price index (French variables are marked by the subscript F).

The BS model assumes that PPP holds for traded goods. If $p_{F,t}^T$ is the price of the French traded good, then the deviation from PPP for traded good of country i, $d_{i,t}$ is:

$$d_{i,t} = e_{i,t} + p_{i,t}^T - p_{F,t}^T. \tag{7.4}$$

Real exchange rate movements can then be decomposed into:

$$z_{i,t} = d_{i,t} + (p_{i,t} - p_{i,t}^T) + (p_{F,t}^T - p_{F,t}). \tag{7.5}$$

Using equation 7.1 we can derive an expression for Δp_{rel}, the change of the relative price of tradables:

$$\Delta p_{rel} = \Delta p^T + \gamma(\Delta \beta^T q^T - \Delta q^N), \tag{7.6}$$

and we can simplify real exchange rate movements into the following expression:

$$\Delta z_{i,t} = \Delta d_{i,t} + \gamma_i(\beta_i^T \Delta q_{i,t}^T - \Delta q_{i,t}^N) - \gamma_F(\beta_F^T \Delta q_{F,t}^T - \Delta q_{F,t}^N), \tag{7.7}$$

which means that changes in the real exchange rate can be decomposed into deviations from PPP in the tradables sector plus changes in relative productivities in country i and France.

7.5.2   The data

Data availability is a big issue when estimating the Balassa-Samuelson model, as we need data on a sectoral basis. We use the latest available data from Eurostat. The sectoral breakdown of the data was done following Alberola and Tyrväinen (1998). We have proxied productivity by labor productivity, as measures of total factor productivity are subject to discussion (see Pilat, 1996). The following series have been used:

	Standard BS model (β_i^T)	Standard error	Cointegrated?
Austria	0.93	(0.09)	No[79]
Belgium	0.99	(.175)	Yes
Finland	0.90	(0.04)	Yes
France	0.95	(0.03)	Yes
Germany	1.05	(0.02)	Yes
Italy	0.90	(0.12)	No
Netherlands	1.16	(0.10)	Yes
Spain	1.66	(0.88)	Yes

Table 7.5   Coefficients of the BS model

- Output (GDP at constant prices), y_i;
- Number of employees, l_i;
- Productivity, $q_i = y_i/l_i$;[78]
- Value-added deflator, p_i (as CPI is not available at sectoral levels).

The following sample periods have been used to compute the β_i^T coefficients of the BS model (annual data): Austria 1976-1996; Belgium 1970-1996; Finland 1970-1996; France 1970-1997; Germany 1960-1997; Italy 1970-1997; the Netherlands 1977-1995; Spain 1970-1994 (further details on the data can be found in appendix C.4. We have decided not to report estimates for Luxembourg, as its economic structure is heavily distorted due to a number of factors (e.g. the strong service and banking sector and special tax arrangements), and we cannot report estimates for Ireland and Portugal, as either data at the sectoral level was unavailable or the sample period was too short for meaningful estimates of long-run effects).

7.5.3   Estimating the Balassa-Samuelson model

As starting point we have to estimate the Balassa-Samuelson model. Given the non-stationarity of most variables, cointegration techniques were employed (I(1) was assumed following the theory). We use the ECM-VAR suggested by Johansen (1991), the number of lags was determined using the Schwartz criteria (using the Akaike criteria did not significantly improve the estimation). For comparison we also estimated the model using the Fully Modified Estimation (FME) method of Phillips and Hansen (1990). Our Johansen estimates of equation 7.1 are reported in Table 7.5 (for details on the estimation procedure and sensitivity analysis see Maier and Dieppe, 2002).

While Alberola and Tyrväinen (1998) have rejected the standard Balassa-Samuelson model for the euro area, our estimates are more in favor of the model. For most countries cointegration could not be rejected using the trace and eigenvalue tests for the Johansen estimation. The exceptions were Austria and Italy. For Austria cointegration was found using residual based Augmented Dickey-Fully tests for the FM estimations at the 5 per cent level. For Italy, cointegration was not rejected at only the 10 per cent level. This could be due to structural breaks or could suggest model failure. Assessing the results, they are generally very similar across countries supporting the Balassa Samuelson hypothesis. The results are reported for the Johansen estimation in Table 3. In all cases the coefficient for traded productivity (β^{Tr}) is significant, and positive. This is robust across estimation methods. In particular, for the Johansen estimation the null hypothesis that the coefficient is greater than or equal to 1 is not rejected for all countries, with Finland being the only exception. This finding should be treated with care as it is not supported using FME estimation. Nonetheless, the coefficients are robust across estimations being greater than 0.85 for all countries.

Sensitivity analysis was also done including using different sample periods, different lag lengths, and different compositions of tradables and nontradables. It was found that the results were sensitive to the assumptions and thus less robust. Thus, while in general the Balassa-Samuelson model could not be rejected, the results appear to be sensitive to the data set, the assumptions made and the estimation period.

a)   Decomposition of real exchange rate movements

In figure 7.6 we have plotted the real exchange rate movements for the countries in our sample against France, the numméraire country. On the one hand we observe that some countries (Germany, the Netherlands, Finland, Austria) have maintained relatively stable real exchange rates (in particular since the early 1980s), on the other hand countries such as Belgium or Italy have seen large fluctuations.

Our decomposition of real exchange rate movements over the whole sample are reported in table 7.6. We report changes in the real exchange rate in the first column and deviations from PPP in the tradable goods sector in the second. The third column shows our estimated BS effect, and the fourth column is the part of the real exchange rate movements we cannot explain. Following equation 7.7 the table can be read as follows: column (2) plus column (3) should equal column (1), the 'residuals' (1)-(2)-(3) cannot be explained and are reported in column (4).

It is interesting to note the following: Spain has seen a real appreciation, which the Balassa-Samuelson model required, but according to the model the appreciation was 'too low'. This means that the BS model would have required the real exchange rate to change more than it actually did. The BS estimates for the Netherlands would almost perfectly offset the real exchange rate movements, but clearly PPP does not hold in the traded sector, so we

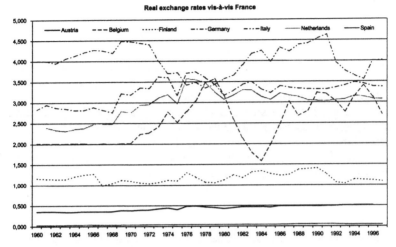

Figure 7.6   Real exchange rate movements

	Δ Real Ex-change Rate	Deviation from PPP (traded goods)	BS Component	Unexplained Movements
Austria	1.110	−0.029	0.003	1.136
Belgium	0.205	−0.139	0.642	−0.298
Finland	0.188	0.642	−0.220	−0.234
Germany	0.602	0.726	−0.246	0.121
Italy	0.143	−0.239	0.597	−0.215
Netherlands	0.808	−0.956	0.622	1.142
Spain	1.298	0.384	2.518	−1.604

Table 7.6   Decomposition of real exchange rate movements

cannot explain that part of the variation. Clearly visible from table 7.6 is also that the (standard) assumption of PPP in the tradables sector is, at least, questionable.

b) Implied inflation differentials

Next, based on our estimated coefficients for the BS model we have calculated annual inflation rates that result from our model and that could prevail in a monetary union. These implied inflation differentials were computed along the following lines: in a monetary union there are no nominal exchange rates. Using the decomposition of inflation differentials (equation 7.5) and assuming that PPP holds in the tradables sector in the long run, we can compute national inflation differential for country i vis-à-vis France using the following:

$$\Delta p_i = \Delta p_G + \gamma_i(\beta_i^T \Delta q_i^T - \Delta_i^N) - \gamma_F(\beta_F^T \Delta q_F^T - \Delta q_F^N). \qquad (7.8)$$

To compute the implied differentials we use the β_i^T-coefficients of the cointegration parameters. In table 7.7 we show implied inflation differentials with France for country i: in the first column we report the average actual inflation rate over the whole sample (in the first row for each country) and averages for smaller subperiods. The second column shows the implied inflation rate that should result in country i if the Balassa-Samuelson model would be the only factor influencing national inflation rates vis-à-vis France. In the last column we report the inflation differentials of country i vis-à-vis France that results from the model, i.e. for the German case calculated as

(*Implied German inflation*) - (*Actual French inflation*).

Estimates over the whole sample period can be found in the first row of each country the second and third row show estimates for more recent subperiods. We see that over the whole sample period French inflation is relatively high (almost 6 per cent). This means that all other implied inflation rates computed for the whole sample period (which are calculated based on that inflation rate) are also somewhat high. This is clearly due to the oil price shock in the 1970s and early 1980s, as inflation rates since 1985 are much lower.

In other words, our calculations for the whole sample period (the first row for each country) tend to be too high. Therefore the second and third row per country is more interesting, as it shows more recent averages. Here we clearly see that (a) the implied inflation differential between France and the other EMU countries is relatively low (expect maybe for the Netherlands and Spain) and (b) it has been decreasing over the last 15 years. This can be interpreted as a sign of economic convergence.

When interpreting this table one has to bear in mind that one of the assumptions underlying these simulations is PPP in the traded goods sector. This is not necessarily a very realistic assumption: in table 7.6 we have shown that deviations from PPP in the tradables sector were – at least for some countries – quite high.

c) Simulated EMU inflation rates

What we are interested in is to simulate inflation rates that would prevail in a monetary union, based on the preceding estimates for the BS model. To do so, we must compute tradables and nontradables prices that would prevail in the euro area countries and then simulate inflation rates for each member country (see also Alberola and Tyrväinen, 1998)

The EMU inflation rate, p_{EUMU} is a weighted average of inflation in the

	Actual Inflation	Implied Inflation	Implied Inflation Differential
Austria	3.625	2.907	−2.900
1985-1989	2.160	1.767	−1.821
1990-1995	3.046	1.883	−0.332
Belgium	5.006	3.546	−2.261
1985-1989	2.407	2.264	−1.324
1990-1995	2.424	1.744	−0.470
Finland	6.735	2.684	−3.123
1985-1989	4.919	1.507	−2.082
1990-1996	2.596	2.704	0.489
France	5.807	-	-
1985-1989	3.588	-	-
1990-1996	2.215	-	-
Germany	2.904	5.561	−0.246
1985-1989	1.265	2.394	−1.194
1990-1996	2.679	2.314	0.099
Italy	8.327	3.501	−2.306
1985-1989	6.215	1.554	−2.034
1990-1997	4.748	2.432	0.217
Netherlands	4.310	3.526	−2.281
1986-1989	0.695	0.892	−2.697
1990-1995	2.532	3.692	1.478
Spain	9.184	5.422	−0.385
1985-1989	6.887	3.027	−0.561
1990-1993	4.757	4.088	1.873

Table 7.7   Implied inflation differentials with France

member countries, where ξ_j are the shares used by the ECB to compute the Harmonized Index of Consumer Prices:

$$\Delta p_{EMU} = \sum_j \xi_j \Delta p_j \qquad (7.9)$$

Using equation 7.6, EMU inflation becomes:

$$\Delta p_{EMU} = \sum_j \xi_j (\Delta p_j^T + \gamma_j (\beta_j^T \Delta q_j^T - \Delta q_j^N)). \qquad (7.10)$$

Under the standard assumption that PPP holds in the tradables sector in the EMU member countries (analytically: $\sum_j \xi_j \Delta p_j^T = p_{EMU}^T$) this last equation can be simplified as follows:

	Simulated Inflation Rates			HICP
EMU Inflation Rate	2.00	1.14	2.90	2.9
Austria	1.00	0.14	1.90	2.5
Belgium	0.86	0.00	1.76	2.9
Finland	1.82	0.96	2.72	2.8
France	1.80	0.93	2.70	2.0
Germany	2.15	1.29	3.05	2.9
Italy	1.55	0.69	2.45	3.0
Netherlands	2.81	1.95	3.71	5.3
Spain	3.21	2.34	4.11	4.0
EMU Tradables Inflation	0.30	−0.57	1.20	-

Table 7.8   Simulated inflation rates for EMU member countries

$$\Delta p_{EMU}^T = \Delta p_{EMU} - \sum_j \xi_j \gamma_j (\beta_j^T \Delta q_j^T - \Delta q_j^N). \qquad (7.11)$$

We can set euro area inflation p_{EMU} at any value, for example at 2 per cent, the maximum inflation the ECB will tolerate in the medium run, and we can compute national inflation rates. This is done by first solving for the European tradables inflation rate p_{EMU}^T, and then computing p^N using

$$\Delta p_i^N = \Delta p_{EMU}^T + \beta_i^T \Delta q_i^T - \Delta q_i^N. \qquad (7.12)$$

Now we have computed the 'European price for tradables', p_{EMU}^T, the 'National price levels for nontradables', p_i^N, and we have chosen a value for euro area inflation. Assuming further that EMU consists only of the countries covered in our sample, we can simulate national inflation rates of the euro area member countries according to equation 7.2 (strictly speaking, as our 'EMU' does not include Ireland and Portugal, our simulations are slightly biased upwards. This effect, however, is very small: the HICP weights add up to 100 per cent, of which we cover about 97 per cent).

Table 7.8 reports the simulated inflation rates, based on estimates for the whole sample period. In the first column, we report results if EMU inflation is set at 2 per cent. We see that all simulated inflation rates are between 1 and 2 per cent, except in Spain where inflation far exceeds the 3 per cent rate. German and Austrian rates are almost identical, which is what we expect, given the close ties between both economies. Note also that the simulated inflation rates for Finland and Italy are relatively low, despite high inflation rates in the past (see table 7.7). Referring back to table 7.6 we see that real exchange rate movements vis-à-vis France were relatively low, which can be explained by frequent adjustments in the nominal exchange rates.

The latest data from Eurostat show that EMU inflation, as measured by the HICP, in April 2001 was 2.9 per cent. We have inserted this figure for p_{EMU} and have computed national inflation rates that would prevail according to our estimates of the BS model. These simulated national inflation rates are reported in the second column of table 7.8. The third column reports actual national inflation rates, taken from the Eurostat website. Strictly speaking, our simulations are based on sectoral deflators, not HICP, as suggested by the use of HICP data from Eurostat. However, the differences between these series are relatively small and should not critically influence our results.

We see a mixed picture. For a number of countries our simulations are surprisingly accurate (Austria, Italy, to some extent also Belgium), whereas for other countries such as the Netherlands or Spain the simulated values differ considerably from the actual values.[80] Germany also has higher inflation rates than our estimates predicted, but this is again mostly due to the distorting impact of the German reunification. We cannot explain the relatively large differences for Finland and France, which are probably mainly due to other factors not incorporated in the model, such as diverging business cycles or the impact of indirect taxation.

All in all, however, we have to conclude that the model is able to explain a fair amount of the inflation differentials. Inflation differentials implied by the Balassa-Samuelson model are 'inevitable' in the sense that the ECB must not worry about them – they are a consequence of economic development and convergence.

7.5.4 Interpretation of the evidence

The question we initially raised was whether diverging inflation rates have – besides the possibly negative economic impact – the potential to amount to an additional threat for the ECB, in the sense that inflation differentials might create additional tension. In the words of the President of the European Central Bank, Wim Duisenberg:

> Significant inflation differences across countries might lead to unsustainable divergences in prices and costs within the euro area or to an unnecessarily tight monetary policy for countries that have achieved price stability.[81]

How should the evidence presented in the preceding sections be interpreted? At first glance, existing inflation differentials in the euro area look quite large. Moreover, Europe's economies are far less integrated than in other monetary unions (e.g. the US), and they lack a common fiscal policy. The standards of living are quite different, and language barriers might obstruct mobility (especially labor mobility), which in turn could mean that economic differences might adjust very slowly. These factors make it unlikely that inflation differentials will disappear quickly.

However, we have shown that current euro area inflation differentials are by no means bigger than those experienced in other monetary unions. We have seen that inflation differentials in the US are persistent, but not permanent, and there is no evidence that in that respect the euro area will be any different. Inflation differentials up to several percentage points can be due to catching-up processes, as estimates of the Balassa-Samuelson model show. Moreover, our simulations show that inflation rates will be divergent, but the magnitude is far from being dramatic: even for Spain, which – according to our estimates – is likely to suffer most from high inflation rates, inflation is greatly reduced, compared to the double digit inflation rates that prevailed until the mid 1980s. Finally, once economic performance of the euro area converges, the differentials due to the BS model will diminish. On a more fundamental level the economies of the euro area are more diversified than in the US, which should make them more robust to sector-specific shocks.

Interpreting the evidence, statistical issues play an important role, too. The ECB uses the Harmonized Index of Consumer Prices (HICP) to get comparable inflation figures in all EMU member countries. As consumption patterns are not the same in all economies, the weights used to construct the national HICP differ. In that regard the example of Ireland has been stressed, where processed food constitutes around 20.5 per cent of the HICP index, while it accounts only for about 13 per cent of the HIPC in the euro area (European Commission, 2001a; European Central Bank, 1999a). Moreover, one has to carefully distinguish between inflation differentials and price level differentials: initial differences in the national price levels at the time the common currency is introduced lead to inflation differentials, as prices follow PPP and converge to the same level. This development is a 'normal consequence' of a monetary union, which means that it will occur at the start of any monetary union.

Furthermore, the selection of price indices is important: as we have seen in section 7.4 the biggest differences occur in those price indices that have the most 'erratic' price components, namely energy and food prices, which are strongly influenced by oil prices or weather conditions. These components are included in the sectoral deflators we have used above. Taking these statistical factors into account we conclude the picture looks much more friendly.

7.6 SUMMARY

In this chapter we have examined the potential political pressure on the European Central Bank, resulting from economic differences: inflation rates in Europe are far from being uniform and inflation differentials have the potential to become a very complicated issue. The example of Ireland, where inflation exceeded 5 per cent in 2000, but which had little impact on EMU inflation, shows the ECB's difficulties. We have shown that within EMU actual inflation differentials are larger than in other monetary unions, such as the US. Although our predicted inflation rates are perhaps not fully compatible with the ECB's target inflation rate of 2 per cent, they are far lower than inflation rates in the pre-EMU era in most European countries. Moreover, one of the most important findings of this chapter is that the hike in inflation rates in 2000/2001 has not led to greater inflation dispersion across the euro area. The current level of inflation differentials should not raise concerns, but can be interpreted (1) as the result of different cyclical positions and (2) the necessary adjustment in some countries to reach more uniform European price levels.

So, we conclude that the ECB should continue to closely monitor the situation, but need not really worry about inflation differentials. We expect EMU inflation differentials to decline further the more the national economies and the standards of living in the euro area converge.

8. The European Context: A Political Assessment

8.1 OVERVIEW

In this chapter we discuss implications for the European Central Bank of our findings of the last chapters. Thorough empirical analysis, as we did for the Bundesbank, is not yet possible for the European Central Bank, since the time span is too short for meaningful economic estimates, but the results so far should allow a fairly accurate description of external pressure. As we have seen current inflation dispersion is not something European monetary policy should be concerned about; and based on that finding we show that political pressure is something the ECB will probably have to worry less about than most previous national European central banks. The main argument is that economic diversity will help the European Central Bank, in that it makes coordination among European governments more difficult. At the same time we expect public support to be quite high. As we explain in the next chapter this conclusion may not continue to hold once the accession countries become full members of the EMU.

Very helpful in this context from an ECB point of view is also the clear mandate for price stability in the Maastricht treaty. Indeed, as we show, the European Central Bank has an unparalleled high degree of statutory independence, which we expect to be a very effective protection against most sources of political pressure.

This chapter is organized as follows: first, we give a brief overview about the institutional framework in which the ECB operates (section 8.2) and its legal status (section 8.3). Then, based on our results of the last two chapters, in sections 8.4 and 8.5 possible political pressure on European monetary policy and public support of the European Central Bank, respectively, are examined.

8.2 THE STRUCTURE OF THE EUROPEAN CENTRAL BANK AND THE EUROSYSTEM

Monetary policy in the EMU member countries has been delegated to the European System of Central Banks (ESCB). It is composed of the European Central Bank (ECB) and the national central banks (NCBs) of all 15 EU Member States. Not all EU members have also introduced the single currency and therefore not all 15 European NCBs participate in the formulation of European monetary policy. For the ECB plus the – currently 12 – NCBs that have introduced the euro the term 'Eurosystem' has been adopted. The Eurosystem is the institution that determines European monetary policy. (European Central Bank, 1999*b*).

The process of decision making in the Eurosystem is centralized through the Governing Council and the Executive Board (see figure 8.1). The Governing Council comprises all members of the Executive Board and the governors of the NCBs of those countries which have adopted the euro. The Executive Board consists of the President, the Vice-President and four other members. They are appointed by common accord of the governments of the Member States at the level of the Heads of State or Government, on a recommendation from the EU Council after it has consulted the European Parliament and the Governing Council of the ECB. Decisions on monetary policy of the Governing Council and of the Executive Board are normally taken by simple majority votes, where each member has one vote ('one member, one vote'). In the event of a tie the President has the deciding vote.

De Haan (1997) provides an overview of its statutory independence and monetary strategy. Wynne (1999) compares the institutional settings of the ECB and the US Federal Reserve. The decision-making process has been criticized for not delivering 'predictable outcomes': 'While 86 per cent of the financial analysts can correctly predict the interest rate steps of the FED the score of ECB analyst's is not higher than 36 per cent.' (Metten, 2001). However, it is somewhat unclear whether this is not more a result of (a) longer experiences with the US Federal Reserve and (b) higher 'manpower', as more analysts focus on the FED than on the ECB.

8.3 THE LEGAL STATUS OF THE EUROPEAN CENTRAL BANK

In the Treaty on European Union the ECB has been granted full constitutional independence:

> ...when exercising their powers and carrying out their tasks and duties, neither the

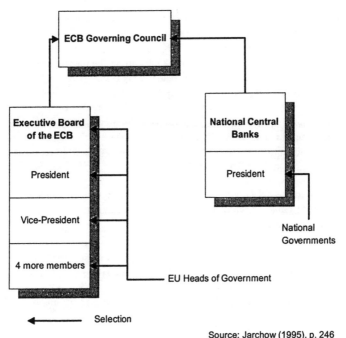

Figure 8.1 The structure of the ECB

ECB, nor any member of its decision making bodies shall seek or take instructions from Community institutions or bodies, from any government of a Member Sate or from any other body.[82]

To ensure security of tenure for members of Executive Board and the governors from national central banks, several provisions have been taken:

- a minimum renewable term of office for governors of five years;
- a minimum non-renewable term of office for members of the Executive Board of eight years;
- removal from office is only possible in the event of incapacity or serious misconduct. Possible disputes are settled by the Court of Justice of the European Communities.

The Treaty on European Union provides that the primary objective of the ECB is to attain price stability. Without prejudice to this primary objective, the ECB is required to support the general economic policies in the EU. 'Should there be any conflict between the objectives to be assessed by the ECB, the objective of price stability will always be paramount.'[83] The ECB has no obligation to announce or obey any targets, but the ECB has announced it will aim at an inflation rate between 0 and 2 per cent in the medium run.

Taking these provisions together, researchers consider the ECB's degree of statutory independence as very high; it

> ... may be regarded as even more independent than the Bundesbank. This is certainly true if one takes into account that in Germany the law, which describes the functions of the Bundesbank can be changed by simple parliamentary majority, whereas in the case of the ECB an unanimous decision of all Member States is required.[84]

We can thus safely conclude that the ECB can be viewed as a very independent central bank. In what follows we sketch actual and potential sources of pressure on and support for the ECB.

8.4   POLITICAL PRESSURE ON THE ECB

History has shown that politicians or certain organized groups might be inclined to put pressure on the ECB. The former German Secretary of Finance, Oskar Lafontaine, who repeatedly asked the ECB to lower interest rates in 1998/99, is just one example. Given the situation of the ECB, what can we say about the chances that these attempts will be successful?

The ECB's basic problem is that one monetary policy will apply to all countries, even though countries (and their economic performance) might differ considerably. Monetary policy will thus fit some countries better than other countries, possibly creating dissatisfaction in countries which would have preferred a different policy stance. In this section we describe possible consequences in all countries.

When analysing public pressure and support it is helpful to distinguish between

- different sources of external pressure and support, i.e. political pressure from national governments, from the European Parliament and organized groups on the one hand,
- and the level of pressure and the direction of pressure, on the other.

Note also that the results strongly depend on the question of how diverse the economies in the euro area are (this issue is discussed in more detail in chapter 7) and the overall economic performance in the euro area.

8.4.1 Governments

First, we look at the direction of pressure. As the ECB is responsible for monetary policy in all EMU member countries, the number of governments involved is obviously considerably higher than in the case of national central banks. We might thus conclude that political pressure might come from more sources than the Bundesbank faced. But will this pressure also be effective and will the level of pressure be high enough to have a significant impact?

The 'traditional' source of political pressure as found in the PBC literature, namely nervous politicians facing an election, has lost most of its threat: first, we have found that elections hardly had any effect on monetary policy in most OECD countries so far. Second, even if we had found a significant electoral impact, in the case of the ECB threats or pressure from politicians would not be very credible:

(a) The ECB is independent. The major reason to assume that the Bundesbank might have feared losing its independence during conflicts with the government was the possibility of changing the Bundesbank Act. At the European level, threats from politicians are not very credible, as any change in the ECB's statute requires unanimous consent of all member countries. This consent will not easily be reached – and certainly not because of national elections in a single EMU member country.

(b) Elections in the EMU member countries do not occur on the same date, typically not even in the same year. Elections to the European Parliament are an exception. However, the political influence of the European Parliament is relatively restricted and so far we do not see that elections to the European Parliament are taken very seriously by national governments. Should – due to upcoming elections – the incumbent government in one member country demand lower interest rates, it is highly unlikely that the other EMU members will tolerate that such a short-run distraction from price stability has any fundamental impact on the ECB's monetary policy.

Vaubel (1999) opposes this second point, hinting at the possibility of a certain 'clustering' of national elections between May 2002 and June 2004. If the members of the ECB Council are partisan in the sense that they want to support the incumbent national government, then, Vaubel argues, they might favor a monetary expansion just before this clustering of elections occurs. However, his analysis is rather weak in this point, as the conclusion only holds under certain conditions: (a) this clustering occurs (in several of these countries early elections have been the rule rather than the exception) and (b) the countries facing an election will also have a majority in the ECB Council. Moreover, the experiences of the Bundesbank council show that a central banker's 'partisan feelings' might be not very pronounced.[85]

We therefore conclude that national elections will not have any significant impact on European monetary policy. This holds in particular if election dates are not systematically coordinated across EMU member countries. Should elections be coordinated or clustered, then the level of political pressure might rise considerably. Yet, the combination of

- a clear mandate for price stability,
- the ECB's independent position and
- the fact that the ECB's legal status can only be changed by unanimous consent of all EMU member countries

makes is very unlikely that the ECB would give in to any political pressure.

Only in the case that Europe is hit by a very severe recession with rising unemployment across all countries, it is not impossible that all national governments might apply 'uniform' pressure on the ECB. Only if in such situation a threat to the ECB's legal status would be credible. Currently, however, we do not see such a situation, and even the sharp economic downturn in 2001 has not led to serious attempts to reduce the ECB's independence. So in our view, we can be very sure that short-run economic difficulties or national 'peculiarities' (e.g. national elections) are highly unlikely to have any impact on European monetary policy.

8.4.2 Pressure groups

The evidence from newspapers we have reported in the chapters 5 and 6 has shown one thing very clearly: interest groups are heterogeneous. Will this tendency continue under the common currency?

Successful pressure groups, on the one hand, are typically rather small and their lobbying provides their members with relatively large benefits. Interest groups with many members and comparatively small benefits, on the other hand, have less lobbying power (this is the 'collective action problem' described in Olson, 1965). If, for example, national tariffs or other trade restrictions are decided by national governments, interest groups such as exporters have strong incentives to use their lobbying power. If, however, these decisions are taken in Brussels, where 'the negotiations pit the export interests in a country directly against the import-competing interest in the same country' (Grossman and Helpman, 1993), an interest group's power decreases.

The source of pressure is related to the number of pressure groups. In the

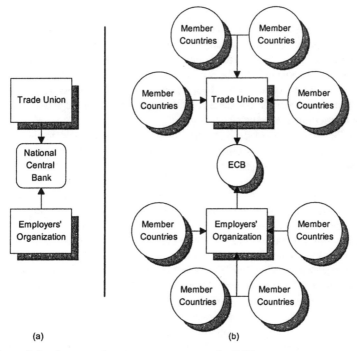

Figure 8.2   Pressure from interest groups on the ECB

EMU a new dimension, namely that of country affiliation, is added. Especially in the short-run, economies are diverse and coordination is difficult. As an example, take the situation in the year 2000: on the one hand, growth was relatively low in countries such as Germany or Italy, so these countries preferred lower interest rates. Ireland and the Netherlands, on the other hand, faced relatively high inflation rates and would prefer a tighter monetary policy. Even if national interest groups were homogenous, it would therefore be highly unlikely that European interest groups could agree on a common 'preferred monetary policy stance'. We thus predict that the diversity within the euro area will help protect the ECB from strong pressure.

We have visualized this situation in figure 8.2, where we have assumed that only two pressure groups exist. Assume both have clear objectives: the trade unions want expansive monetary policy, the employer's organizations demand tighter monetary policy. Figure 8.2 (a) shows the situation as it was in any EMU member country before the introduction of the euro: the national central banks faced two pressure groups that coordinate interests from their members and formulate (more or less) clear demands of what will best suit their interest.

Since the introduction of the euro, things have become more complicated for the pressure groups. This is shown in figure 8.2 (b): at the European level they not only have to coordinate possibly diverging interests from their members in each country, they also have to coordinate possibly diverging interests between their national counterparts. The formulation of a common 'group interest' with respect to monetary policy has become more difficult for pressure groups at the European level. At the same time this facilitates the ECB's task, as less pressure will be the result.

In the long-run two scenarios are possible: first, one could imagine that pressure groups realize that their strength grows if they unite. Second, it is also possible that diverging interests prevent such a movement. In the latter case the number of organized groups putting pressure on the ECB might rise in absolute terms, compared to the case of a national central bank. But a growing number of pressure groups need not mean that they are effective, on the contrary, the more diverse their interests are, the more it is likely that their desired policy stances will differ and the less effective their pressure becomes.

If monetary policy has the same effects in all euro area member states and if they are relatively similar in economic terms, then economically, they will move (more or less) in unison. This means that, for example, recessions occur not just in one member country, but in all countries, all countries similarly suffer from high inflation rates etc. Provided that the preference structures among different European countries are somewhat similar, interest groups will find it rather easy to coordinate their wishes and demands across countries. If, however, monetary policy affects different countries differently, then this coordination across countries becomes more difficult.

So the likelihood of pressure groups to effectively unite depends on the degree of economic diversity. Diversity is a problem for the ECB, as it questions the 'one monetary policy fits all countries'-approach, but it also facilitates the ECB's task. As an example of the difficulties for interest groups to agree on one policy stance at the European level, we briefly sketch the situation for trade unions in Europe. To increase their power at the European level trade unions engage in the European Trade Union Confederation (ETUC), which in October 1998 consisted of 65 national trade union organizations from 28 countries and 14 European Industry Federations with a total of 59 million members.[86] Its members are by far the most representative national trade unions.

Goetschy (1996) illustrates the challenges faced by the ETUC:

> In view of the diversity of interest, claims had to fulfill a unifying role and could only remain very general. The basic dilemma in setting the agenda was the following: claims had to be acceptable to a maximum of members and ought not to interfere too much with issues of national controversy.[87]

To make matters even more complicated for pressure groups at the European level, new coalitions of interest groups might arise: all German interest groups vs. all Irish interest groups, e.g. Irish trade unions unite with Irish employers to demand higher interest rates. Possibly, frequent coalitions of different national interest groups make the formulation of a common 'European interest group policy' with respect to monetary policy almost impossible. Note that this argument holds in particular for monetary policy and does not exclude the possibility of coordination in other fields, say, trade unions agree on common minimum labor standards etc.

The discussion about the reduction of working hours can serve as an example. Originally this issue was thought to be a unifying claim, but when the discussion shifted to more concrete modalities of the reduction the issue quickly became a fairly conflictual item: the Nordic unions did not really believe that it would help to create jobs, and the German and the British unions were favoring a solution of reduced working hours without pay cuts, while the French and Italian unions were more flexible on that point. In the document *Jobs and Solidarity at the Heart of Europe* the reduction of working hours was considered as major tool in the fight against unemployment, but still the Nordic unions continued to stick to their earlier views (Goetschy, 1996).

Given the difficulties of bundle diverging interest, some studies identified the diminishing role and authority of union confederations even at national levels, compared to sectoral unions (Bridgford and Stirling, 1994 and Hyman and Ferner, 1994). This again may lead to a higher number of interest groups, but at the same time makes them less effective.

In conclusion pressure groups have to form a united front across regions to be powerful. However, there is no reason to believe that pressure groups will be less heterogeneous in the broader European context than within a single country. At present, we do not see any 'broad' organized group at European level, able to combine diverging interests of different interest groups and having a powerful effect on the ECB's monetary policy. We thus predict that the number of pressure groups will rise, but pressure on the ECB will be more diverse and, therefore, less effective.

8.4.3 Countries

Talking about political consequences we also have to consider the possibility that in one country the government and interest groups 'join forces' and unite to demand changes in monetary policy. This could arise as a consequence of economic diversity, for example if a country is particularly affected by an external shock. Might we expect that countries could blame the ECB for inflation differentials and put political pressure on the ECB?

The ECB's main task is to keep inflation low. If it fails on this point, criticism is likely. So far the country with the highest inflation rate has been Ireland. If political pressure on the ECB is applied, it should come from that country. However, the common conception within the European Union seems to be that not the ECB but Ireland's fiscal policy has to be blamed for creating high inflation rates: Ireland's decision to cut indirect taxes, for instance, has been sharply criticized for further fueling the already strong economic growth and being pro-cyclical and expansionary.[88]

At a more fundamental level, this issue shows that the European Economic and Monetary Union may create the wrong incentives: if a member country conducts a successful economic policy and manages to achieve high growth rates, it may get punished for not 'adjusting downwards' to lower euro area growth. This may result in political tension – but these tensions occur between EMU member states and need not have an impact on European monetary policy.

Political pressure on the ECB has not resulted, at least not so far: low inflation countries have not pushed for higher interest rates, which does not come as a surprise. We also observe, however, that no such request came from Ireland either, the country that suffers most from high inflation. Clearly, Europe's monetary policy has to focus on overall inflation rates and not particularly on Irish inflation, but once the Irish government was criticized for creating high inflation, it would have been easy for the Irish government to point at the ECB as culprit. The fact that this has not occurred is a good sign.

So we cannot rule out the possibility that all organized groups from one country (including the government) might demand changes in the European monetary policy, for example in the presence of an asymmetric shock. However, monetary policy is hardly the right economic instrument to solve these problems. Therefore we expect that pressure resulting from individual member countries will be rather small.

8.4.4 European institutions: The European Parliament

From a legal point of view, the national governments are potentially the main threats to the ECBs independent position: any change to the Maastricht treaty requires unanimous consent of the national countries. Other European institutions such as the European Commission or the European Parliament have no direct possibility to influence the ECB's degree of statutory independence. Pressure groups consist of voters, which is the reason why national governments might listen to them and which is why indirectly they may have an impact on monetary policy – but other European institutions do not even have this indirect impact.

Still, in the European context the European Commission and the European Parliament are important players and therefore deserve a closer look. The

ECB's accountability, for instance, is reflected above all in the Maastricht treaty by the fact that the President or other members of the Executive Board may by heard by the European Parliament (article 109b.3 of the Maastricht Treaty). Also, the ECB is required to publish an annual report on its monetary policy, which is presented to the European Parliament. On that basis a general debate is held. Additionally, following the treaty of Maastricht the European Central Bank must report to the European Parliament at least four times year. And finally, the European Parliament is involved in appointing the members of the Executive Board (see section 8.2).

This frequent dialog between the two institutions is considered as very important by the ECB. From a democratic point of view the European Parliament represents the European public. In particular for a young institution such as the ECB it is very important to gain credibility, for which the European Parliament is an important 'ally'.

In terms of political pressure, what can we expect from the European Parliament? Basically, it faces a similar situation as interest groups: it will be quite difficult to coordinate interests across countries or common interests. So in that respect the positive conclusion of the previous section also holds for the European Parliament. Elections to the European Parliament are the only ones that occur within a very small period across all Europe. So potentially a booming economy at European election eve might be in the interest of the European Parliament. However, for this to be a credible threat to the ECB's independent status the European Parliament lacks power: As we have said changing the Maastricht Treaty requires consent of the national governments, not the European Parliament.

To summarize, we do not see a major potential for conflicts between the European Parliament and the European Central Bank: it will be difficult for the European Parliament to coordinate interests across countries and elections do not pose a serious danger to the ECB's legal status. Indeed, so far the European Parliament has been a major source of support to the European Central Bank.

However, we have to remind you that should Europe be hit by a very severe recession, we cannot exclude the possibility that national governments could potentially agree on changing the Maastricht Treaty. In such a situation it is difficult to predict the position of the European Parliament.

8.5 PUBLIC SUPPORT FOR THE ECB

What can we say about public support? Does the same conclusion hold as for pressure, namely that it will be less effective?

As before, the key to answer this question lies in the fact that European economies are quite diverse and that the single European monetary policy will lead to quite different economic results in the member countries. As with external pressure this implies that while some countries profit from the ECB's policy, others might 'suffer'. Second, an important factor is the approval of European Union in general.

8.5.1 Support resulting from economic diversity

Basically, like external pressure public support gains a new dimension. This is best illustrated for interest groups: in the EMU support will not only come from different pressure groups within one country, but will most probably also be spread between countries. This also holds for national governments and in particular for the European Parliament.

We have shown that the influence of pressure groups is likely to decrease, as interests become more diverse. This means that the fraction of the European population represented by a certain organized group becomes smaller. In simple terms, if 11 countries are in a boom and one country is in recession, the chances that monetary policy responds to the demands of that particular country are small. A similar reasoning holds for interest groups. Example: at national level, trade unions represent a certain fraction of all workers. At European level, for example German trade unions represent a smaller fraction of all workers, as French or Irish workers might have other interests regarding monetary policy. Thus the scope for small, but well organized groups, to influence monetary policy has been reduced. Moreover, existing economic diversity of the euro area members makes coordination for public pressure even more difficult, or, in turn, may increase public support for the ECB.

As we have seen in the previous chapter, pressure triggers public support. This can all the more be expected the smaller an organized group, the more group-specific the request and the stronger its members demand changes in monetary policy.

8.5.2 Support resulting from increased approval of the European Union

Clearly, support for the ECB will also depend on (a) people's beliefs about prospects for the economic situation and (b) support for the European Union in general. To judge the latter, the Eurobarometer survey, a survey carried out in all European countries and asking standardized questions about the EU, is quite helpful. The Eurobarometer survey 54 shows quite a positive picture:[89] the majority of people take a favorable view of membership of the European Union, as 50 per cent of the citizens consider it to be a good thing (+1 per cent in comparison with spring 2000), whereas 14 per cent take the opposite view. In each of the Member States, positive views outnumber negative views, and there was an increase in positive opinion in four Member States.

In reply to the question about the benefit derived from membership of the Union, the answers remained unchanged: 47 per cent of citizens think that their country has benefited, while 32 per cent take the opposite view. Perhaps even more important is that 55 per cent of Europeans support the single currency, whilst 37 per cent are against it. These figures might appear low in absolute terms, but approval is rising (support for the euro in the Eurobarometer Autumn 2000 survey was up again by 5 percentage points). This means that confidence in European institutions – and thus support of them – is likely to be growing. Finally, we can assume that approval in particular of the European Central Bank and the new European currency will increase sharply, once the new coins and banknotes have been introduced.

Other European institutions also showed increasing rates of approval: The steady increase in the European public's general perception of the importance of the European Central Bank has already been presented in the introduction (section 1.2), but also the level of confidence in the European Commission, which stood at 40 per cent in spring 1999 and 45 per cent in the previous Euro-barometer survey, rose to 46 per cent in autumn 2000. The level of confidence in the Commission exceeds 50 per cent in eight Member States.

To summarize, the distributive effects of monetary policy, combined with possibly different fiscal policies (which remain under national control) are diverse. We can thus expect that if some people suffer from, say, high unemployment and demand lower interest rates, other organized groups from other regions within the EMU (who currently benefit from low inflation) will support the central bank. This is all the more relevant as Europe is heterogeneous and its economic performance varies across the Member States. We thus predict that public support will rise and help strengthen the ECB's position.

8.6 SUMMARY

In this chapter we have examined the situation of the European Central Bank. We have shown that the ECB's statutory independence is very high – it might even be considered as being more independent than the Bundesbank. This strong position should be helpful during conflicts with governments or interest groups.

Next, we have examined the likelihood that pressure from outside might be applied on the ECB. We have shown in previous chapters that the influence of elections on national monetary policy has often been overrated, and it is indeed very unlikely that national elections will have any impact on the ECB's monetary policy at all. Moreover, the ECB is in the relaxed position of a supra-national central bank that does not face coordinated elections, so high pressure from all European governments before elections is not something we expect.

In chapter 5 we showed that pressure groups are very heterogeneous. There is no reason to believe that this will change in the future: indeed, the task of European pressure groups might even become more complicated, as interests in the different national pressure groups might diverge, due to, for example, diverging growth or inflation rates. It is quite unlikely that European interest groups will be more homogeneous than German interest groups were, which potentially will facilitate the ECB's task.

Summarizing the above, our conclusion is that we expect pressure to be less effective, while we do not believe that the ECB will enjoy less support for its policies than national central banks. Instead, it is quite likely that pressure from one sector and/or one country will provoke strong supportive reaction from other sectors and/or countries.

This allows the ECB to focus on economic needs more than on pressure from different interest groups. Taking these factors together, the ECB is today probably in an even more comfortable position than any European national bank has ever been.

9. The Impact of EMU Enlargement

9.1 OVERVIEW

Currently, the EMU comprises 12 member states. In December 1997 talks on membership were announced with the Czech Republic, Cyprus, Estonia, Hungary, Poland and Slovenia. Other countries (Bulgaria, Latvia, Lithuania, Malta, Romania, Slovakia and Turkey) might join the EU at a later stage (since Cyprus and Malta applied for membership, it would be more correct to talk about 'Eastern and Southern European Countries', even though one usually refers to them as 'Eastern Accession Countries'). In principle, each new EU member is a potential candidate for EMU. In this chapter we investigate what EU enlargement might imply ·for the European Central Bank. Our concern throughout this part of the study is with implications for Europe's monetary union rather than implications for the EU in general. For instance, the impact of the accession countries on agricultural policy – thought undoubtedly a very important and difficult issue – will not be examined in detail. Moreover we examine the impact of 'quick EMU enlargement', which is what would happen if the accession countries joined today. This assumption is made to avoid the uncertainties regarding the future economic development of the candidate countries.

There are several fundamental factors that distinguish the analysis of EMU enlargement to the East from the previous two chapters on the existing monetary union. The accession countries have not only to meet economic entrance criteria and secure the functioning of a market economy strong enough to cope with the competitive pressure within the European Union, but they also have to fulfill political tasks such changing their legal system to guarantee human rights, augmenting their institutional framework to secure democracy or protecting minorities. In that respect Eastern enlargement differs markedly also from the UK or Denmark joining EMU, as those countries – though not member of the European Monetary Union – are already members of the European Union, whereas the accession countries also have to adopt the *acquis communautaire*, that is the legal and economic framework of the EU.

The main economic consequences of Eastern EMU enlargement arise from a strong increase in economic diversity. Compared to the economic power of current EMU members, the accession countries are much weaker and they need to catch up to current EMU levels very quickly. This is the main economic challenge of EMU enlargement – one that is quite different from what we experience today. Indeed, our analysis reveals that a high degree of initial convergence is necessary to reduce external pressure on the ECB and to ensure a high degree of public support.

The final decision on Eastern EMU enlargement will be a political one, not exclusively based on economic needs. But obviously an adoption of the euro in the accession countries will have important economic and political implications. In what follows those consequences are examined: in the sections 9.2 and 9.3 we look at the economic and political consequences, respectively. However, as the EMU grows this also affects the decision-making process within the ECB. In section 9.4 we evaluate the current proposals to reform the decision making in the ECB's Governing Council. Finally, in section 9.5 the main points of this chapter are summarized.

9.2   ECONOMIC CONSEQUENCES OF EMU ENLARGEMENT

Currently, 13 countries have applied for EU membership. Table 9.1 summarizes some key information on the candidate countries (source: Eurostat): in terms of EU population the candidate countries represent 45 per cent, but only 7 per cent of its GDP. The high degree of economic divergence is apparent, with GDP per head varying between 5.400 to 18.500 PPS (compared to 22.530 PPS in the EU), inflation rates ranging from 0.9 to 54.9 per cent, growth rates from 1.6 to 7.2 per cent and unemployment between 4.9 and 19.1 per cent in 2000. According to recent calculations of the European Commission, EU enlargement will decrease the average income in the EU by about 13 per cent.

Most of these countries can be characterized as small open economies, as they are very open to international trade. Data from 1998 show that with the exception of Poland and Romania the averge of exports and imports of goods and services as share of GDP – a common measure for the degree of openness – was above 40 per cent and exceeded 80 per cent in some small countries such as Estonia and Malta (European Central Bank, 2000b).

Before candidate countries are allowed to enter the euro area they have to participate for at least two years in the European Exchange Rate Mechanism ERM II, the fixed exchange rate system set up for non-euro area members with fixed parities and wide bands of currently +/- 15 per cent (de Grauwe and Lavrac, 1999 and Szapáry, 2001). Still, the general expectation is that countries applying for EU membership have to introduce the euro quickly.[90] The entrance criteria for EMU enlargement for the candidate countries are not finalized, but we might assume that similar to the Maastricht criteria some

Data from 2000	Population	GDP/capita in PPS	Unem- ployment	GDP growth	Inflation rate
Bulgaria	8 191	5 400	16.2	5.8	10.3
Cyprus	755	18 500	4.9	4.8	4.9
Czech R.	10 278	13 500	8.8	2.9	3.9
Estonia	1 439	8 500	13.2	6.9	3.9
Hungary	10 043	11 700	6.6	5.2	10.0
Latvia	2 424	6 600	14.2	6.6	2.6
Lithuania	3 699	6 600	15.6	3.3	0.9
Malta	388	11 900	6.5	5.0	2.4
Poland	38 654	8 700	16.3	4.0	10.1
Romania	22 456	6 000	7.0	1.6	45.7
Slovakia	5 399	10 800	19.1	2.2	12.7
Slovenia	1 988	16 100	6.9	4.6	8.9
Turkey	64 818	6 400	6.6	7.2	54.9
EU	376 455	22 530	8.2	2.4	2.1

Table 9.1   Key information on the candidate countries

economic 'pre-requisites' must be fulfilled. Therefore, we first examine the candidate countries' performance on the basis of these critera.

a)   The candidate countries and the Maastricht critera

The aim of the convergence criteria is to achieve some form of economic convergence, which means first and foremost macroeconomic stabilization, but also a reduction of economic disparity between the euro area and the accession countries. A high degree of convergence facilitates the ECB's task, as then the single monetary policy better fits the needs of the individual member countries.

The convergence critera set out in the Maastricht Treaty focus on four economic variables: inflation rates, long-term interest rates, fiscal deficit ratios and public debt ratios. Table 9.2 displays the differences between the reference value and the actual values for each accession country and each criterion for the year 2000 (source: Schweickert, 2001). Positive values show the need for further convergence, while negative values indicate that the criteria have already been fulfilled. It turns out that most candidate countries have already made good progress towards convergence; additional comparisons with some existing EMU members (not reported) show that the Baltic states and Slovenia even outperform Greece or Portugal.

However, the Maastricht critera might blur the picture somewhat by focusing on few economic variables. It has been argued that the Maastricht critera are not really appropriate to measure convergence efforts for accession countries: for instance, countries with high growth rates of GDP typically face the need for

	Inflation rate	Interest rate	Fiscal deficit	Public debt
Reference Value	2.8	7.3	3.0	60.0
Bulgaria	7.4	−2.3	−1.5	35.5
Czech Republic	1.3	0.4	2.2	−31.0
Estonia	1.2	−0.2	−1.9	−49.0
Hungary	7.1	1.7	0.0	10.5
Latvia	0.6	3.1	−1.1	−49.4
Lithuania	−1.3	0.9	−0.1	−33.7
Poland	7.2	5.7	−0.6	−16.3
Romania	41.1	36.1	0.5	−28.7
Slovak Republic	9.3	0.4	2.5	−33.0
Slovenia	6.2	5.7	−2.0	−35.0

Table 9.2   Convergence of the accession countries: the Maastricht criteria

real appreciation, either by exchange rate revaluation or higher inflation rates. Therefore, it cannot be excluded that either the inflation or the fixed exchange rate criterion is missed. Moreover, from an economic point of view fully functional goods and capital markets are more important for the functioning of a currency union than fiscal and monetary convergence.

In what follows we focus on two main issues: economic dispersion and the distribution of the countries around the mean. The latter is particularly important with regard to external pressure or public support: for the position of the ECB a scenario where half of the countries is moving in one direction and the other half in the opposite direction is considerably worse than a situation where most of the countries (except one or two outliers) concentrate around the mean.

b)   Economic dispersion
The main difficulty for monetary policy in a currency union is that economic booms are typically associated with high inflation rates and thus require relatively high interest rates, whereas in recessions monetary policy is more expansionary to stimulate the economic recovery. Moreover, if inflation differentials translate into different inflation expectations, inappropriate nominal wage responses might be the consequence. This could foster wage-price spirals, which would further increase inflation differentials. The more EMU members differ in their cyclical position, the more difficult is it to determine the appropriate interest rate level.

Economic dispersion investigates differences in inflation and growth rates between the accession countries and the euro area. It is for instance possible that the business cycle in the accession countries is not in line with the euro area cycle. Second, the economic implications of external shocks could be

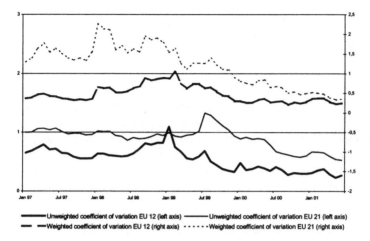

Unweighted coefficient of variation EU 12 (left axis) ——— Unweighted coefficient of variation EU 21 (left axis)
— Weighted coefficient of variation EU 12 (right axis) · · · · · · Weighted coefficient of variation EU 21 (right axis)

Figure 9.1   Inflation rates of the candidate countries

systematically different in the accession countries, leading to a boom in the current euro area and a recession in the accession countries. In what follows we give a brief overview over recent empirical findings and add our own results where necessary.

We have shown in section 7.5 that economic dispersion of the current EMU member states is comparable to that experienced previously in other monetary unions. If the accession countries joined very quickly, this would change substantially. In table 9.3 we review some recent empirical studies for the EU accession countries. It turns out that so far all economic evidence indicates that economic dispersion would sharply increase if the accession countries joined 'today'.

To visualize the impact of EMU enlargement on inflation rates we use unweighted scaled standard deviations as a measure for economic dispersion (scaled standard deviations, also known as coefficients of variation, are computed by dividing the standard deviation by the mean). They take into account the mechanical increase in standard deviation, caused by an increase in the mean. This seems appropriate here, given the big differences in inflation rates. In figure 9.1 we compare the current euro area (EU 12) with the situation after the candidate countries have joined: the EU 21 is the current euro area plus Cyprus, Czech Republic, Estonia, Hungary, Latvia, Lithuania, Poland, Slovakia and Slovenia (we decided to leave out Bulgaria and Romania: both countries had inflation rates above 100 per cent, which we regard as temporary distortions).

We see that (a) both coefficients are higher for the EU 21 than for the EU 12 (the unweighted is more than twice as high) and (b) that the impact on the

Study	Methodology and main findings
Frenkel et al. (1999)	Structural VARs to examine differences in demand and supply shocks between EMU members and (a) countries that are EU members, but not EMU members, (b) EFTA countries and (c) accession countries. Results suggest that EMU enlargement towards the accession countries would entail 'significantly higher' costs than EMU enlargement towards countries of the other two groups.
European Bank for Reconstruction and Development (2000)	Analysis of institution building and capital markets with the use of convergence indicators. Convergence is more advanced for goods markets than for capital markets, institutional and capital market convergence towards the standards set by the EMU members has yet to be achieved.
Eichengreen and Ghironi (2002)	Growth model for the average annual rate of growth per capita income on a cross section of countries, forecasting the period 1999-2006. Unless the accession countries improve their institutional framework, economic divergence between EMU incumbents and new members continues. If institutions are upgraded to EU levels accession countries are likely to grow faster than the present euro area members.
Fidrmuc and Korhonen (2002)	VAR models to test the degree of correlation of supply and demand shocks. The correlation of supply shocks greatly varies across countries, and, turning to demand shocks, only Hungary displays a high correlation with the euro area.
Schweickert (2001)	Cost/Benefit analysis; Slovenia and Hungary yield the highest net benefits, the net benefits are lowest for Romania, Latvia, Lithuania and Bulgaria.
Wagner (2002)	Theoretical model; quick EMU entry might result in high costs for some accession countries due to real divergence (or slow real convergence).

Table 9.3   The economic situation of the accession countries

unweighted standard deviation is much larger. The latter is no surprise, given the low economic weight of the candidate countries. Data for the second quarter in 2001 indicate that the unweighted and weighted coefficient of variation increase by more than 112 per cent and 43 per cent, respectively (see table 9.4). This increase is quite substantial and would imply higher inflation dispersion than in the other monetary unions in our sample.

	Unweighted coeff. of variation			Weighted coeff. of variation		
	EU 12	EU 21	Difference	EU 12	EU 21	Difference
1999	0.57	1.06	85%	0.64	1.25	95%
2000	0.36	0.75	108%	0.28	0.66	136%
2001Q1	0.34	0.66	92%	0.37	0.50	36%
2001Q2	0.26	0.56	112%	0.25	0.36	43 %

Table 9.4   Coefficient of variation for the EU 12 and EU 21

c) **What can we say about the distribution of the countries?**

Monetary policy in the euro area focuses on the euro area average. To what extent this policy is appropriate for individual countries depends on the distribution of the countries around the mean.

In order to evaluate the actual distribution, we hypothesize two extreme scenarios (see figure 9.2):

- Only two outliers determine the observed inflation spread and all other member states are located at the average HICP inflation. This is a 'benign case' for monetary policy, since it is appropriate for a large majority of the European countries.

- If the observed inflation spread is caused by two groups of countries, while none is at the union average, monetary policy faces a worst case scenario: if monetary policy is determined using the union average, it fits none of the individual countries – interest rates are too high for one half of the group and too low for the other half.

One of the problems of the standard deviation is that is provides little additional information on the underlying distribution properties, such as the skewness. To visualize the characteristics of the distribution we use a band or 'corridor' for the actual (unweighted) standard deviation (see also Maier and Hendrikx, 2002). This corridor can be computed as follows: at any moment, any particular standard deviation has also been obtained with a certain spread between the highest and the lowest values. Leaving this spread fixed, it is possible to compute a theoretical maximum and minimum for the standard deviation:

- The maximum corresponds to the case in which half of the countries are at the highest value and the rest at the lowest (i.e. the case of the two extreme groupings).

- The value for the minimum standard deviation is obtained when all the countries, except the ones with the highest and lowest values, are at the average (i.e. the case of only two countries with different positions).

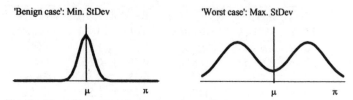

Figure 9.2   Two extreme cases for monetary policy

The first case can be interpreted as the maximum divergence that can be obtained at a certain moment, for a given spread; the second reflects the relatively best scenario in terms of dispersion that could be obtained, with only two countries that differ. The relative position of the actual standard deviation with respect to its theoretical max and min values shows to which of the two scenarios the actual position of the countries around the average is closer.

More formally, the unweighted standard deviation is computed as follows:

$$s_t = \sqrt{\left(\frac{\sum_i (y_{i,t} - \bar{y})^2}{N}\right)},$$

where t denotes the time index, $\bar{y}$ is the mean and N is the number of countries. Inserting values for the maximum and minimum observations ($y_{max,t}$ and $y_{min,t}$, respectively), the maximum standard deviation (half the countries at the highest value and half at the lowest) is computed as:

$$s_{max,t} = \sqrt{\left(\frac{0.5N(y_{min,t} - \bar{y})^2 + 0.5N(y_{max,t} - \bar{y})^2}{N}\right)},$$

the minimum standard deviation (two outliers, the observations of all other countries are equal to the mean) is

$$s_{min,t} = \sqrt{\left(\frac{(y_{min,t} - \bar{y})^2 + (y_{max,t} - \bar{y})^2}{N}\right)}.$$

However, the formulas for the minimum and maximum standard deviation imply an average inflation rate which is different from the actual average inflation. In order to correct for this problem, we have to slightly refine the formulas, so that they return the same average inflation rate for the minimum and maximum standard deviation (see appendix B for details).

The corridor visualizes the distribution of the countries for a given degree of dispersion; i.e. the heterogeneity of the countries at any given point in time becomes apparent. Note that as the spread increases, the corridor for the

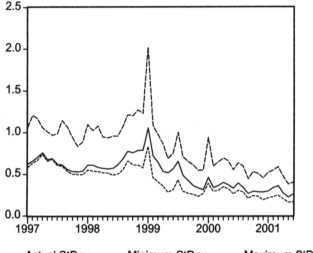

—— Actual StDev ------- Minimum StDev ---- Maximum StDev

Figure 9.3   Corridor for headline HICP for the EU 12

maximum and minimum standard deviation also becomes wider.

First, we examine euro area inflation (figure 9.3). We clearly see that the actual standard deviation is very close to the minimum standard deviation. With regard to inflation the ECB is thus in a very comfortable position, or, put differently: the situation in the euro area is currently characterized by few outliers, not two different groups of countries. This holds all the more since the actual standard deviation has not moved away from the minimum standard deviation since the introduction of the euro: before the launch of the single currency each national central bank was autonomous. Bound by the Maastricht treaty, all governments and central banks aimed at keeping inflation low. There-fore, a certain harmonization of inflation rates could have been expected until the launch of the euro in 1999. However, since the adoption of the single cur-rency, one European monetary policy has been applied to these countries. One might assume that a single monetary policy might have reinforced tendencies for inflation rates to move in different directions, as monetary policy can less be tailored to fit the national needs. Yet, the introduction of the euro has not resulted in a tendency to cluster in different 'groups'.

As a sidestep, this tool also allows us to examine the effect of the three EU member countries currently not members of the euro area (Denmark, Sweden and the UK) introducing the euro. We see in figure 9.4 that the impact in terms of convergence is relatively limited: the standard deviation basically remains close to the minimum level, though the spread is somewhat higher (in particular

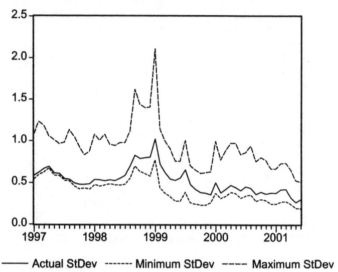

——— Actual StDev ------- Minimum StDev - - - - Maximum StDev

Figure 9.4   Corridor for headline HICP for the EU 15

since 2000). The main reason is that in terms of inflation these three countries
are rather similar to the euro area. This also holds for the UK, whose business
cycle is traditionally more in line with the US than with the euro area (Wynne
and Koo, 2000): in this case having an autonomous monetary policy apparently
helps to reduce the differences between euro area and UK inflation.

The picture changes quite dramatically when the accession countries are
included in our analysis. Figure 9.5 shows the corridor for the 'EU 21', that
is the EU 12 plus the candidate countries (again we decided to leave out
Bulgaria and Romania). We observe that the spread increases quite sharply,
and the actual scaled standard observation moves on average somewhat closer
to the maximum. How big the changes are becomes even clearer if the corridor
for the EU 12 and the measure of dispersion for the candidate countries are
plotted in one graph: we see in Figure 9.6 that the *actual* scaled standard
deviation of the EU 24 in many cases is even higher than the *worst case* scaled
standard deviation for the EU 12. Additional analysis (not reported) showed a
relatively clear distinction between a group of low inflation countries (basically
current EMU members and Cyprus, Czech Republic, Lithuania and Latvia)
with inflation rates ranging from 1 per cent to 5 per cent, and a group of high
inflation countries with inflation rates between 8 per cent to 12 per cent.

In other words: if the candidate countries joined today, even the worst possible dispersion for a given spread of the current euro area would not be sufficiently 'positive' to describe the new situation. This implies that a monetary

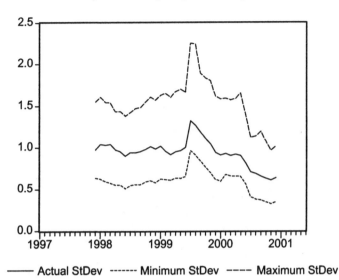

—— Actual StDev ------- Minimum StDev ---- Maximum StDev

Figure 9.5   Corridor for headline/interim HICP for the EU 12 plus candidate countries

policy stance, orientated at the euro area aggregate, might not be appropriate for the accession countries.

Note, however, that we are using the unweighted scaled standard deviation to compute this corridor. The impact on the weighted standard deviation is certainly less apparent, since these countries would enter the euro area with low (initial) weights. This corridor cannot be computed for weighted standard deviations and therefore one might argue that excessive weight is placed on outliers. We have tried to take that criticism into account by leaving out Bulgaria and Romania, the two countries with the highest inflation rates. Adding those to the corridor would considerably worsen the picture. Still, for the sentiments in the accession countries the unweighted standard deviation is the best representation, as high national inflation in, say, Poland or Slovakia hurts people in these countries – and it is not really a relief for Polish people to know that your own bad situation only accounts for a low percentage of euro area inflation!

Moreover, while the economic impact of the accession countries might be rather limited, politically it is not. An economic weight of only about 5 per cent in terms of GDP contrasts sharply with a political weight of about 30 per cent of future EMU population. This means that while economically the impact of the candidate countries on the formulation of the European monetary policy stance is relatively limited, the number of people potentially suffering from too high or too low interest rates might be significant. To visualize the difference

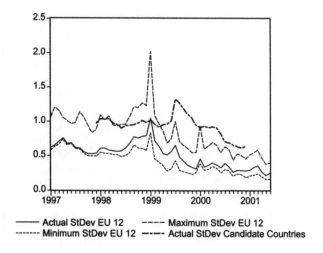

Figure 9.6   Comparison of the corridor for headline/interim HICP for the EU12 plus candidate countries

between the economic and political weights of the accession countries we plot the percentage covered in terms of GDP and population weights within a corridor of +/- 1 per cent of HICP inflation (see figure 9.7). We see that the difference between the EU 12 and the EU 23 in terms of economic weight is relatively small (upper part of figure 9.7), both are moving up or down simultaneously. However, the comparision with population weights (lower part of figure 9.7) reveals that while on average 80 per cent of EU 23 GDP lies within a corridor of +/- 1 per cent of HICP inflation, the percentage of EU 23 population covered is sharply lower (the minimum is below 45 per cent!).

d) Interpretation of the evidence
There are two possible interpretations of these findings: first, one could argue that divergent monetary policies are an important source of inflation differentials. This could be the case if monetary policy is used to stabilize output, possibly at the cost of temporarily higher inflation. Then reducing the number of autonomous monetary policies by introducing a common currency (or letting the candidate countries join the euro area) would reduce inflation dispersion. Inflation dispersion across the EU 12 plus the candidate countries would decrease after they join, because the single European monetary policy would remove divergent monetary policy stances as source of inflation differentials.

A second interpretation, however, would be less optimistic. Theoretically, an

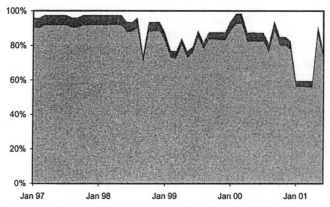

Distribution around EMU-inflation measured in GDP weights

■ ±1.0 percentage point EMU12 ▨ ±1.0 percentage point EMU23

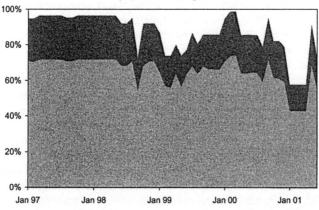

Distribution around EMU-inflation measured in population weights

■ ±1.0 percentage point EMU12 ▨ ±1.0 percentage point EMU23

Figure 9.7   Economic and political weight of the accession countries

autonomous monetary policy, in combination with flexible exchange rates, is a good tool to stabilize the economy in the face of external (asymmetric) shocks. Allowing the exchange rate to float protects an economy from spill-overs and could lead to more stable inflation rates than a common monetary policy. Following this line of thought, one would expect lower, not higher inflation dispersion, if every country has its own monetary policy, which can be designed to fit the need of its own economic situation. Obviously, this holds all the more the more diverse the countries are. According to this second interpretation we would expect inflation dispersion to further rise, once the candidate countries join the EMU.

So joining the euro area could reduce inflation dispersion to the extent that this dispersion is caused by divergent monetary policies. If all candidate countries would attach the same weight to keeping inflation rates low, inflation dispersion of the EU 21 should not be dramatically higher than in the EU 12. Currently, inflation rates in the candidate countries are on average higher than in the euro area – not really a surprise, given the big economic challenges in the Eastern accession countries.

From the point of view of European monetary policy these structural differences are quite big. If the candidate countries joined today, this might have rather important implications. During their catching-up processes the accession countries are very likely to have higher inflation rates than the euro area, because of the Balassa-Samuelson effect, and because price levels are much lower in the candidate countries and will most likely adjust upwards. So on the one hand accession countries have to grow faster to converge on the same economic levels (price levels or per-capita income), which on the other hand means that growth differentials and inflation rate differentials are inevitable. This makes the ECB's task more complicated.

What will be the main source of this additional growth in accession countries to overcome the structural differences? A popular argument, as formulated by Baldwin et al. (2001), is that accession countries will demand higher inflation rates to grow faster. However, regarding overall inflation in the euro area in our view this argument does not hold: if indeed high inflation fosters economic growth (which is *not* what most empirical studies find![91]), then current EMU members and accession countries would both profit, and as the accession countries would not grow relative to the current euro area members, the economic gap would not be closed. This was only the case before the new members access the EMU, as only then they can use an autonomous monetary policy and have relatively higher inflation rates to simulate growth – once they are 'in', this possibility does not exist anymore. It is possible that accession countries might want to experience higher inflation rates in their countries, due to the Balassa-Samuelson effect. But this only reinforces our argument that currently EMU accession is not an economic improvement for most candidate countries.

Instead, additional growth must result from other policy options. Fiscal policy could be one alternative, but is restricted by the Stability and Growth Pact and can only contribute in a very limited way. By the same argument, substantial EU subsidies are quite unlikely, given the tight budget situation in most incumbent euro area members. The other alternative is labor market policy or structural improvement and upgrading the candidate countries' institutional framework. This task is not facilitated by the need to liberalize capital markets, which is on the one hand part of the *acquis communautaire*, but which on the other hands increases the probability to attract volatile capital flows.

In our view the main threat for European monetary policy does not result from inflation differentials, but from the distribution of the countries around the mean. In the most extreme case of two groupings of countries, one experiencing a recession and deflation and the other facing a economic boom with very high inflation rates, focusing on the aggregate level effectively means that monetary policy suits no individual member country: interest rates are too low for the boom countries to fight inflation and too high for the recession countries to foster economic growth. This may undermine the acceptance of European monetary policy, certainly in the medium- and long run. This point is covered in more detail in the next section, when we talk about political consequences of EMU enlargement.

To summarize, economic dispersion between the euro area and the candidate countries is currently very high. Economic convergence is likely to increase relatively quickly, for instance due to increases in trade between the candidate countries and the EMU (there is a growing literature on the effect of having a common currency on trade, e.g. Rose, 2000, and Rose and Frankel, 2002. Lasser and Schrader, 2002, show that the trade patterns of the Baltic states helped to increase integration into the Western European economy, Hallett and Piscitelli, 2002 use a theoretical model to show that due to trade integration smaller economies are likely to convergence). Still, unless intial convergence is high, EMU enlargement might entail high economic costs – less for the euro area, but first and foremost for the accession countries. As the candidate countries have a small weight in the euro area aggregate, European monetary policy can hardly tailor its single monetary policy to fit the needs of these countries.

Even though fast accession to EU may be politically desirable, on economic grounds we currently cannot find convincing arguments for quick accession. In our view, EMU accession currently makes little economic sense – not for the euro area, but for most candidate countries. Should we conclude that the candidate countries should not join the euro area at all? No, the picture is quite likely to change in the medium term: as, for instance, trade links between the EMU countries and the accession countries increase and capital markets become more integrated, it is quite likely that over time also business cycle correlation increases. Also to the extent that monetary policies were used for other purposes than to keep inflation low, the elimination of national monetary policies in the candidate countries might foster economic convergence. This benefit is gained from joining the ERM II. So in a medium-run perspective even the candidate countries might enjoy not just political, but also economic, benefits from joining the euro area.

9.3   POLITICAL CONSEQUENCES FROM EMU ENLARGEMENT

9.3.1   Consequences of increased economic dispersion

We have seen that if the accession countries joined today, economic dispersion would greatly increase in the future due to EMU enlargement. A higher degree of inflation dispersion potentially pulls monetary policy in different directions. Although economic convergence is likely to be much higher when EMU enlargement finally takes place, examining a 'quick enlargement' scenario is interesting to show the consequences of missing initial convergence. It also shows why quick accession might not be the most desirable option for European monetary policy. As we have explained in section 7.2, monetary policy in a monetary union cannot take into account inflation differentials in its policy formulation. Still, increased economic diversity might increase political pressure on the European Central Bank.

From the ECB's point of view EMU enlargement entails two main immediate consequences, resulting from an increase in economic diversity. First, inflation rates in EU accession countries are on average somewhat higher than in the euro area. The main reasons for that are unclear: the Balassa-Samuelson effect certainly plays an important role here, though its magnitude is debatable (according to de Broeck and Slok, 2001, estimates range from 0.8-1.6 percentage points).[92] But apart from that it might also be the case that national central banks in the accession countries were tempted to use monetary policy to pursue more ambitious growth targets. As a result, it will be one of the main tasks for the ECB to bring inflation expectations (which also determine wage negotiations) down in the accession countries to be more in line with EMU inflation rates to avoid wage-price spirals, which would set the ground for permanent (structural) deviations.

Second, accession countries have to catch-up to the euro area level quickly. As discussed in the last section, their options are very limited: fiscal policy is restricted by the Stability and Growth Pact, and structural policies and welfare gains from trade liberalization will take a long time. So at least in the short run, to provide economic growth, from the perspective of an accession country, monetary policy may seems to be a very promising policy option. Still, the European Central Bank has been very explicit that it will not change its monetary policy strategy to facilitate entrance of the new members:

> Whatever the intensity of the Eurosystem's involvement in the enlargement process, we will always focus on the maintenance of price stability *in the euro area*. Hence, any arrangements or other forms of co-operation with accession countries will be without prejudice to the Eurosystem's independence and our primary objective.[93]

9.3.2 Consequences for public pressure and support

From a public choice perspective EMU enlargement clearly goes beyond purely economic areas. Of interest is the impact of EMU membership on national interest groups and the government. Obviously, the constraints under which the government operates changes significantly – the discretion of national policymakers is sharply reduced (Bofinger, 1998). Areas of major change include the following:

- A country can no longer determine its own trade policy, but is obliged to keep its markets open vis-à-vis other members. Restrictions on non-members can only be imposed as a part of the EU's general trade policy.
- Subsidies to national industries are heavily restricted.
- Financing of public sector deficits by the central bank is not allowed.
- Restrictions on capital movements vis-à-vis other member countries, but also third member countries, are abolished. Safeguard measures can only be decided by the European Council.

The last two point means that countries have to compete for funds in a completely integrated financial markets, or, put differently, public debtors no longer possess monopsony position in the domestic national financial market. By accepting these constraints the balance between policymakers and national interest groups in the accession countries changes significantly: national policymakers have less to 'offer' to interest groups, as in important policy fields their hands are tied.

To analyse the situation of interest groups, let us look at a simple example first: trade policy. The traditional tools of trade policy are no longer available at the country level, as decisions on tariffs and subsidies will be taken in Brussels. This means that the demand for protection in candidate countries is also likely to decline – simply because certain measures are no longer available at the national level. Similarly, pressure to change interest rates in candidate countries will cease immediately, once they adopt the euro. Therefore, Bofinger (1998) concludes that EMU enlargement entails massive shifts in political power in the accession countries, from which traditionally weak interest groups (consumers, exporters) might benefit, whereas relatively stronger interest groups (such as import-competing firms) might lose. Therefore, pressure from organized groups is likely to decrease at the national level and to shift to the European level. There organized groups face the same problems as described in chapter 8: pressure is likely to be less effective, due to coordination problems across interests and countries.

By similar reasoning, the effectiveness of pressure from interest groups on European monetary policy will decrease, even though the number of sources, as compared to the current level, might increase. So the reasoning of chapter 8 still holds, in fact, it becomes even stronger, due to the strong diversity of the enlarged euro area. Similarly, national governments currently have the ability to exert pressure on national central banks (a possibility, which at least some governments actively use),[94] but once the candidate countries have introduced the euro, this political pressure becomes ineffective.

Translated into our terminology of public pressure and public support, the basic findings of chapter 8 are confirmed: we expect a relatively high degree of public support, whereas political pressure on the ECB will be lower than that on the respective national central bankers. However, one important reservation has to be made: the current level of economic dispersion is so high, that if the accession countries joined today, in some regions or countries the benefits of joining EMU are rather debatable. As a consequence, public support in these countries or regions is likely to decline, whereas external pressure could increase. As the political weight in these regions far exceeds the economic weight, people in the accession countries might feel that their situation is not adequately reflected in the European monetary policy stance.

Additionally, adjustment mechanisms such as labor migration or fiscal redistribution could be evoked, entailing either massive outflows of human capital, or massive transfers from the EU, or both. Currently, the EU does not seem willing to adopt either possibility. Therefore, we argue that the main danger of EMU enlargement is not political pressure on the European Central Bank, the main difficulty lies in the acceptance of monetary policy: even if two distinct 'groups' of countries emerge, with one requiring tighter monetary policy and the other one requiring monetary ease, European monetary policy must still target the euro aggregate. But if the economic differences are too big, acceptance of European monetary policy will suffer, as people realize that the single monetary policy is not suitable for their region or country.

What could be the consequence? Feldstein (1997) takes a rather controversial position by predicting that EMU could potentially lead to war, as exit of EMU is not foreseen in the Maastricht Treaty.

A critical feature of the EU in general and the EMU in particular is that there is no legitimate way for a member to withdraw. This is a marriage made in heaven that must last forever. But if countries discover that the shift to a single currency is hurting their economies and that the new political arrangements are also not to their liking, some of them will want to leave. The majority may not look kindly on secession...[95]

If one does not want to go as far as Feldstein, two other recent experiences from countries that either share or shared a common currency are insightful.

- Former Czechoslovakia split into the Czech Republic and Slovakia in January 1993, but to mitigate the economic effects of the split both countries agreed to retain their common currency for at least six months (Fidrmuc et al., 1999). However, the monetary union lasted less than six weeks. According to Fidrmuc et al. (1999) the main factors contributing to the failure were low integration of the currency union and the absence of fiscal transfers. But while Feldstein (1997) argues that lack of proper exist mechanisms might lead to disaster, Fidrmuc et al. (1999) stress the importance of high barriers to exit as a important measure to stabilise EMU during 'rough times'. Moreover, an important reason for the break-up was lack of political commitment. Clearly, the break-up of Czechoslovakia was not only due to economic difficulties, but also to political factors. Yet, for those two countries the benefit of having two separate currencies are rather limited. Once economic difficulties mounted, breaking up the currency union was probably also fostered by nationalistic motives.

- Preceding the reunification, Germany introduced a common currency in the GDR. Despite huge financial transfers throughout the 1990s (and despite institutional upgrading, high labor migration etc.), East German regions still belong to the poorest in current euro area (source: EU Competitiveness Report 2001, for more information on the economic consequences of the German re-unification see also Hunt, 2000). Germany's growth rates sharply declined, and the country moved from being one of the fastest growing European countries since the 1950s to one of the least growing countries in the EU in the 1990s. This despite the fact that all the theoretical pre-requisites for successful monetary union were given and that labor mobility – due to the common language – was probably higher than it will ever be in the rest of Europe!

This is not to say that EMU enlargement immediately endangers the European Monetary Union, simply because monetary policy might not fit the needs of the accession countries.[96] Again we have to remind you that the previous analysis is based on the scenario that the candidate countries join 'today', i.e. that no further convergence takes place prior to EMU enlargement. But the preceding analysis shows the potential dangers of currency unions, where economic convergence is very low. So in that sense the main result of the analysis is that initial economic convergence is an important requirement prior to EMU accession.

Furthermore, we have to distinguish between political motives, leading to EU accession, and economic motives, leading to EMU accession. Accession to both Unions should be treated as two separate issues. Clearly, political motives are important factors for the candidate countries to join the European Union, and we do not expect that any candidate country might wish to leave the European Union, once they have joined. Few people would consider leaving the European Union only on the grounds that monetary policy was not to their liking. Here other economic and political considerations from participation in the EU play an important role.

Currently, public support for the European Union is high in the accession countries: according to the latest Eurobarometer survey (Autumn 2000) more than 65 per cent of all citizens above 18 years in the 13 accession countries favor membership in the European Unions. Counting only those citizens who would actively vote in a referendum, the majority is even larger (79 per cent), though with significant regional differences: Rumania and Bulgaria have the highest rate of approval (97 and 95 per cent, respectively), while people in Malta (53 per cent), Estonia and Lithuania with 59 per cent and Poland (67 per cent) are a bit more skeptical. Still, relatively speaking political pressure on European monetary policy is likely to increase and public support will decrease, if economic diversity exceeds a certain level. Therefore, entry to the currency union should be based on economic convergence, simply because the performance of Europe as a whole depends on the appropriateness of European monetary policy for all member countries. So despite quick accession to the European Union being politically desirable, accession to the European Monetary Union should be based on economic fundamentals.

Going back to the German example again, Frijters et al. (2001) have measured life satisfaction in East and West Germany and provide evidence that – despite the economic problems – life satisfaction in East Germany has steadily increased since the German reunification. It is unclear to what extent the absolute improvement in standards of living is the driving force behind this, but, *ceteris paribus*, the increase in happiness should also increase the support for the currency union, despite the huge regional disparities. In some respect, the German reunification is comparable with quick EU and EMU accession of the candidate countries. If E(M)U enlargement results in a similar improvement in the standards of living in the accession countries, we might expect that approval for both EU and EMU membership remains high.

9.4 INSTITUTIONAL CONSEQUENCES OF EMU ENLARGEMENT

In this last section of this chapter we turn away from the economic or political analysis and focus on institutional issues. One of the most immediate consequences of EMU enlargement will be that decision making in the European Central Bank will become more difficult. Monetary policy decisions are taken in the Governing Council, which at present consists of the following members: six members of the Executive Board and 12 national central bank governors. They all have one vote, equaling a total of 18 votes (for comparison: the US Federal Reserve has 12 board members, the Bank of England nine and Canada seven). If eventually all the accession countries plus Britain, Denmark and Sweden join EMU, this could amount to a total of 33 members. As Eichengreen and Ghironi (2002) illustrate it: 'Imagine that every member is allowed to make a 15 minute opening statement. It would then take a day to dispense with the opening ceremonies'![97]

In section 7.2 we examined the potential role of monetary policy in a monetary union. Based on economic arguments we concluded that monetary policy should focus on the aggregate, not on national or regional developments. In an enlarged EMU this is all the more important, since economic diversity will increase sharply.

For the decision-making process in the Governing Council the behavior of the national central bank governors is crucial, as they form the majority. Here two possible scenarios might be distinguished:

- They might view themselves as representatives of their home country. In this case they are more concerned about national inflation at home and less about inflation in the euro area. As a result, the decision making in the ECB Governing Council is a 'bargaining process', subject to any kind of coalition forming: the accession countries, for instance, might opt for relatively loose monetary policy to stimulate growth. If they 'join forces' with the southern EMU members, they might have a majority in the Governing Council, despite the fact that their economic power may be less than, say, 30 per cent of the euro area.[98]

- The national central bank governors might also view themselves as 'Europeans', only concerned about developments in the euro area. Such a situation might be preferable on economic grounds, but requires a strict discipline of the national central bank governors. It also implies that criticism on European monetary policy might increase from countries suffering from quite different levels of inflation or growth rates. So this scenario requires very good communication of the ECB, but also of the national central banks, to explain the monetary policy decisions. A strong position of the Executive Board, which is most likely to focus on the euro area, is also preferable.

The current decision-making process in the ECB's Governing Council is largely based on the second scenario: as a result of the 'one member, one vote' voting system in the Governing Council small countries are heavily overrepresented. Luxembourg, for example, has the same weight in the Governing Council as Germany or France. The rational behind this system is to avoid central bankers being more concerned about national interests than the euro area average: 'A system of weighted voting ... would have fostered the thinking that the governors were just national representatives and not equal members of a collegiate body charged with formulating a common policy.'[99]

If the decision-making process is not fundamentally changed, the weight of the national central bank governors in the Governing Council will decrease, relative to the weight of the national central bankers. If national central bankers care less about the euro area average than the Governing Council, but more about the situation in their own country, this could have an impact on the ECB's monetary policy stance: as the weight of the Governing Council (and thus the euro area as a whole) decreases relative to the weight of the national governments (which translates into national interest), coalition forming among the national governors is facilitated.

So as a result of EMU enlargement the ECB could be following a policy less focused on the need of a majority of the countries, but not necessarily on the euro area average. In that sense national demands could become more important than monetary policy for the entire euro area.[100] How likely is such a scenario?

It requires that the decision-making process as such remains unchanged, in particular that the weight of the Executive Board decreases. It also assumes a certain 'struggle' in the Governing Council between the Executive Board on the one hand (assumed to focus more on the euro area) and the national central bankers (assumed to focus more on the needs of their country), and a possibly changing coalitions within the Governing Council. Only in these cases will EU enlargement lead to changes in the ECB's policy stance.

If national central bank governors indeed value the situation in their home country higher than the euro area average, the scope for this 'struggle' between the Executive Council and the national central banks increases. The likelihood of such a situation strongly depends on the ability of the Executive Board (which is assumed to focus on the euro area average) to shape the ECB's policy stance – and on the trade links between the EMU members, because if the 'big' members suffer, as monetary policy focuses on the need of the small countries, growth in the small countries will also be affected if trade links are strong.

De Haan et al. (2002) have examined the voting behavior in the Bundesbank Council and show that regional differences play a role in dissent voting. With regard to the ECB this could mean that central bankers coming from, e.g. a country with low inflation and low growth, could be more inclined to advocate a cut in interest rates than colleagues from high inflation countries. In this case, the decentralized structure of the ECB could turn out to be a disadvantage. This issue will become less important the more business cycles within the euro area converge.

Moreover, the fact that different researchers advocate very different and not compatible scenarios (e.g. Baldwin et al. (2001) assume the ECB might follow high inflation policies due to the accession countries, whereas Eichengreen and Ghironi (2002) rather fear that accession countries might '... demand anti-inflationary interest hikes that choke off expansion in the rest of Euroland'[101]) shows (a) a high degree of uncertainty about the future behavior and the motives of the accession countries and (b) that all these fears are highly speculative. In our view it is quite unlikely that EMU enlargement will lead to such a 'struggle' between the Executive Board and the other Governing Council members we believe the ECB will continue to focus on the euro area average, as it has done so far. Nevertheless, for purely practical purposes the decision-making process has to be altered to facilitate coordination and monetary policy formulation. Several proposals have been made:[102]

1. Votes could rotate among council members, as is currently done in the Federal Reserve in the United States.

2. Single council members represent groups of countries. This IMF-like constituency system has also been implemented in Germany after the reunification.[103]

3. Voting could be entirely delegated to an independent group, such as the Executive Board – this option thus means stripping the national central bank governors of their voting power.

4. The voting power of the Executive Board could be increased to reduce the relative impact of regional issues.

5. The mandate for the ECB could be limited to achieve inflation targets set e.g. by the Ecofin Council.

To solve the large-numbers problem a reduction of the number of voting members in the Governing Council is needed, while the regional-interest problem can be overcome by reducing the number of national central bank governors.

Giving the Executive Board additional votes would help to reduce the importance of regional issues, but would not solve the large-number problem.[104]

Delegating voting to an independent group would be the 'cleanest' solution, but is probably the least feasible politically. Moreover, it would weaken the accountability of the ECB's monetary policy if national central bankers (who are accountable to their domestic polities) were not allowed to take part in the decision-making process. A constituency system would not foster the thinking of central bank governors that they are Europeans, not representative of national governments.

The last option, the Ecofin Council setting inflation targets, would remove the ECB's goal independence. This would provide a framework for interest-rate decisions, but would not address the large-number problem. This can be solved by a constituency-system, which would certainly speed up decisions. The German experience, however, shows that such reorganization is politically difficult; moreover, if, for example, one Governing Board member represents very similar countries, the regional-interest problem remains.

So in our view the best solution is a rotating system, as is currently practiced by the Federal Reserve. Currently, this also seems to be the ECB's preferred solution.[105] However, two main difficulties are associated with that option: first, European countries are used to permanent representation at the Governing Council, so they might resist that move. Second, 'the representatives of the countries in which Europe's predominant financial centers are located are a source of information on financial-market conditions. Requiring them to rotate off the Council might therefore impede the flow of information to the ECB.'[106] This issue can be solved by granting some members permanent seats in the Governing Council. The main advantage of the system, however, namely that every country is represented similarly (i.e. has to rotate after a similar period) would then be lost. Moreover, a possible 'clustering' of countries with possibly similar regional interest cannot fully be excluded, even though its possibility is greatly reduced.

To conclude, EMU enlargement greatly increases potential problems for European monetary policy by increasing the number of potential coalitions and outcomes that might arise from an increased number of participants in the policy-decision process. To what extent these potential issues translate into actual problems remains to be seen.

To solve the immediate impact on the decision making we favor a rotating system. This would at the same time reduce the large-number problem and the possibility that regional issues might dominate European monetary policy.

9.5 SUMMARY

We have seen in chapter 7 that economic divergence of the current euro area is not something one should worry about, but economic convergence will become a major topic, once the candidate countries are members of the euro area. We argue that these countries currently are economically very different, both in terms of growth rates (GDP growth or inflation rates) and levels (GDP per capita and price levels). Adjustment of growth rates and levels at the same time is not possible.

In our view quick EMU enlargement it is not economically favorable for the candidate countries – not from the perspective of the euro area, but based on their own economic interests. However, the decision on EMU enlargement will be a political one, and for political reasons a quick accession might be preferable. Our analysis has shown that a strong increase in economic diversity could translate into mounting economic pressure on the ECB. Again we have to remind you that we examined a scenario where the candidate countries join 'today'. To some extent this is a scenario of 'maximum divergence', as we might expect that economic convergence between the current euro area and the accession countries will increase prior to EMU enlargement. Still, our analysis highlights the need for high initial convergence, as otherwise political and public support in some regions or countries might sharply decrease.

So far the ECB's position on these issues is relatively clear: the task of monetary policy is to guarantee price stability, structural issues are the task of fiscal, structural or institutional policies. Currently, we do not see any changes to that position, so in our view the impact of EU enlargement on the ECB's monetary policy stance should be fairly limited. Still, the magnitude of the growth and inflation differentials pose new challenges for the external communication of the ECB. No one expects the candidate countries to immediately have the same growth and inflation rates as the current euro area members. Still, the ECB needs to explain clearly why inflation and growth differentials persist and to what extent this is an issue for European monetary policy.

Quite fundamental, however, will be the implications of EU enlargement for the decision-making process of the ECB. Here, the solution will also give indication whether the members of the Governing Council view themselves more as 'Europeans' or as delegates of their own country. If the latter was the case, the decision making (and the outcome) might suffer from national feelings.

10. Conclusion

10.1 OVERVIEW

For many years, the relationship between the government and the central bank has been one of the prime objects of interests in the political-economy literature. Does the government interfere with monetary policy? Were political business cycles created, because politicians want to increase their chances of being re-elected? These questions have been the subject of debates, not just in Germany, but also elsewhere.

We have examined the role of politics in monetary policy. We have analysed various central banks, but our first objective was to study the Deutsche Bundesbank, a central bank that has commonly been viewed as prototype for an independent central bank. Also, it has served as role model for central banks in many other countries, including the European Central Bank. One of the main reasons why politicians made central banks independent was to send a credible signal of commitment to sound monetary policy – which is not compatible with abuse of monetary policy for short-run (e.g. electoral) purposes. If even this central bank was subject to frequent manipulation before elections, or if German politicians had easy access to monetary policy to foster their ambitions, then the whole concept of central bank independence should perhaps be reconsidered.

Our results show that the attention that the political business cycle has received, was, at least with regard to monetary policy, unwarranted. We find indications that elections are important, but certainly not as influential as the PBC hypothesis suggests. There were times of pressure, but neither the Bundesbank, nor most other central banks have given in. Therefore, we have shifted the focus to other interesting areas: first constructing better indicators for conflicts, which has led to the new pressure indicator, and second, examining not only the potential impact of the government, but also of other pressure groups. However, pressure is not the only external influence on the Bundesbank: we have shown that public support is an important variable, too. Looking at the ECB we have checked whether inflation differentials have the potential to trigger additional pressure from organized groups or governments. Finally, we extended our focus beyond the EMU by examining the candidate countries, analysing both for economic and political implications.

179

The purpose of this final chapter is to summarize our main findings, point to unanswered questions and offer some suggestions for further research.

10.2 MAIN FINDINGS

In this study we have estimated several models for political pressure. The general hypothesis tested was that – even in the case of central banks with a high degree of statutory independence – politics might have an impact on monetary policy. We wanted to investigate how this impact might look. In doing so, we have followed two approaches, cross-country studies where possible, and country-specific tests where necessary.

In chapter 2 we have given a review of existing studies on the Bundesbank. We have shown that some questions have not been fully answered and that there is room for improvements. One of the issues that deserved a closer look was how monetary policy should be measured. Based on our discussion of the institutional setting we have proposed two main measures of monetary policy: short-term interest rates as proxy for effective monetary policy, and monetary policy indices as proxy for a central bank's rhetoric.

In chapter 3 we have used short-term interest rates to show for a panel of 14 OECD countries that elections have had little, if any, impact on monetary policy. Country-specific tests were also carried out in chapter 4 to investigate the influence of politics on the rhetoric of the Bundesbank, the Bank of Japan and the US Federal Reserve. Again, we conclude that the impact of non-economic factors was small, albeit we have seen clear signs of political pressure in the rhetoric of the German central bank. This political pressure, however, did not translate into a different stance of monetary policy.

One of the difficulties we encountered here was the definition of political pressure. Existing indicators had several shortcomings, most of which we tried to overcome by introducing a new 'pressure indicator'. This indicator, based on reports demanding changes of monetary policy as found in three German newspapers, allowed us to differentiate between pressure from different sources. It is shown that of all the groups we have examined only the financial sector had a significant impact on the Bundesbank's policy. The government did not significantly interfere with German monetary policy.

This finding is confirmed in chapter 6 where we introduced public support. We have shown that government support for the Bundesbank was high across time, and we have pointed to the fact that conflicts between the government and the Bundesbank mostly occurred about institutional issues, such as the creation of the EMS, but relatively rarely about the current policy stance. Econometrically, we were able to show that a high degree of public support can – at least partly – offset pressure from organized groups.

The chapters 7 and 8 offered an outlook for the European Central Bank. We have analysed economic dispersion in the euro area and have examined inflation differentials as a potential new source of pressure. Moreover, based on the interpretation of our results in the European context, we conclude that the ECB is in a very comfortable position: we expect less pressure, more support, and even the issue of diverging inflation rates has shown to be less reason to worry about than a first glance at current European inflation rates might suggest.

Finally, in chapter 9 we have highlighted the main consequences from EMU enlargement. If the candidate countries join, economic convergence will drop significantly. This means that the single monetary policy will be less appropriate for an enlarged EMU. Consequently, not only will the task for European monetary policy be more complicated, but increased economic dispersion even has the potential to undermine the long-run support for the currency union.

Based on the econometric evidence we presented, a mixed picture of the Deutsche Bundesbank emerges: certainly very independent when we talk about governmental influence, perhaps less independent when we look at the impact of the financial sector. Political pressure on the European Central Bank potentially comes from more directions, but is likely to be less efficient. This will help the ECB to gain credibility and secure the support for the single currency in the long run. Quick EMU enlargement, however, might reverse this positive impact.

Six main conclusions of this study emerge:

1. From our cross-country tests we can safely conclude that the impact of elections on short-term interest rates can be neglected. As we believe that this is the best way to measure monetary policy, we can conclude that the standard PBC model is not supported by the evidence obtained from analysing the behavior of central banks. Therefore, we can completely reject this model for monetary policy.

   This does not exclude the possibility that central banks are subject to pressure or postulates that pressure is absent in monetary policy before elections. But we think that the timing of elections has no impact on the central bank's implemented policy stance. This finding is not only confirmed for Germany; our panel tests for 14 OECD countries showed no electoral impact.

2. Our analysis of central banks' rhetoric showed that there might have been situations before elections when the Bundesbank rhetoric differs from the policy it is implementing. This is not only a clear sign of the pressure central banks face, but it also shows that the Bundesbank used the possibility to deviate from its announced policy stance, presumably

to calm down politicians before elections. However, the implementation of the German monetary policy was not significantly influenced by elections. For the Federal Reserve and the Bank of Japan a similar political impact was not found.

3. In view of these results we can safely conclude that the hypothesis of PBCs in monetary policy has been completely refuted. Given the simplicity of this model, this does not necessarily come as a surprise. Indeed, from our analysis of the Bundesbank we conclude that more sophisticated indicators of political pressure, also of pressure from interest groups in general, are needed. We have shown that better indicators can give a more detailed picture of the factors influencing German monetary policy. Based on evidence in the newspapers we have found that the influence of the financial world could be crucial. Little is known about the exact role of financial institutions and the relationship between central banks and commercial banks and therefore clearly warrants further research.

4. We have shown that support of a central bank was a significant element of Germany's monetary policy. We have found that high public support is important as it can offset pressure from other groups. Practically, if we augment traditional reaction functions by adding a support component, we can make better forecasts. Moreover we were able to show that support among all major German interest groups was high: the more the Bundesbank was criticized, the stronger the supportive reaction from organized groups and, perhaps most important, from the government. Again, further research and probably also international evidence is needed to clarify how support of central banks exactly influences monetary policy.

5. Our analysis of the ECB shows that it possesses all the requirements (especially a very independent legal status) for a successful low-inflation policy. We expect political pressure to be lower, as interest groups have difficulties to coordinate their interest, and a high degree of public support.

    Currently, inflation rates diverge in the euro area, but experiences from other monetary unions show that these differentials are likely to decrease as business cycles converge. New estimates of the Balassa-Samuelson model showed that inflation differentials are less problematic than they might appear at first glance. Inflation dispersion is currently not influenced by the level of inflation rates. Overall, the degree of economic convergence in the euro area can be considered as very high.

6. On economic grounds, quick EMU enlargement is not desirable. Not for current EMU members, since the candidate countries are economically

small compared to the incumbents, and therefore the euro area aggregate will not change dramatically. But for the candidate countries quick accession means that their growth prospects are seriously limited: they cannot use an autonomous monetary policy, fiscal policy will be restricted by the Stability and Growth Pact and exchange rates will be fixed. Growth must thus mainly result from institutional improvements and structural policies. While this is certainly a solid basis for high growth in the long run, in the short run economic disparities are less likely to diminish.

Should the candidate countries join early, severe problems for the candidate countries might arise: due to their diversity the single European monetary policy will be less appropriate for their needs. This has the potential to undermine political and public support for the currency unions. Therefore we recommend a slow accession strategy.

10.3 DISCUSSION

The question of whether political pressure on central banks occurs – and maybe even has a significant impact – remains a strongly debated one. However, based on our findings we have to conclude that the discussion, at least partly, focused on the wrong issues: if politics has a significant impact on monetary policy, it is certainly not at fixed (electoral) intervals, at least not in the countries we have examined in this study. But, if this is not the case, when do governments try to influence central banks?

A point we could not really answer in this study is the question when pressure occurs. We have seen that pressure is neither significantly related to election dates, nor to diverging policy stances. Most economists would probably have named these factors as key determinants for (political) pressure, yet in the German case they were not the prime cause for conflicts.

Related to that question is the problem that international evidence on public support is unavailable. Empirically, we were able to show that pressure causes supportive actions, but does this only occur in Germany, or can similar reactions also be observed in other countries? What about support for the central bank in high-inflation countries? Here not only international evidence would be helpful, but clearly, one of the things that misses in this study is a theoretical model explaining why and when public support of a central bank occurs. Here too further research is warranted.

At a more fundamental level, what one might expect from the public choice literature is that the government formulates an opinion about the current monetary policy stance, interest groups have perhaps different demands etc. We have found that this is not the case: no institution or interest group we have examined has had a *single* opinion, all groups were heterogeneous, and governmental pressure was not even significantly related to elections! This is not quite what could have been expected from the literature; the picture we found was less black-and-white than previous studies suggested.

The impact of the financial sector on monetary policy clearly deserves more attention. The fact that – despite using different methodologies and quite different classification of what the 'financial sector' comprises – both Havrilesky (1993) and this study have found a significant influence of financial institutions on monetary policy can be interpreted as a clear sign that this relationship needs further research.

One thing should be pointed out: our study should not lead to the conclusion that there were hardly any conflicts between the Bundesbank and the government. Instead we have to differentiate between conflicts about the 'correct' economic policy and conflicts about institutional matters: our inspection of newspapers clearly showed that if conflicts between government and Bundesbank arose in the past, it was in most cases about institutional setup. These conflicts, however, are not reported in any of these indicators, as they are not directly related to economic policies. Heipertz (2001) covers the conflicts surrounding the German reunification and European Monetary Union. He concludes that the Bundesbank has always recognized that these issues were decided in a political process. Two examples might illustrate this point.

- After the plans for the European Monetary System became public in the late 1970s, the Bundesbank opposed requirements of unlimited purchase of foreign currency, as this would undermine its ability to autonomously determine the German monetary policy. This was a veritable conflict between the government and the central bank, but the issue was not about lowering or raising interest rates, but the conflict arose from the potential threat to the autonomous institutional setting of the Bundesbank.

- Similarly, the so-called 'Goldwar Issue' in 1998 arose, when former Secretary of Finance, Theo Waigel, demanded revaluation of the Bundesbank's gold reserves. This would have raised the Bundesbank's profits, which, in turn, would have reduced the government's budget deficit and would have helped to fulfill the Maastricht criteria for entering in the European Economic and Monetary Union. The Bundesbank considered the demand as potential threat to its autonomous status and refused.

Both conflicts were not about the stance of monetary policy, but more about the independent status of the Bundesbank. Of course, making the Bundesbank more dependent could ultimately lead to changes in monetary policy, but as there were not direct consequences for monetary policy, these conflicts were not relevant for our econometric studies.

In the introduction we have explained our reason for focusing on the Bundesbank as prime object to study: it has been the most independent central bank, at least before the ECB was set up. We have said that if our investigation of external pressure on the Bundesbank shows that the Bundesbank's policy was not as free of external influences as it should have been, given its independent status, then the whole concept of central bank independence should be reconsidered. Our study has shown a mixed picture: when we talk about government influences, the Bundesbank has managed to pursue an independent policy, has never hesitated to enter a conflict with the government and has not given in. Yet, it would be wrong to conclude that external factors did not influence German monetary policy, as the impact of the banking sector shows. Our point here is that a high degree of statutory has protected the Bundesbank from governmental influences, which was the aim of making the Bundesbank independent.

So what we find is that this concept of high statutory independence has worked, at least in the German case, and there is no reason to believe that it should not work in other countries, too. In that respect, the recent trend to make central banks more independent can only be welcomed.

Notes

1. Alesina and Summers (1993), p. 159.
2. Muscatelli (1998), p. 530.
3. See Grilli et al. (1991), p. 367.
4. A different definition of central bank independence has been proposed by Debelle and Fischer 1995. They distinguish between 'goal independence' and 'instrument independence', the former implying that a central bank is free to set its own targets, whereas the latter means that a central bank is given control over monetary instruments and is allowed to use them. See also Bofinger et al. (1996), p. 183-185.
5. 'Ultimately, any democratically elected government whose views are in line with public opinion can discipline the central bank by reducing either its personnel or policy independence.' Berger and Schneider (2000), pp. 44-45.
6. For the following countries the results were taken from Eijffinger and Van Keulen (1995): Austria, Denmark, Finland, New Zealand, Norway, Portugal, Spain.
7. LVAU is the unweighted legal-independence index.
8. The measure is the sum of the indices for political and economic independence. The index for political independence alone is shown in parentheses.
9. Source: Eijffinger and de Haan (1996), p. 23.
10. Participants in the Eurobarometer survey were asked to what extent nine European institutions played an important role in the life of the European Union (the other European institutions included the European Parliament, the European Commission etc.) The exact figures for the European Central Bank were as follows: Eurobarometer 51 (Spring 1999) 62 per cent, Eurobarometer 52 (Autumn 1999) 65 per cent, Eurobarometer 53 (Spring 2000) 66 per cent and Eurobarometer 54 (Autumn 2000) 68 per cent.
11. See Forder (1996), pp. 43-44.
12. Interestingly, following the usual approach, in its early stages the Bundesbank (or better: *Bank deutscher Länder*) would appear to be anything but independent: the bank's decisions were subject to the explicit consent of the Allied Banking Commission, a branch of the Allied High Commission in Germany. In spite of the law, the bank operated in a very favorable institutional setting until the formal end of the Allied jurisdiction in 1951 (see Berger 1997a).
13. This chapter is largely based on Maier and de Haan (2000). Reprinted by permission of Routledge, London.
14. We will call this behavior 'opportunistic', following the terminology commonly found in the literature. Note, however, that some authors (e.g. Cargill and Hutchison, 1991) call this behavior 'manipulative', while 'opportunistic' is used for governments that try to dissolve the parliament to gain maximum advantage if the economic climate is favorable.
15. An interesting offspring of the conflict models is the 'theory of optimal central-bank bashing' (see Waller, 1991): if a central bank does not produce the administration's preferred money-inflation outcome, it might get bashed. In the future, the chances of the administration to get its desired policy will increase the higher the reputation for bashing. See also Kane (1980).
16. Cowart (1978), p. 300.
17. Indeed, various authors question whether there is any evidence at all for regular fluctuations

around a slowly changing trend (see Knot and de Haan, 1996). The same critique holds, of course, for the change of the federal full employment budget balance as percentage of GDP as used by Berger (1997a) and Berger and Schneider (2000). Employing this concept also on a monthly and quarterly basis as these authors do is even more questionable. (To be fair to these authors, is has to be noted that they employ annual, quarterly and monthly data and that their results are stable across frequencies.)

18. Still, over its 24 years of money targeting, the average absolute deviation from the target mid-point amounted to only 1.7 percentage points, as Houben (1999) points out.

19. Note that we have corrected for the jump in the growth rates after the reunification.

20. Similar statements can be found in von Hagen (1998), p. 453.

21. Goodhart (1994), pp. 1426-27.

22. Boschen and Mills (1995) were the first to develop such an index for the US; Dominguez (1997) has used the same methodology to construct her indices for Germany and Japan.

23. See Giersch et al. 1992, pp. 125-84.

24. As the working paper version is much longer and contains important findings which are not included in the published version of the paper, we refer to both versions.

25. However, Lang and Welzel claim that setting the dummy equal to zero for 1973 and 1974 (which seems more correct) does not alter their results significantly.

26. In his reply, Vaubel (1998) argues, however, that including the elections of 1990 and 1994 the evidence based on the non-parametric test supports his hypothesis (11 observations supporting the hypothesis against 4 rejecting it). See also Berger and Woitek (1998a).

27. This view is supported by Bernanke and Mihov (1997). These authors examined which variable the Bundesbank actually targets and reason that the behavior of the Bundesbank might better be described as nominal income targeting.

28. Lohmann assigns each council member the party code (ranging from -2 to 3) of the federal or Land government that originally appointed him. The dummy is one if the sign of the median voter in the Bundesbank council equals the sign of the party control of federal government.

29. The variable is constructed as follows: $w*$election period dummy$+(1-w)*$election period dummy$*$supportive Bundesbank majority dummy; where w denotes the proportion of Bundesrat members supporting the federal government.

30. See Vaubel (2002), p. 2.

31. The following abbreviations are used: CM: Conflict model; PBC: Political Business Cycle Theory; PT: Partisan Theory; PPT: Party Preference Theory; PT*: Alesina et al. (1992) version of the Partisan Theory; RPBC and RPT: Political Business Cycle Theory and Partisan Theory with rational expectations, respectively.

32. This argument has been put forward by Frey and Schneider (1981) and Berger and Schneider (2000).

33. Forder (1999), p. 25.

34. Note that the choice of the CBI measure is not crucial for our results. Indeed, we also ran estimates with other measures of statutory CBI (for instance the indices developed by Grilli et al., 1991, and Eijffinger and Schaling, 1993), but this did not qualitatively change our implications.

35. Here we follow Clark et al. (1998), p. 99-100.

36. The bias of the OLS estimator disappears since the number of time periods is large, see Kennedy (1998), p. 149-150.

37. When estimating the model the log is preferable on econometric grounds: in our estimations, the disturbances are assumed to be normally distributed, thus having positive and negative values. While the interest rate can only be positive, the log of the interest rate can take on negative as well as positive values and thereby fits the model assumptions better. Note, however, that the results are not affected by the log transformation.

38. These findings were first reported in Leertouwer and Maier (2001)

39. If we use the plain nominal interest rate instead of the log even the coefficient for a 12-months pre-election period is insignificant. Other tests confirmed that the election coefficient for Japan lacks robustness. Japan is a special case, as elections are endogenous in Japan. This means that the parliament can call elections when the ruling party experiences a favorable situation.

Further information on the political institutions in Japan will be given in section 4.5.

40. Note that we skip the estimation results for the lagged interest rates, which were highly significant. The lag length j is 4, the number of observations $n = 444$.

41. Since our focus is on a specific set of 14 countries instead of drawing the countries randomly from a large population, a fixed effects model is the appropriate specification here, see Baltagi (1995), p. 10

42. Beck (1991), p. 27.

43. As pointed out in section 2.3 cases of doubt arise when two instruments are used in opposing directions. Then the monthly bulletins of the Bundesbank can give valuable information about their intentions, as typically either 'inflationary pressures' are stressed or 'the need for higher growth' is highlighted.

44. The original sample period was 01:1977-12:1993, in Maier (1999) the Bundesbank index is extended to 01:19691-02:1998. This chapter is largely based on Maier (2000).

45. The estimation of an ordered logit model requires that the index starts with 0. Therefore, it is impossible to assign 0 to neutral monetary policy, as has been done in previous studies.

46. We have corrected the jump in the growth rate of M3 after the German reunification by adding a dummy variable when detrending the series.

47. For Germany the sample period is restricted since the net production index for West Germany is only available until 12:1994. In fact for all German time series data availability is a problem in the 1990s, where one often has to combine different macroeconomic series to get longer and more recent samples. However, similar results can be obtained for the period 01:1969-02:1998.

48. However, the values of the coefficients have to be interpreted cautiously (Greene, 1997), which is why we do not estimate the magnitude of the electoral effect. Running regressions without the elections in 1972 and 1983 which were called earlier we obtained similar results.

49. Since the rhetoric of the Bundesbank stresses the importance of monetary targeting, we also estimated all models for the annual growth rate of M3 instead of the consumer price index as an additional robustness check. With one exception, this did not change our results substantially. The use of the central bank money stock instead of M3 delivered similar results. However, only seasonally adjusted figures for the central bank money stock are available, therefore we have preferred to use data for M3.

50. In additional estimates not reported here we have excluded the Bretton Woods period. This lowered significance of the coefficients $Post12$ and $Post18$ to the 10 per cent level, $Post24$ became insignificant.

51. It is interesting to note that if we drop the one-period lag for the Bundesbank index the $\zeta POLGOV_t$ dummy becomes highly significant. We estimated all models with and without lagged dependent variable as economic theory cannot give a clear recommendation whether to include the lag or not. While this in general did not change our results, this is the only exception. However, Frey and Schneider (1981) as well as Berger and Schneider (2000) include a lagged dependent variable. Therefore, we still think the model still has to be rejected.

52. The same procedure has also been used by Lohmann (1998) to reproduce Vaubel's results in a regression analysis.

53. Note the rapid succession of two election in 10:1979 and 06:1980.

54. For the period up to late 1979 and from 1983 onwards, the FED closely controlled the federal funds rate. Only during the 'Volcker disinflation period' from late 1979 to late 1982 the FED targeted directly non-borrowed reserves, with the federal funds rate moving freely. Earlier studies on US monetary policy, i.e. Bernanke and Blinder (1992) or Sims (1992) recommend using the federal funds rate as indicator for monetary policy. See also Kalyvitis and Michaelides (2001).

55. We also get insignificant results for the $AltPBC - 1_t$ and $AltPBC - 2_t$ variables (results not reported), and our results do not depend on whether the Bretton Woods System is included or not.

56. Posen (1993), p. 48-49.

57. Havrilesky (1993), p. 40.

58. See also Maier et al. (2002), on which this chapter is largely based.

59. To deal with this problem we have changed our pressure variables into simple -1, 0, 1 variables, i.e. if there is any (independent of size) pressure for monetary ease the variables are -1; any pressure for higher rates means +1, otherwise the variable is 0. This did not change our basic findings.

60. In table 5.1 the financial sector consists of commercial banks, savings banks, credit cooperatives and bank organization. The export-oriented employers organization comprises statements from *Bundesverband der Industrie (BDI)* and the *Bundesvereinigung der Arbeitgeber (BDA)*, the domestic-oriented employers organization consists of *Deutscher Industrie- und Handelstag (DIHT)* and the Chambers of Commerce. Finally, abbrevation 'HB' stands for the newspaper *Handelsblatt*.

61. Lohmann (1992) describes a framework where a central bank is generally 'independent', but if large economic shocks occur the government has the possibility to overrule the central bank's decisions. The central banker anticipated this, and thus will always set monetary policy such that overruling is never necessary. One could argue that this is what we see here: before elections the central bank anticipates that if it does not deliver the desired monetary policy, the government will overrule its decision. Therefore the central bank sets monetary policy accordingly, thereby also avoiding pressure as our new indicator measures it.

    However, three objections can be made: first, we have seen that elections have an impact on the Bundesbank's rhetoric, but have no economic effects on the Bundesbank's policy. Second, the Bundesbank has never hesitated to alert the public, if its autonomy was threatened. Third, its legal status makes overruling not impossible, but very difficult and potentially very costly for the incumbent.

62. However, his empirical findings have to be interpreted cautiously, see de Haan and van't Hag (1995).

63. Note that some of the estimated newspaper coefficients tend to become quite large. This merely reflects the fact that few observations are available at the disaggregated level.

64. Havrilesky (1993), p. 273.

65. For more information about 'stability culture' see Hayo (1998), Winkler (1999) or Deutsche Bundesbank (1998b).

66. Significant at the 13 per cent level, the coefficient $Pressure_{t-2}$ is significant at the 1 per cent level.

67. Estimation bias is not a big worry in this case, as our estimates show that the coefficients of the economic variables change little after the inclusion of political variables.

68. See Maier and Knaap (2002), on which this chapter is largely based.

69. See Pierce and Rebeck (2001), p. 442.

70. Walton and Deo (1999), p. 7.

71. European Central Bank (2001b), p. 58.

72. 'Under the skin of anz international economist lies a deep-seated belief in some variant of the PPP theory of exchange rates.' Dornbusch and Krugman (1976), p. 540.

73. European Commission (2001b, p. 6.

74. European Central Bank (1999c), p. 51.

75. Data for the German Länder was provided by de Haan et al. (2002), data for the Spanish provinces was provided by Alberola and Marques (2000) and Wynne and Koo (2000) provided regional data for the US. In the case of the US the analogy of a 'monetary union between regions' used to be even stronger as the notes issued by the different FED districts used to be different.

76. This topic has been covered in several ECB publications, see European Central Bank (1999a), p. 35, European Central Bank (2000a), European Central Bank (2000c) and European Central Bank (2001a).

77. We have decided not to use Germany, the largest EMU member, as numméraire, due to the structural break in the data after the German reunification. However, the results reported for the decomposition of real exchange rate movements are quite sensitive to the selection of the numméraire country. See Maier and Dieppe (2002) for more details and additional results.

78. As is commonly done in the Balassa-Samuelson literature, labour productivity is measured as 'output per worker'. More appropriate would be 'output per hour', but data on working hours

was only available for certain countries.

79. For FME the relationship is cointegrating.
80. Note, however, the following when interpreting the simulated values: For the Netherlands (1) the sample period is very short (nine observations); (2) as the share of part-time work is relatively high, our measure of productivity might be biased; (3) in 2001 indirect taxes were substantially increased. According to the Dutch Central Bank this led to an increase of inflation of approximately 1 per cent. Taking these factors into account, our simulations for the Dutch inflation rate are fairly good. Our estimates for Spain suffer from the fact that our sample period runs only until 1993. This means that we cannot capture the strong decline in Spanish inflation since the early 1990s.
81. W. Duisenberg, 'Conditions for the Success of EMU', Speech delivered in Pamplona, 14. November 1997.
82. European Central Bank (1999*b*), p. 57.
83. European Central Bank (1999*b*), p. 56.
84. De Haan (1997), p. 413-414.
85. After all, Berger and Woitek (1997*a*) and Neumann (1998) have shown that the voting behavior of the member of the Bundesbank Council was not compatible with Vaubel's hypothesis (section 2.4.2). Moreover, we have shown in section 5.5 that pressure is not significantly related to elections.
86. These are the latest figures published on the ETUC's website. See http://www.etuc.org/ for more information.
87. See Goetschy (1996), p. 255.
88. E.g. the 'Neue Züricher Zeitung online' from the 13th of March, 2001 and the 'Wall Street Journal' from the 12th of February, 2001 both report that European Union finance ministers blame Ireland for failing to follow the EU's anti-inflation policies.
89. Eurobarometer survey No 54 was conducted in November and December 2000 among more than 16 000 citizens of the European Union. All results were taken from the website of Eurobarometer survey 54, http://europa.eu.int/comm/dg10/epo/eb/eb54/highlights.html.
90. According to an article in the newspaper *Volkskrant* from 7.1.2002, Günther Verheugen, responsible for EU enlargement in the European Commission, has argued that future EU members must agree on introducing the euro. This is to avoid the difficulties associated with Denmark, Sweden and the UK not being part of the euro area.
91. See Eijffinger and de Haan (1996) and Berger et al. (2001) for overviews.
92. On the 'Frankfurt European Banking Congress 2001' on November, 23 2001 the governor of the Polish Central Bank, Balcerowicz, estimated that the BS effect accounts for roughly 1 percentage point in Polish inflation rate. This announcement is somewhat surprising, given that from his position Poland can only benefit if the general perception is such that the BS effect could play an important role. Due to lack of empirical data (and the short estimation period) we could not verify this statement.
93. Christian Noyer, 'Some ECB views on the accession process', Speech delivered on the occasion of The Central Eastern European Issuers & Investors Forum, Vienna, 17 January 2001.
94. Central banks in the Czech Republic and Poland were under severe pressure from the government to lower interest rates. The Polish Central Bank even openly declared that it had never been under such political pressure before, violating the own constitution and EU regulations. See the articles 'Attacken auf osteuropäische Zentralbanken', *Neue Zürcher Zeitung* from 21.12.2001 and 'Warschau tastet Autonomie der Notenbanken an', *Handelsblatt* from 4.1.2001.
95. Feldstein (1997), p. 61 and p. 70.
96. In particular we would like to stress that EMU enlargement and the discussion about 'dollarization' in Latin America – although both roughly cover the topic of joining a currency union – are not comparable. The *Lehman Brothers Eurasia Group Stability Index* tries to measure stability of emerging markets, based on political and economic factors (they account for 60 per cent and 40 per cent of the index value, respectively). Their index runs from 0 to 100 (100 being the 'most stable') and shows that the candidate countries are more stable than the Latin American countries: for example the ratings for Hungary and Poland (74 and 71, respectively)

compare favorably with the rating for Argentine (47) and Brazil (64).

97. Eichengreen and Ghironi (2002), p. 31.
98. One might argue that such a situation frequently occurs in the Council of the European Union in Brussels, where national interest often dominate European policies.
99. See Thygesen (1990), p. 10-11.
100. This issue has been examined on theoretical and game-theoretical grounds. See Baldwin et al. (2001), Chapter 6. For a different position see Bindseil(2001).
101. Eichengreen and Ghironi (2002), p. 30.
102. For a more extensive discussion see Baldwin et al. (2001) and Eichengreen and Ghironi (2002).
103. After the German reunification a restructuring of the decision-making process was necessary, as otherwise the Bundesbank Council would have expanded to 26 members. This problem was solved by merging several *Land* central banks. See also appendix 10.3 on Germany's institutional system.
104. Moreover, the ECB seems reluctant to adopt such a solution, as few days before the Nice Summit in December 2000 the ECB issued a statement reminding political leaders that 'the core constitutional principle of government of the monetary policy of the ECB is 'one member, one vote'.' See Eichengreen and Ghironi (2002), p. 31.
105. ECB President Duisenberg: 'In all likelihood ... it will go in the direction of the system currently used by the Federal Reserve system, where there is some sort of rotation scheme.' Quoted after Reuters, 'Council may see rotating scheme with new members', 21.11.2001.
106. Eichengreen and Ghironi (2002), p. 33.

A. Germany's Institutional Setting

Some sections in this book require some specific information about Germany's institutional setting, e.g. to judge how political hypotheses should be tested and in interpreting the results of previous studies.

A.1 GERMANY'S POLITICAL SYSTEM

Germany is a federal state with 16 *Bundesländer*. Each Bundesland has its own government. Germany's multi-party system usually leads to coalitions, both at national and Land levels. Since the end of the Second World War, Germany has been a politically very stable country, as relatively few political shifts occurred at the federal level:

- The center-right Christian Union Parties (CDU/CSU) dominated federal government until 1966.
- In December 1966 a Grand coalition of the CDU/CSU and the Social Democratic Party (SPD) came in power. This is a first shift to the left.
- In October 1969 the SPD formed a government with the liberal Free Democratic Party (FDP) as 'junior partner'. This is a second shift to the left.
- In September 1982 the CDU/CSU and the FDP formed a coalition. This is a shift to the right.
- Since October 1998 the federal government is formed by a leftist coalition of the SPD and the Green Party. This is another shift to the left (this period is not included in any of the studies reviewed here).

All in all, this makes that only five political 'regimes' can be distinguished in Germany since 1945. The main problem is how to treat the period of the Grand coalition (Dec. 1966–Oct. 1969).

For coding political regimes, several possibilities have been used:

- Alesina and Roubini (1990; 1992) used a dummy that is +1 during a right wing government, -1 if a left wing government is in office and 0 otherwise. The shift to the left during the Grand coalition from 1966 to 1969 is counted as -0.5 for the first two periods (instead of -1.0), and a shift to the right is assumed in 1972, which Alesina and Roubini also counted as -0.5 (instead of -1.0). However, this shift to the right in 1972 is controversial, if not wrong, as Neumann (1989) and Berger and Woitek (1997*b*) argued.[1]

- Lohmann (1998) uses a 'party code' for the federal government, which is supposed to cover the degree political ideology might be implemented. For instance a CDU/CSU government has a lower value (-2) than a CDU/CSU-FDP coalition (-1). The party code ranges from -2 to +3. The drawback of this method is that the party code assumes a linear relationship, i.e. the difference between a CDU/CSU-FDP coalition and a CDU government is implicitly assumed to be as great as the difference between a SPD-government and a coalition between the SPD and the Green Party.

- Berger and Woitek (1997*b*) construct a party index that takes two values, either 'right majority government' or 'left majority government'. The Grand coalition is treated as a leftist government, but Berger and Woitek also point out that excluding this period does not alter their results.

The German parliamentary system at the federal level consists of two chambers of parliament: the Bundestag, which is chosen through Federal elections, and the Bundesrat, whose members are appointed by the Land governments. In general, the Bundesrat contributes to every law, but the intensity of the contribution differs subject to two types of laws: the so-called *Einspruchsgesetz* is an act of the Bundestag to which the Bundesrat can only object. However, the Bundestag can overrule this decision by simple majority. Thus a law can be adopted against the will of the Länder. For bills that touch the interests of the Länder, the consent of the Bundesrat is obligatory (*Zustimmungsgesetz*).

There have been various conflicts about the question of whether certain laws require the consent of the Bundesrat. It is unclear whether the consent of the Bundesrat is required for changes in the law governing the Bundesbank: the Bundesrat declared the Bundesbank Law to be *zustimmungspflichtig* during the discussion about the change of the law after unification. However, given the position of the Federal Constitutional Court, this cannot be considered legal (Amtenbrink, 1999; for a different view see Lohmann, 1998). Anyhow, a change of the Bundesbank law is more likely to happen if the same party holds the majority in both the federal parliament and the Bundesrat, because under divergent party control changes are more difficult. This justifies a close

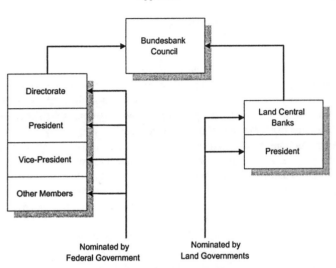

Figure A.1   The structure of the Deutsche Bundesbank

inspection of the role of the Bundesrat, as it has been undertaken by Lohmann (1998).

A.2   THE STRUCTURE OF THE DEUTSCHE BUNDESBANK

The composition of the Bundesbank council (*Zentralbankrat*), the supreme policy-making body of the Bundesbank, reflects Germany's federal structure. It consists of up to eight members of the Directorate and the presidents of the Land central banks (*Landeszentralbank*) (see figure A.1). Before unification each state seated a bank, but the integration of five new states made a restructuring necessary. First, with 16 banks decision making would have become more difficult. Second, the relative weight of the Land central banks in the Zentralbankrat would have increased, which the Bundesbank Directorate opposed. It was therefore decided to create state-overlapping banks, thereby reducing the total number of Land central banks to nine (previously 11).[2]

The Directorate consists of the President and the Vice-President of the Bank and up to six other members. They are all nominated by the Federal government and are appointed by the President of the Federal Republic for eight (not less than two) years, which is considerably longer than the regular term period for a government (four years). The presidents of the Land central banks are nominated by the Land governments. Bundesbank council decisions are taken by simple majority vote.

A.3   Aims and instruments of the Deutsche Bundesbank

Until the start of EMU, the Bundesbank regulated the amount of money in circulation and of credit supplied to the economy with the aim of safeguarding the currency. In addition, the bank had the obligation to support the government's economic policy if this did not prejudice the primary objective of price stability. At the same time, the central bank in Germany was completely independent of any instructions from government; it could consult the government but was under no obligation to agree with it.[3] Government representatives had the right to attend meetings of the Zentralbankrat, but not to vote. From historical and anecdotal evidence, however, it is known that despite this independence a number of public conflicts between government and the central bank occurred (see e.g. Berger and de Haan, 1999).

The Bundesbank was not under any obligation to agree, obey or announce any targets. The federal government was responsible for decisions about the exchange rate regime. Therefore, during the Bretton Woods era, German monetary policy was subordinate to exchange rate policy. Although the Bundesbank tried to gear its monetary policy towards domestic price stability as much as possible, there was little room for an independent, domestically oriented interest rate policy.

Monetary targeting played a crucial role in German monetary policy since 1975. Since 1988 the Bundesbank employed a broad monetary aggregate (M3), which consists of notes and coins in circulation, sight deposits, time deposits for less than four years and savings deposits at statuary notice, as the target for its monetary policy. Before, a weighed aggregate, the central bank money stock (*Zentralbankgeldmenge*, ZBG) was used.[4]

Initially, the Bundesbank announced a fixed target for money growth. However, this appeared to be too ambitious, as it turned out that it was not possible to exactly fine-tune the growth of the targeted aggregate. From 1979 on, the Bundesbank started to announce so-called target zones. The target for the following year was announced at the end of each year, when the Bundesbank also announced whether it was aiming for the upper or lower half of the target zone. Sometimes this also happened in the course of a year.

The Bundesbank was provided with a wide range of instruments.[5] By setting its official rates and using liquidity policy instruments (mainly minimum reserve policy) the Bundesbank had the ability to steer money market rates. Its most important instruments were:

Minimum reserve regulations were introduced in 1948. Banks were obliged to hold a specific percentage of certain liabilities as non-compensated balances at the central bank. The reserve percentages varied according to the degree of liquidity of the bank's liabilities. This instrument increases the effectiveness of the other instruments, especially open market operations, and puts an automatic brake on monetary expansion: any increase in sight deposits, time deposits or saving accounts leads immediately to an increase in the amount of required reserves, leading to an automatic tightening of money market conditions. Up to the beginning of the 1980s, the Bundesbank actively manipulated the minimum reserve rates in order to steer monetary conditions.

Discount facilities were the most important monetary instruments targeted at refinancing of commercial banks and often used to signal a major change in the policy stance. It enabled banks to borrow a fixed maximum amount of money from the Bundesbank. This credit must be backed by trade bills. The discount rate normally was the floor for short-term interest rates in the money market. Changes in the discount facility could either be a change in the discount rate, or in the rediscount quotas.

Lombard facilities were the second most important instrument for refinancing policy. The lombard rate usually was the ceiling for interest rates in the money market. It was a relatively expensive end-of-day facility, making it possible for banks with an acute liquidity shortage to obtain central bank money.

Open market operations were carried out during the 1960s and 1970s in an attempt to neutralize inflows of liquidity from abroad. Of increasing importance, however, were the open market transactions under repurchase agreements. Starting in the early 1970s with domestic bills as collateral (*Wechselpensionsgeschäfte*), the scope of this instrument was widened in 1979, when the Bundesbank developed the instrument of repurchase agreements in fixed-interest securities (*Wertpapierpensionsgeschäfte*, popularly known as 'repos'). After February 1985, this developed into the most important instrument of monetary policy, as it became the leading instrument for steering short-term interest rates in the money market.

B. The refined 'corridor' for the standard deviation

As explained in chapter 9, there are some difficulties associated with this simple form of the indicator: the formulas for the minimum and maximum standard deviation imply an average inflation rate, which is different from the actual average inflation. In order to correct for this problem, we have to slightly refine the formulas, so that they return the same average inflation rate for the minimum and maximum standard deviation.

For the minimum standard deviation we have to insert an inflation rate y^*, that corresponds to the inflation rate for all countries except the two outliers. For the maximum standard deviation, the countries should not be divided into two equal groups, but into a group α with the lowest value and a group $(1 - \alpha)$ with the highest. Therefore, we have to correct the formulas for the $s_{min,t}$ and $s_{max,t}$ as follows:

$$s_{min,t} = \sqrt{\left(\frac{(y_{min,t} - \bar{y})^2 + (y_{max,t} - \bar{y})^2 + (N-2)(y_t^* - \bar{y})^2}{N} \right)}, \qquad (B.1)$$

where

$$y_t^* = \frac{N\bar{y} - y_{min,t} - y_{max,t}}{N-2},$$

and

$$s_{max,t} = \sqrt{\left(\frac{\alpha N(y_{min,t} - \bar{y})^2 + (1 - \alpha)N(y_{max,t} - \bar{y})^2}{N} \right)}, \qquad (B.2)$$

where

$$\alpha = \frac{\bar{y} - y_{max,t}}{y_{min,t} - y_{max,t}}.$$

C. Data sources

C.1 INTEREST RATES AS INDICATORS FOR MONETARY POLICY

We have primarily used monthly data from IFS statistics on industrial production, inflation and the short-term interest rate (line 60B). Additional data has been provided by the following national central banks: Denmark, Sweden, UK and New Zealand. For Germany we have used data from Deutsche Bundesbank (1998a). Data for the United States has been obtained from the FRED database.

Growth rates have been computed as the change in the log of the raw series and have been detrended if necessary. All computed series were stationary.

The election dummy is +1 eleven months before the election and during the election month, and 0 otherwise. The dummy for central bank independence is +1 if the level of central bank independence is above-median, and 0 otherwise. The dummy for monetary policy autonomy is +1 if monetary policy autonomy is absent, and 0 otherwise.

The sample period differs for each country due to data availability. The following data were available: Austria 1967:1-1997:12; Australia 1969:7-1996:06; Belgium 1960:1-1997:12; Canada 1975:1-1997:12; Denmark 1972:1-1997:12; France 1964:1-1997:12; Finland 1972:10-1997:12; Germany 1960:1-1997:12; Italy 1971:1-1997:12; Japan 1960:1-1997:12; Norway 1971:8-1997:12; Spain 1974:1-1997:12; Sweden 1965:12-1997:12; UK 1960:1-1997:12; United States 1960:1-1997:12; New Zealand 1973:1-1997:12. Due to lack of election data, the sample period for Canada reduces to 1975:1-1996:07. Due to lack of democratic elections, the sample period for Spain reduces to 1977:1-1997:12.

C.2 MONETARY POLICY INDICES AS INDICATORS FOR MONETARY POLICY

Growth rates are computed as the change in the log of the raw series and have been detrended if necessary. All computed series were stationary. The OC_t dummy to cover the impact of the oil crisis is +1 between 01:1974-12:1975 and 01:1978-12:1981 and 0 otherwise.

Germany The following series have been taken from Deutsche Bundesbank (1998*a*) (Bundesbank codes in brackets): M3 (TU0800), CPI (UU0062), day-to-day rate (SU0101) and the unemployment rate for West Germany (UU0299). The net production index was directly provided by the Bundesbank, we get quantitatively similar results if we use the production index from the Bundesbank CD-ROM (UU02NA). M3 has been corrected for the German reunification.
Election dates have been taken from the webserver of the German parliament http://www.bundestag.de.

Japan The following economic data for Japan was taken from Datastream: The consumer price index, total production index, the Tokyo call money market rate for overnight loans, M1 and the non-seasonally adjusted unemployment rate.
Election dates were kindly provided by the Japanese Embassy in Bonn, Germany.

United States All data has been taken from the Federal Reserve Economic Data-webserver http://www.stls.frb.org/fred/index.html. We have used non-seasonally adjusted data for M1, M3 and the consumer price index for all urban consumers. Seasonally adjusted data has been used for the total production index and the unemployment rate. Election dates have been taken from the TIME 'Almanac of the 20th Century' CD-ROM.

All models of chapter 4 have been estimated with EVIEWS 3.1.

C.3 THE NEWSPAPER INDICATORS FOR 'PRESSURE' AND 'SUPPORT'

These data sets were build during a stay at the *Hamburgisches Welt-Wirt-schafts-Archiv* (HWWA archive) in Hamburg, Germany. Gathering the data was done by screening all articles related to the Bundesbank or monetary policy in the newspapers 'Frankfurter Allgemeine Zeitung' (FAZ), 'Handelsblatt' (HB) and 'Die Welt' for the period 1/1960-12/1998. For each article the following characteristics were noted: The main actors, the main statements ('who wants what') and the date of appearance.

Classification of the Data Two hypothetical examples of 'typical' article can illustrate the procedure. First, consider an article such as: 'The trade union ABC has expressed its concern about high unemployment, therefore they suggest that the Bundesbank should lower interest rates quickly'. This shows a demand for monetary ease from the trade unions. Second, an article such as

'The employer's association welcome the recent cut in interest rates, but insist on further steps by the central bank to reduce unemployment' also shows a demand for monetary ease, in this case from the employers' organization. Each newspaper article was classified into one of the following categories, based on the following origins:

Government Statements from the ruling party.

Financial sector Commercial banks, bank organizations, savings banks and credit cooperatives.

Trade associations Statements from the export-oriented trade organizations *Bundesverband der Industrie* (BDI), *Bundesvereinigung der Arbeitgeber* (BDA) and statements from trade organizations, where the exact source is unknown.

Industry Statements from the domestic-oriented trade organization *Deutscher Industrie- und Handelstag* (DIHT) and the Chambers of Commerce.

Trade Unions All statements of trade unions.

Other Statements from journalists, Council of Economic Advisors, economic researchers or research institutes, but also supra-national organizations such as the European commission or the IMF. In some cases (especially in comments) it is expressed that the Bundesbank experiences pressure from unspecified source ('The Bundesbank is asked to lower the interest rates' or 'The demand for monetary ease becomes more frequent'). These statements are also counted as 'other opinions'.

Coding of the articles for the pressure indicator Articles demanding a more restrictive monetary policy were counted as +1, each article calling for monetary ease was counted as -1. The news indicator for each category then consists of the simple sum of pluses and minuses. This closely follows Havilesky's methodological approach. If an approval statement contains also a demand for further policy measures ('We are glad the interest rates were lowered, but this was only a first step. Further policy measures are necessary'), then such a statement was classified as pressure and counted in one of the categories above.

Coding of the articles for the support indicator For the 'support index' we counted all articles expressing approval of current Bundesbank policy as +1. The time series then consists of the simple sum of the pluses.

C.4   THE EUROPEAN CONTEXT: AN ECONOMIC ANALYSIS

We use Eurostat data for the following sample periods: Austria 1976-1996; Belgium 1970-1996; Finland 1970-1996; France 1970-1997; Germany 1960-1997; Italy 1970-1997; the Netherlands 1977-1995; Spain 1970-1994.

The raw data consists of annual GDP data for the traded and the nontraded sector, from which implicit value-added deflators were computed. The sectoral breakdown was done following Alberola and Tyrväinen (1998):

- Traded goods sector: Manufacturing industry + Transportation
- Non-traded goods sector: The rest of the economy, excluding Agriculture and Public Sector.

Employment has been mesured as number of employed persons, as data on working hours was not available for most countries.

Data for the German Länder was provided by de Haan et al. (2002), data for the Spanish provinces was provided by Alberola and Marques (2000) and our data set for Spain has been augmented by data taken from Alberola and Tyrväinen (1998) Wynne and Koo (2000) provided regional data for the US.

Finally, the HICP inflation figures were taken from the Eurostat webserver.

C.5   THE IMPACT OF EMU ENLARGEMENT

For the candidate countries 'interim HICP' was used for the following sample periods (monthly data): Czech Republic, Estonia, Hungary, Lithuania, Romania, Slovenia 1996:1-2001:10; Bulgaria 1997:01-2001:5; Latvia 1997:12-2001:11; Poland 1997:1-2001:6; Slovakia 1996:1-2000:12.

All data was taken from Eurostat.

---

1. Karl Schiller, a social democrat and head of both the department of commerce and the treasury department, resigned in June 1972. When the SPD/FDP coalition government was re-elected in 1972, the department of commerce went to the liberals (the social democrats kept the treasury department). This event does not qualify as major political change. See Berger and Woitek, 1997*b*.
2. See also Jarchow (1995), p. 48.
3. BbankG 1957, Art. 12: 'Without prejudice to the performance of its functions, the Deutsche Bundesbank shall be required to support the general economic policy of the Federal government. In exercising the powers conferred on it by this Act, it shall be independent of instructions from the government.'
4. The Bundesbank used, rather arbitrarily, the constant minimum reserve percentages as of

January 1974. The formula for the central bank money stock was as follows: *Central Bank Money Stock* = C + (0.166 * *Sight Deposits*) + (0.124 * *Time Deposits*) + (0.081 * *Savings Accounts*).

5. This part draws on Boonstra (1997). For an extensive treatment of the German monetary policy see also Jarchow (1995), Issing (1996), Mishkin and Posen (1997) and Deutsche Bundesbank (1995).

Bibliography

Ahking, Francis W. and Stephen M. Miller (1985), 'The relationship between government deficits, money growth and inflation', *Journal of Macroeconomics*, **7 (4)**, 447–467.

Akaike, Hirotsugu (1969), 'Fitting autoregressive models for prediction', *Annals of the Institute of Statistical Mathematics*, **21**, 243–247.

Akaike, Hirotsugu (1970), 'Statistical predictor identification', *Annals of the Institute of Statistical Mathematics*, **22**, 203–217.

Alberola, Enrique and Jose M. Marques (2000), 'On the relevance and nature of regional inflation differentials: The case of Spain', *Bank of Spain Discussion Paper*.

Alberola, Enrique and Timo Tyrväinen (1998), 'Is there scope for inflation differentials in EMU? An empirical evaluation of the Balassa-Samuelson model in EMU countries', *Bank of Finland Discussion Papers*.

Alesina, Alberto (1987), 'Macroeconomic policy in a two-party system as a repeated game', *Quarterly Journal of Economics*, **102 (3)**, 651–678.

Alesina, Alberto (1988), 'Macroeconomics and politics', in S Fischer (ed.), *NBER Macroeconomics Annual*, Cambridge, Mass: MIT Press.

Alesina, Alberto and Lawrence H. Summers (1993), 'Central bank independence and macroeconomic performance: Some comparative evidence', *Journal of Money, Credit and Banking*, **25 (2)**, 151–62.

Alesina, Alberto and Nouriel Roubini (1990), 'Political cycles in OECD economies', *NBER Working Paper Series*.

Alesina, Alberto and Nouriel Roubini (1992), 'Political cycles in OECD economies', *Review of Economic Studies*, **59**, 663–688.

Alesina, Alberto, Gerald D. Cohen and Nouriel Roubini (1992), 'Macroeconomic policy and elections in OECD countries', *CEPR - Discussion Paper Series*.

Alesina, Alberto, Nouriel Roubini and Gerald D. Cohen (1997), *Political Cycles and the Macroeconomy*, Cambridge, Mass.: MIT Press.

Allen, Stuart D. (1986), 'The Federal Reserve and the electoral cycle', *Journal of Money, Credits and Banking*, **18 (1)**, 88–94.

Amtenbrink, Fabian (1999), *The Democratic Accountability of Central Banks*, Oxford: Hart Publishing.

Andreas Andrikopoulos, John Loizides and Kyprianos Prodromidis (2002), 'Fiscal instruments, political business cycles and the EMU: Some stylized facts', *mimeo*.

Angeloni, Ignazio, Anil Kashyap, Benoit Mojon and Daniele Terlizze (2002), 'Monetary transmission in the euro area: Where do we stand?', *mimeo*.

Artis, Michael J. and Wenda Zhang (1999), 'Further evidence on the international business cycle and the ERM: Is there a European business cycle?', *Oxford Economic Papers*, **51**, 120–132.

Asea, Patrick K. and W. Max Corden (1994), 'The Balassa-Samuelson model: An overview', *Review of international economics*, **2 (3)**, 191–200.

Balassa, Bela (1964), 'The purchasing power parity doctrine: A reappraisal', *Journal of Political Economy*, **72**, 584–96.

Baldwin, Richard E., Erik Berglor, Franceso Giavazzi and Mika Widgren (2001), *Nice Try: Should the Treaty of Nice be ratified?*, London: CEPR.

Balkhausen, Dieter (1992), *Gutes Geld und schlechte Politik. Der Report über die Bundesbank*, Düsseldorf.

Baltagi, Badi H. (1995), *Econometric analysis of panel data*, Chichester: John Wiley.

Barro, Robert J. and David B. Gordon (1983), 'A positive theory of monetary policy in a natural rate model', *Journal of Political Economy*, **91 (4)**, 589–610.

Basler, Hans-Peter (1978), 'Die wirtschaftspolitischen Zielpräferenzen der Deutschen Bundesbank: Eine empirische Analyse des Zentralbankverhaltens für die Zeit von 1958 bis 1974', *Kredit und Kapital*, **11**, 84–108.

Baum, Thomas M. (1983), 'Empirische Analyse der Bundesbankautonomie', *Konjunkturpolitik*, **29**, 163–186.

Beck, Nathaniel (1991), 'The FED and the political business cycle', *Contemporary Policy Issues*, **9**, 25–38.

Berger, Helge (1997*a*), 'The Bundesbank's path to independence: Evidence from the 1950s', *Public Choice*, **93 (3-4)**, 427–453.

Berger, Helge (1997*b*), *Konjunkturpolitik im Wirtschaftswunder. Handlungsspielräume und Verhaltensmuster von Bundesbank und Regierung in den 1950 Jahren*, Tübingen: Mohr Siebeck.

Berger, Helge and Friedrich Schneider (2000), 'The Bundesbank's reaction to policy conflicts', in Jakob de Haan (ed.), *History of the Bundesbank: Lessons for the ECB*, London: Routledge, pp. 43–66.

Berger, Helge and Jakob de Haan (1999), 'A State within the State? An event study on the Bundesbank', *Scottish Journal of Political Economy*, **46 (1)**, 17–39.

Berger, Helge and Ulrich Woitek (1997*a*), 'How opportunistic are partisan German central bankers? A note on the Vaubel-Hypothesis', *European Journal of Political Economy*, **13 (4)**, 807–822.

Berger, Helge and Ulrich Woitek (1997*b*), 'Searching for political business cycles in Germany', *Public Choice*, **91**, 179–197.

Berger, Helge and Ulrich Woitek (1998*a*), 'Biased or just conservative? Further observations on the Bundesbank's preferences', *mimeo, University of München*.

Berger, Helge and Ulrich Woitek (1998*b*), 'Does conservatism matter? A time series approach to central banking', *CESifo Working Paper*.

Berger, Helge and Ulrich Woitek (2001), 'Money demand rather than monetary policy: The German political business cycle', *European Journal of Political Economy*.

Berger, Helge, Sylvester C. W. Eijffinger and Jakob de Haan (2001), 'Central bank independence: Update on theory and evidence', *Journal of Economic Surveys*, **15 (1)**, 3–40.

Bernanke, Ben S. and Alan S. Blinder (1992), 'The federal funds rate and the channels of monetary transmission', *American Economic Review*, **82 (4)**, 901–921.

Bernanke, Ben S. and Ilian Mihov (1997), 'What does the Bundesbank target?', *European Economic Review*, **41**, 1025–1053.

Bierens, Herman J. (1997), 'Testing the unit root with drift hypothesis against nonlinear trend stationarity, with an application to the US price level and interest rate', *Journal of Econometrics*, **81**, 29–64.

Bindseil, Ulrich (2001), 'A coalition-form analysis of the 'one country-one vote' rule in the governing council of the European Central Bank', *International Economic Journal*, **15 (1)**, 141–164.

Bofinger, Peter (1998), 'The political economy of the Eastern enlargement of the EU', in Barry Eichengreen (ed.), *Forging an integrated Europe*: University of Michigan Press, pp. 273–325.

Bofinger, Peter, Julian Reischle and Andrea Schächter (1996), *Geldpolitik: Ziele, Institutionen, Strategien und Instrumente*, München: Vahlen.

Boonstra, Wim W. (1997), 'Germany: Building a reputation of monetary stability', in Wim W. Boonstra and Sylvester C. W. Eijffinger (eds), *Banks, financial markets and monetary policy*, Amsterdam: NIBE.

Boschen, John F. and Leonard O. Mills (1995), 'The relation between narrative and money market indicators of monetary policy', *Economic Inquiry*, **33 (1)**, 24–44.

Bridgford, Jeff and John Stirling (1994), *Employee relations in Europe*, London: Blackwell.

Broeck, M de and T Sloeck (2001), 'Interpreting real exchange rate movements in transition countries', *IMF Working Paper*.

Burdekin, Richard C.K. (1987), 'Cross-country evidence on the relationship between central banks and governments', *Journal of Macroeconomics*, **9 (3)**, 391–405.

Canova, Fabio (1995), 'The economics of VAR models', in Kevin D. Hoover (ed.), *Macroeconomics: Development, Tensions and Prospects*, Dordrecht: Kluwer Academic Publishers, pp. 57–97.

Canzoneri, Matthew, Robert Cumby and Behzad Diba (1999), 'Relative labor productivity and the real exchange rate in the long run: Evidence for a panel of OECD countries', *Journal of International Economics*, 47, 245–266.

Canzoneri, Matthew, Robert Cumby, Behzad Diba and Gwen Eudey (2000), 'Productivity trends in Europe: Implications for real exchange rates, real interest rates and inflation', *mimeo*.

Cargill, Thomas F. and Michael M. Hutchison (1991), 'Political business cycles with endogenous election timing: Evidence from Japan', *Review of Economics and Statistics*, **73 (4)**, 733–39.

Cargill, Thomas F., Michael M. Hutchison and Takatoshi Ito (1997), *The Political Economy of Japanese Monetary Policy*, Cambridge, Mass.: MIT Press.

Cecchetti, Stephen G., Nelson C. Mark and Robert J. Sonora (2000), 'Price level convergence among United States cities: Lessons for the European Central Bank', *NBER Working Paper Series*.

Ciccarelli, Matteo and Alessandro Rebucci (2001), 'The transmission mechanism of European monetary policy: Is there heterogeneity? Is it changing over time?', *Bank of Spain Working Paper*.

Clarida, Richard and Mark Gertler (1996), 'How the Bundesbank conducts monetary policy', *NBER Working Paper Series*.

Clark, William R. and Mark Hallerberg (2000), 'Mobile capital, domestic institutions, and electorally-induced monetary and fiscal policy', *American Political Science Review*, **94 (2)**, 323–346.

Clark, William R., Usha N. Reichert, Sandra L. Lomas and Kevin L. Parker (1998), 'International and domestic constraints on political business cycles in OECD economies', *International Organization*, **51 (1)**, 87–120.

Clements, Benedict, Zenon G. Kontolemis and Joaquim Levy (2001), 'Monetary policy under EMU: Differences in the transmission mechanism?', *IMF Working Paper*.

Cowart, Andrew T. (1978), 'The economic policies of European governments, part I: Monetary policy', *British Journal of Political Science*, **8**, 285–311.

Cukierman, Alex (1992), *Central Bank Strategy, Credibility and Independence*, Cambridge, Mass.: MIT Press.

Cukierman, Alex, Steven B. Webb and Bilin Neyapti (1992), 'Measuring the independence of central banks and its effect on policy outcomes', *World Bank Economic Review*, **6 (3)**, 353–98.

Debelle, Guy and Stanley Fischer (1995), 'How independent should a central bank be?', in Jeffrey C. Fuhrer (ed.), *Goals, Guidelines and Constraints Facing Monetary Policymakers*: Federal Reserve Bank of Boston Conference Volumes, pp. 195–221.

Demopoulos, George, George Katsimbris and Stephen Miller (1987), 'Central bank policy and the financing of government budget deficits: A cross-country comparison', *European Economic Review*, **31 (5)**, 1023–1050.

Deutsche Bundesbank (1995), *The Monetary Policy of the Bundesbank*, Frankfurt/Main.

Deutsche Bundesbank (1998*a*), *Fünfzig Jahre Deutsche Mark - Monetäre Statistiken 1948-1997 auf CD-ROM*, München: Vahlen.

Deutsche Bundesbank (1998*b*), 'Stellungnahme des Zentralbankrats zur Konvergenzlage in der Europäischen Union im Hinblick auf die dritte Stufe der Wirtschafts- und Währungsunion', *Informationsbrief zur Europäischen Wirtschafts- und Währungsunion*.

Dickey, David A. and Wayne A. Fuller (1979), 'Distribution of the estimates for autoregressive time series with a unit root', *Journal of the American Statistical Association*, **74**, 427–431.

Dickey, David A. and Wayne A. Fuller (1981), 'Likehood ratio statistics for autoregressive time series with a unit root', *Econometrica*, **49 (4)**, 1057–1072.

Dolado, Juan J., Tim Jenkinson and Simon Sosvilla-Rivero (1990), 'Cointegration and unit roots', *Journal of Economic Surveys*, **4 (3)**, 249–273.

Dominguez, Kathryn M. E. (1997), 'Do the G-3 countries coordinate monetary policy?', in Benjamin J. Cohen (ed.), *International Trade and Finance: New Frontiers for Research: Essays in Honor of Peter B. Kenen*, Cambridge: Cambridge University Press. (Kennedy School of Government, Harvard University)

Dornbusch, Rüdiger and Paul Krugman (1976), 'Flexible exchange rates in the short run', *Brookings Papers on Economic Activity*, **3**, 537–575.

Eichengreen, Barry and Fabio Ghironi (2002), 'EMU and enlargement', *mimeo*.

Eijffinger, Sylvester C. W. and Eric Schaling (1993), 'Central bank independence in twelve industrial countries', *Banca Nazionale del Lavoro Quarterly Review*, **184**, 1–41.

Eijffinger, Sylvester C. W. and Jakob de Haan (1996), 'The political economy of central bank independence', *Princeton Special Papers in International Economics*.

Eijffinger, Sylvester C. W., Maarten van Rooij and Eric Schaling (1996), 'Central bank independence: A paneldata approach', *Public Choice*, **89**, 163–182.

Eijffinger, Sylvester C.W. and Martyn Van Keulen (1995), 'Central bank independence in another eleven countries', *Banca Nazionale del Lavoro Quarterly*, **192**, 39–83.

Els, Peter van, Alberto Locarno, Julian Morgan and Jean-Pierre Villetelle (2001), 'Monetary policy transmission in the euro area: What do aggregate and national structural models tell us?', *European Central Bank Working*

Paper.

Engel, Charles and John H. Rogers (1996), 'How wide is the border?', *The American Economic Review*, **86 (5)**, 1112–1125.

European Bank for Reconstruction and Development (2000), *Transition Report 2000: Employment, Skills and Transition*, London.

European Central Bank (1999*a*), 'Inflation differentials in a monetary union', *Monthly Bulletin*, **10**, 36–45.

European Central Bank (1999*b*), 'The institutional framework of the European System of Central Banks', *ECB Monthly Bulletin*, **7**, 55–63.

European Central Bank (1999*c*), 'Longer-term development and cyclical variations in key economic indicators across euro area countries', *Monthly Bulletin*, **8**, 33–54.

European Central Bank (2000*a*), 'An analysis of price developments: The breakdown of the overall HICP into its main components', *Monthly Bulletin*, **12**, 28–29.

European Central Bank (2000*b*), 'The Eurosystem and the EU enlargement process', *ECB Monthly Bulletin*, **2**, 39–51.

European Central Bank (2000*c*), 'Inflation differentials within the euro area', *Monthly Bulletin*, **12**, 32–34.

European Central Bank (2001*a*), 'Decomposing overall HICP developments since early 1999', *Monthly Bulletin*, **6**, 37–38.

European Central Bank (2001*b*), 'The economic policy framework in EMU', *Monthly Bulletin*, **11**, 51–65.

European Commission (1999), 'Autopreise in der Europäischen Union am 1. November 1998 – Unterschiede deutlich niedriger', *DN: IP/99/60*.

European Commission (2001*a*), 'Dg ecfin: Policy issues related to macroeconomic differences in the euro area'.

European Commission (2001*b*), 'Economic reform: Report on the functioning of Community product and capital markets'.

Fatás, Antonio (1997), 'EMU: Countries or regions? Lessons from the EMS experience', *European Economic Review*, **41**, 743–751.

Feldstein, Martin (1997), 'EMU and international conflict', *Foreign Affairs*, **76 (6)**, 60–73.

Fidrmuc, Jan and Iikka Korhonen (2002), 'Optimal currency area between the EU and accession countries: The status quo', *mimeo*.

Fidrmuc, Jan, Julius Horvath and Jarko Fidrmuc (1999), 'Stability of monetary unions: Lessons from the break-up of Czechoslovakia', *Transition Economics Series, Institute for Advanced Studies, Vienna*.

Forder, James (1996), 'On the assessment and implementation of 'institutional' remedies', *Oxford Economic Papers*, **48**, 39–51.

Forder, James (1999), 'Central bank independence: Reassessing the measurements', *Journal of Economic Issues*, **33 (1)**, 23–40.

Frenkel, Michael, Christiane Nickel and Günter Schmidt (1999), 'Some shocking aspects of EMU enlargement', *Deutsche Bank Research Note*.

Frey, Bruno S. and Friedrich Schneider (1981), 'Central bank behaviour: A positive empirical analysis', *Journal of Monetary Economics*, 7, 291–315.

Frijters, Paul, John P. Haisken-DeNew and Michael A. Shields (2001), 'The value of reunification in Germany: An analysis of changes in life satisfaction', *IZA Discussion Paper*.

Froot, Kenneth A. and Kenneth Rogoff (1995), 'Perspectives on PPP and long-run real exchange rates', in Gene M. Grossman and Kenneth Rogoff (eds), *Handbook of International Economics, vol. III*, North-Holland: Elsevier Science, pp. 1647–1688.

Froyen, Richard T., Thomas Havrilesky and Roger N. Waud (1997), 'The asymmetric effects of political pressures on U.S. monetary policy', *Journal of Macroeconomics*, 19 (3), 471–493.

Geweke, John, Richard Meese and William Dent (1983), 'Comparing alternative tests of causality in temporal systems', *Journal of Econometrics*, 21 (1), 161–194.

Giannaros, Demetrios S. and Baharat R. Kolluri (1985), 'Deficit spending, money, and inflation: Some international empirical evidence', *Journal of Macroeconomics*, 7 (3), 401–417.

Giersch, Herbert, Karl-Heinz Paqué and Holger Schmieding (1992), *The Fading Miracle: Four Decades of Market Economy in Germany*, Cambridge: Cambridge University Press.

Goetschy, Janine (1996), 'The European Trade Union Confederation and the construction of European unionism', in Peter Leisink, Jim van Leemput and Jacques Vilrokx (eds), *The challenges to trade unions in Europe: innovation or adaptation*, Bodmin, Cornwall: Hartnolls Limited, pp. 53–73.

Goldberg, Pinelopi K. and Frank Verboven (2001), 'Market integration and convergence to the law of one price: Evidence from the European car market', *NBER Working Paper*.

Goodhart, Charles A. E. (1994), 'What should central banks do? What should be their macroeconomic objectives and operations?', *The Economic Journal*, 104, 1424–1436.

Gouriéroux, Christian (1997), *ARCH models and financial applications*, New York and Heidelberg: Springer.

Grauwe, Paul de and Vladimir Lavrac (1999), 'Challenges of European Monetary Union for Central European Countries', in Paul de Grauwe and Vladimir Lavrac (eds), *Inclusion of Central European Countries in the European Monetary Union*, Dordrecht: Kluwer, pp. 1–12.

Greene, William H. (1997), *Econometric Analysis*, New Jersey: Prentice Hall.

Gregorio, José de, Alberto Giovanni and Holger C. Wolf (1994), 'International evidence on tradables and nontradables inflation', *European Economic Re-*

view, **38**, 1225–1244.

Grilli, Vittorio, Donato Masciandaro and Guido Tabellini (1991), 'Political and monetary institutions and public financial policies in the industrial countries', *Economic Policy*, **13**, 341–392.

Grossman, Gene M. and Elhanan Helpman (1993), 'The politics of free trade agreements', *NBER Working Paper*.

Haan, Jakob de (1997), 'The European Central Bank: Independence, accountability and strategy: A review', *Public Choice*, **93**, 395–426.

Haan, Jakob de and Gert Jan van't Hag (1995), 'Variation in central bank independence across countries: Some provisional empirical evidence', *Public Choice*, **85**, 335–351.

Haan, Jakob de and Laurence Gormley (1997), 'Independence and accountability of the European Central Bank', in Mads Andenas, Laurence Gormley, Christos Hadjiemmanuil and Ian Harden (eds), *European Economic and Monetary Union: The Institutional Framework*, Dordrecht: Kluwer, pp. 333–353.

Haan, Jakob de, Helge Berger and Robert Inklaar (2002), 'Is the ECB too decentralized?', *mimeo*.

Hallett, A. Huges and Laura Piscitelli (2002), 'Does trade integration cause convergence?', *Economics Letters*, **75**, 165–170.

Hamada, Koichi and Fumio Hayashi (1985), 'Monetary policy in postwar Japan', in Albert Ando (ed.), *Monetary Policy in Our Times*, Cambridge, Mass.: MIT Press.

Harvey, Andrew C. (1990), *The econometric analysis of time series*, Cambridge, Mass.: MIT Press.

Haskel, Jonathan and Holger Wolf (2001), 'The law of one price – a case study', *CESifo Working Paper*.

Havrilesky, Thomas (1993), *The Pressures on American Monetary Policy*, Norwell, Mass. and Dordrecht: Kluwer Academic.

Hayo, Bernd (1998), 'Inflation culture, central bank independence and price stability', *European Journal of Political Economy*, **14**, 241–263.

Heipertz, Martin Karl Georg (2001), 'How strong was the Bundesbank?', *CEPS Working Documents*.

Hibbs, Douglas A. (1977), 'Political parties and macroeconomic policy', *American Political Science Review*, **71 (4)**, 1467–1487.

Hochreiter, Eduard and Georg Winckler (1995), 'The advantages of tying Austria's hands: The success of the hard currency strategy', *European Journal of Political Economy*, **11**, 83–111.

Houben, Aardt (1999), 'The Evolution of Monetary Strategies in Europe', PhD thesis: University of Groningen.

Hsiao, Cheng (1981), 'Autoregressive modelling and money-income causality detection', *Journal of Monetary Economics*, **7**, 85–106.

Hsieh, David A. (1982), 'The determination of the real exchange rate: The productivity approach', *Journal of International Economics*, **12**, 355–362.

Hunt, Jenifer (2000), 'Why do people still live in EastGermany?', *mimeo*.

Hyman, Richard and Anthony Ferner (1994), *New Frontiers in European industrial relations*, London: Blackwell.

Inklaar, Robert and Jakob de Haan (2001), 'Is there really a European business cycle? A comment', *Oxford Economic Papers*, **53**, 215–220.

Issing, Ottmar (1996), *Einführung in die Geldpolitik*, München: Vahlen.

Ito, Takatoshi and Jin Hyuk Park (1988), 'Political business cycles in the parliamentary system', *Economics Letters*, **27**, 233–238.

Jarchow, Hans-Joachim (1995), *Theorie und Politik des Geldes II: Geldpolitik*, Göttingen: Vandenhoeck & Ruprecht.

Johansen, Soren (1991), 'Estimation and hypothesis testing of cointegration vectors in Gaussian vector autoregressive models', *Econometrica*, **59** (**6**), 1551–1580.

Johnson, David R. and Pierre L. Siklos (1994), 'Political effects on central bank behaviour: Some international evidence', in Pierre L. Syklos (ed.), *Varieties Of Monetary Reforms*, Dordrecht: Kluwer Academic Publishers.

Judson, Ruth A. and Ann L. Owen (1999), 'Estimating dynamic panel data models: A guide for macroeconomists', *Economics Letters*, **65**, 9–15.

Kalyvitis, Sarantis and Alexander Michaelides (2001), 'New evidence on the effects of US monetary policy on exchange rates', *Economics Letters*, **71**, 255–263.

Kane, Edward J. (1980), 'Politics and FED policymaking: The more things change, the more they remain the same', *Journal of Monetary Economics*, **6**, 199–211.

Kawai, Masahiro (1980), 'Exchange rate-price causality in the recent floating period', in David Bigman and Teizo Taya (eds), *The functioning of floating exchange rates. Theory, evidence, and policy implications*, Cambridge: Ballinger, pp. 189–211.

Kennedy, Peter (1998), *A Guide to Econometrics*, Oxford: Blackwell Publishers.

Kirchgässner, Gebhard and Werner W. Pommerehne (1997), 'Public spending in federal states', in Pantelis Capros and Daniele Meulders (eds), *Budgetary Policy Modelling: Public Expenditures*, London: Routledge.

Knot, Klaas and Jakob de Haan (1996), 'Fiscal policy: Theory and measurement', in Klaas Knot, *Fiscal Policy and Interest Rates in the European Union*, Cheltenham: Edward Elgar.

Laaser, Claus-Friedrich and Klaus Schrader (2002), 'Europea integration and changing trade patterns: The case of the Baltic states', *Kiel Institute of World Economics Working Paper*.

Lang, Günther and Peter Welzel (1992), 'Budgetdefizite, Wahlzyklen und

Geldpolitik: Empirische Ergebnisse für die Bundesrepublik Deutschland 1962-1989', *Jahrbuch für Nationalökonomie und Statistik*, **210 (2)**, 72–85.

Leertouwer, Erik and Philipp Maier (2001), 'Who creates Political Business Cycles? (Should central banks be blamed?)', *European Journal of Political Economy*, **17 (3)**, 445–463. Reprinted by permission of Elsevier Science from 'Who creates political business cycles?' by Erik Leertouwer and Philipp Maier, European Journal of Political Economy, 17 (3).

Lelyveld, Iman van (1999), 'Inflation or unemployment? Who cares', *European Journal of Political Economy*, **15**, 463–484.

Lohmann, Susanne (1992), 'Optimal commitment in monetary policy: Credibility versus flexibility', *American Economic Review*, **82 (1)**, 273–286.

Lohmann, Susanne (1997), 'Partisan control of the money supply and decentralized appointment powers', *European Journal of Political Economy*, **13**, 225–246.

Lohmann, Susanne (1998), 'Federalism and central bank independence: The politics of German monetary policy, 1957-92', *World Politics*, **50 (3)**, 401–446.

Maier, Philipp (1999), 'Pressure on the Bundesbank?', *Germany Institute Amsterdam Working Paper Series*.

Maier, Philipp (2000), 'Pressure on the Bundesbank?', *Kredit und Kapital*, **4**, 1–30. Reprinted by permission of Duncker & Humblot from 'Pressure on the Bundesbank?' by Philipp Maier, Kredit und Kapital, 4, 1–30.

Maier, Philipp and Alistair Dieppe (2002), 'Analyzing inflation differentials in EMU member countries', *mimeo*.

Maier, Philipp and Jakob de Haan (2000), 'How independent is the Bundesbank really? A survey', in Jakob de Haan (ed.), *History of the Bundesbank: Lessons for the ECB*, London: Routledge, pp. 6–42.

Maier, Philipp and Maarten Hendrikx (2002), 'Implications of EMU enlargement for European monetary policy: A political economy view', *mimeo*.

Maier, Philipp and Thijs Knaap (2002), 'Who supported the Deutsche Bundesbank?', *Journal of Policy Modeling*. Reprinted by permission of Elsevier Science from 'Who supported the Deutsche Bundesbank?' by Philipp Maier and Thijs Knaap, Journal of Policy Modeling, forthcoming, Copyright 2002 by the Society for Policy Modeling.

Maier, Philipp, Jan-Egbert Sturm and Jakob de Haan (2002), 'Political pressure on the Bundesbank: An empirical investigation using the Havrilesky approach', *Journal of Macroeconomics*. Reprinted by permission of Elsevier Science from 'Political Pressure on the Bundesbank: An empirical investigation using the Havrilesky approach' by Philipp Maier, Jan-Egbert Sturm and Jakob de Haan, Journal of Macroeconomics, forthcoming.

Marsh, David (1992), *The Most Powerful Bank: Inside Germany's Bundesbank*, New York: Times Books.

Metten, Alman (2001), 'ECB krigt meer effect met minder bestuurders', *Financieele Dagblad*.

Mihov, Ilian (2001), 'Monetary policy implementation and transmission in the European Monetary Union', *Economic Policy*, 33, 371–406.

Mishkin, Frederic S. and Adam S. Posen (1997), 'Inflation targeting: Lessons from four countries', *NBER Working Paper*.

Missong, Martin and Philippe Herrault (1990), 'Eine kritische Analyse internationaler Vergleiche von Zentralbankreaktionsfunktionen am Beispiel Deutschland-Frankreich', *Schweizerische Zeitschrift für Volkswirtschaft und Statistik*, **126 (4)**, 567–581.

Mueller, Dennis C. (1989), *Public Choice II*, Cambridge: Cambridge University Press.

Muscatelli, Anton (1998), 'Optimal inflation contracts and inflation targets with uncertain central bank preferences: Accountability through independence?', *The Economic Journal*, **108**, 529–542.

Neumann, Manfred J. M. (1989), 'Politics and business cycles in industrial democracies: A comment', *Economic Policy*, **8**, 90–92.

Neumann, Manfred J. M. (1993), 'Die Deutsche Bundesbank als Modell für eine Europäische Zentralbank? Koreferat zu Roland Vaubel', in Dieter Duwendag and Jürgen Siebke (eds), *Europa vor dem Eintritt in die Wirtschafts- und Währungsunion*, Berlin: Duncker and Humblot, pp. 81–95.

Neumann, Manfred J. M. (1998), 'Geldwertstabilität: Bedrohung und Bewährung', in Deutsche Bundesbank (ed.), *Fünfzig Jahre Deutsche Mark, Notenbank und Währung in Deutschland Seit 1948*, München: Beck, pp. 309–346.

Neumann, Manfred J. M. and Susanne Lohmann (1987), 'Political business cycles in industrialized democratic countries: A comment', *Kyklos*, **40**, 568–572.

Nordhaus, William D. (1975), 'The political business cycle', *Review of Economic Studies*, **42**, 169–190.

Obstfeld, Maurice and Kenneth Rogoff (1996), *Foundations of International Macroeconomics*, Cambridge, Mass.: MIT Press.

Olson, Mancur (1965), *The logic of collective action*, Cambridge: Harvard University Press.

Paldam, Martin (1997), 'Political business cycle', in Dennis C. Mueller (ed.), *Perspectives on Public Choice: A Handbook*, Cambridge: Cambridge University Press, pp. 342–370.

Parsley, David C. and Shang-Jin Wei (2000), 'Explaining the border effect: The role of exchange rate variability, shipping costs, and geography', *Journal of International Economics*.

Perron, Pierre (1989), 'The great crash, the oil price shock, and the unit root hypothesis', *Econometrica*, **57 (6)**, 277–301.

Persson, Torsten and Guido Tabellini (1990), *Macroeconomic Policy, Credibility and Politics*, London: Harwood Academic Publishers.

Phillips, Peter C.B and Bruce E. Hansen (1990), 'Statistical inference in instrumental variables regression with I(1) processes', *Review of Economic Studies*, **57 (1)**, 99–125.

Pierce, Thomas J. and Ken Rebeck (2001), 'Short-run monetary policy and the macroeconomic environment', *Contemporary Economic Policy*, **19 (4)**, 434–443.

Pilat, Dirk (1996), 'Labour productivity levels in OECD countries: Estimates for manufacturing and selected service sectors', *OECD Working Paper*.

Posen, Adam S. (1993), 'Why central bank independence does not cause low inflation: There is no institutional fix for politics', in Richard O'Brien (ed.), *Finance and the international economy 7, the Amex Bank Review Prize Essays*, Oxford and New York: Oxford University Press, pp. 41–54.

Posen, Adam S. (1995), 'Declarations are not enough: financial sector sources of central bank independence', *NBER Macroeconomics Annual*, **10**, 253–274.

Rogers, John H. (2001), 'Price level convergence, relative prices, and inflation in Europe', *International Finance Discussion Papers*.

Rogers, John H., Gary Clyde Hufbauer and Erika Wada (2002), 'Price level convergence and inflation in Europe', *mimeo*.

Rogoff, Kenneth and Anne Sibert (1988), 'Elections and macroeconomic policy cycles', *Review of Economic Studies*, **55**, 1–16.

Romer, Christina D. and David H. Romer (1989), 'Does monetary policy matter? A new test in the spirit of Friedman and Schwartz', *NBER Macroeconomics Annual*, pp. 121–170.

Rose, Andrew K. (2000), 'One money, one market: Estimating the effect of common currencies on trade', *Economic Policy*, **15 (30)**, 7–46.

Rose, Andrew K. and Jeffrey Frankel (2002), 'An estimate of the effect of common currencies on trade and income', *Quarterly Journal of Economics*.

Samuelson, Paul A. (1964), 'Theoretical notes on trade problems', *Review of Economics and Statistics*, **46**, 145 – 54.

Schultes, Dieter (1996), 'Geldmengenziele und diskretionäre Elemente der Politik der Bundesbank', *Kredit und Kapital*, **29 (1)**, 54–89.

Schweickert, Rainer (2001), 'Assessing the advantages of EMU enlargement for the EU and the accession countries: A comparative indicator approach', *Kiel Institute of World Economics Discussion Paper*.

Siklos, Pierre L. and Martin T. Bohl (2002), 'Quantifying conflicts between the Bundesbank and the Federal Government', *mimeo*.

Sims, Christopher A. (1992), 'Interpreting the macroeconomic time series facts: The effects of monetary policy', *European Economic Review*, **36**, 975–1000.

Sinn, Hans-Werner and Michael Reutter (2001), 'The minimum inflation rate for Euroland', *NBER Working Paper*, **8085**, 32–34.

Smyth, David J. and Susan Washburn Taylor (1992), 'Inflation-unemployment trade-offs of Democrats, Republicans, and Independents: Empirical evidence on the partisan theory', *Journal of Macroeconomics*, **14 (1)**, 47–57.

Soh, Byung Hee (1986), 'Political business cycles in industrialized democratic countries', *Kyklos*, **39**, 31–46.

Strauss, Jack (1996), 'The cointegrating relationship between productivity, real exchange rates and purchasing power parity', *Journal of Macroeconomics*, **18 (2)**, 299–313.

Sturm, Jan-Egbert, Jan P.A.M. Jacobs and Peter D. Groote (1999), 'Output effects of infrastructure investment in the Netherlands 1853-1913', *Journal of Macroeconomics*, **21**, 355–380.

Suardi, Massimo (2001), 'EMU and asymmetries in monetary policy transmission', *Economic Papers, European Commission, Brussels*.

Summers, Robert and Alan Heston (1991), 'The Penn World Table (Mark 5): An expanded set of international comparisons', *Quarterly Journal of Economics*, **106**, 327–68.

Szapáry, György (2001), 'Maastricht & the choice of exchange rate regime in transition ecountries during the run-up to EMU', *European Network of Economic Policy Research Institutes Working Paper*.

Taylor, John B. (1992), *Monetary policy rules*, Chicago: University of Chicago Press.

Thornton, Daniel L. and Dallas S. Batten (1985), 'Lag-length selection and tests of granger causality between money and income', *Journal of Money, Credit, and Banking*, **17 (2)**, 164–178.

Thygesen, Niels (1990), 'Monetary management in a monetary union', *mimeo*.

Vaubel, Roland (1997), 'The bureaucratic and partisan behaviour of independent central banks: German and international evidence', *European Journal of Political Economy*, **13**, 201–224.

Vaubel, Roland (1998), 'Reply to Berger and Woitek', *European Journal of Political Economy*, **13**, 823–827.

Vaubel, Roland (1999), 'The future of the Euro: A public choice perspective', *Universität Mannheim Discussion Paper*.

Vaubel, Roland (2002), 'Comment on Susanne Lohmann 'Federalism and central bank independence: The politics of German monetary policy, 1957-92'', *mimeo*.

von Hagen, Jürgen (1998), 'Geldpolitik auf neuen Wegen (1971-1978)', in Deutsche Bundesbank (ed.), *Fünfzig Jahre Deutsche Mark: Notenbank und Währung in Deutschland Seit 1948*, München: Beck, pp. 439–473.

Wagner, Helmut (2002), 'Pitfalls in the European enlargement process – financial instability and real divergence', *Deutsche Bundesbank Discussion*

Paper.

Waller, Christopher J. (1991), 'Bashing and coercion in monetary policy', *Economic Inquiry*, **19**, 1–13.

Walsh, Carl E. (1997), 'Inflation and central bank independence: Is Japan really an outlier?', *Monetary and Economic Studies*, **15 (1)**, 89–117.

Walton, David and Stephane Deo (1999), 'Limit to inflation convergence in Euroland', *Global Economics Paper*.

Wei, Shang-Jin and David C. Parsley (1995), 'Purchasing power disparity during the floating rate period: Exchange rate volatility, trade barriers and other culprits', *NBER Working Paper Series*.

Winkler, Bernhard (1999), 'Is Maastricht a good contract?', *Journal of Common Market Studies*, **37 (1)**, 39–58.

Wynne, Mark A. (1999), 'The European System of Central Banks', *Economic Review*, pp. 2–14.

Wynne, Mark A. and Jahyeong Koo (2000), 'Business cycles under monetary union: A comparison of the EU and US', *Economica*, **67**, 347–374.

Zarnowitz, Victor (1992), *Business Cycles: Theory, history, indicators, and forecasting*, Chicago: University of Chicago Press.

Author Index

Subject Index